1989

Reading Nietzsche

Vita S Solomon

Reading Nietzsche

Edited by

Robert C. Solomon
and
Kathleen M. Higgins

New York   Oxford
OXFORD UNIVERSITY PRESS
1988

Oxford University Press

Oxford New York Toronto
Delhi Bombay Calcutta Madras Karachi
Petaling Jaya Singapore Hong Kong Tokyo
Nairobi Dar es Salaam Cape Town
Melbourne Auckland

and associated companies in
Berlin Ibadan

Library of Congress Cataloging-in-Publication Data
Reading Nietzsche / edited by Robert C. Solomon and Kathleen M.
Higgins.
p. cm.
Bibliography: p.
Includes index.
ISBN 0-19-504858-X
1. Nietzsche, Friedrich Wilhelm, 1844–1900. I. Solomon, Robert
C. II. Higgins, Kathleen Marie.
B3317.R35 1988
193—dc19   88-15609

Printing (last digit): 9 8 7 6 5 4 3 2 1

Printed in the United States of America
on acid-free paper

For Tim, Colleen, Jeanine, Maureen, and Jim

For Andy and Jon

Preface

In February of 1985, the College of Liberal Arts and the philosophy, German, and literature departments of the University of Texas at Austin sponsored a symposium on the subject "Reading Nietzsche." Behind the conference was the recognition of Nietzsche's renewed importance, not just as a rediscovered topic or tool for intellectual criticism for scholars but as a profound source of inspiration for students. Students were reading him whether or not he was required reading in courses. Students were discussing him, taking his side, even when the scholarly opposition turned against them. But reading and interpretating Nietzsche is not so easy as it seems, and while there may be no one way of getting Nietzsche "right," it was clear that there were many, many ways of getting him clearly wrong. Nevertheless, the enthusiasm was and is there. It was that enthusiasm—and the confusion about interpretation—that prompted the conference.

We decided, against the current wave of scholarly attempts at an overall synthesis, not to focus on Nietzsche's ideas as such. There are currently quite a few studies of this sort. They try, some insightfully, others merely desperately, to capture the central theme and characterize the dominant style of Nietzsche's work. But, unlike Rousseau, who famously (and probably falsely) declared that his entire career was the development of one single idea, Nietzsche was above all an experimentalist, who tried out ideas as he tried on styles, not so much later rejecting them as moving beyond them, occasionally reaching back and borrowing from them. There is no Nietzschean *überhaubt*, no single theme, and those that are most often promoted to fill this role—the *übermensch*, the will to power, and eternal recurrence—do not bear even slight scholarly scrutiny. There are, of course, grand and personal concerns that permeate Nietzsche's work—the nature of morality, the pathetic motives of much moral and Christian thinking, the historical role of Socrates, the Greeks, and Jesus—but there is hardly a single theme or set of themes that tie the entire corpus together. Indeed, Karl Jaspers was not entirely wrong when he wrote (in 1936) that one had not thoroughly read Nietzsche until, for every claim, he or she had also found the contradiction. Nietzsche shifted from idea to idea, from style to style, and, while his work certainly adds up to a lifelong masterpiece, his philosophy is not of a piece.

It is for that reason, as well as for pedagogical reasons, that we organized the conference around Nietzsche's individual works, and not around his ideas as such. Students read one book at a time, and their impressions of Nietsche are built one book at a time. Even those who take upon themselves the courageous task of reading through every volume have a chance to think about one book at a time, and sometimes one book has little obvious relation to the book that Nietzsche wrote just before or just afterward. We decided, therefore, to deal with each book separately—and to treat some with suspicion (notably those that Nietzsche did not actually publish, and, in one notorious case, that he did not even write). Moreover, we have organized the book according to what seemed to be the order in which most students tend to read Nietzsche, with such accessible works as *On the Genealogy of Morals* first, rather than by way of the usual chronological or biographical organization. This effort results in a few oddities, but the advantages far outweigh the disadvantages and it results in a far more readable volume.

We would like to offer special thanks to Robert King, our Dean of Liberal Arts at Texas, for his sponsorship and support, to our contributors who made the conference so lively and rewarding and the preparation of this volume so enjoyable and edifying, to our editor Cynthia Read for her encouragement and patience, to Grace Killan for help with the typescript, and to Lissa Anderson for her now infamous Nietzsche-Wagner cake.

Austin, Texas   K. M. H.
July, 1987   R. C. S.

Contents

Abbreviations

Unless otherwise noted, citations from Nietzsche's writings are identified by the acronyms of their English titles, Arabic numbers referring to the paragraphs or sections in which the passages appear. Where appropriate, Roman numerals indicate the parts of the works.

Citations listed are based on the texts as they appear in the Colli-Montinari *Kritische Gesamtausgabe* (KGA) or the *Kritische Studienausgabe* (KSA), unless otherwise noted.

PTA Philosophy in the Tragic Age of the Greeks
BT The Birth of Tragedy, in *The Basic Writings of Nietzsche* (New York: Random House, 1968)
SE Schopenhauer as Educator
HH Human, All Too Human
D Dawn (or Daybreak)
GS The Gay Science (New York: Random House, 1974)
Z Thus Spoke Zarathustra, in *The Portable Nietzsche* (New York: Viking, 1968)
BGE Beyond Good and Evil, in *The Basic Writings*
GM On the Genealogy of Morals, in *The Basic Writings*
TI Twilight of the Idols, in *The Portable Nietzsche*
A The Antichrist, in *The Portable Nietzsche*
EH Ecce Homo, in *The Basic Writings*
WP The Will to Power (New York: Random House, 1968)

Chronology of Nietzsche's Works

1844 Nietzsche born (October 15).

1872 *The Birth of Tragedy* published.

1873 Two of the *Untimely Meditations* published: *David Strauss, the Confessor and Writer* and *On the Advantage and Disadvantage of History for Life*.

1874 The third *Untimely Meditation, Schopenhauer as Educator*, published.

1876 The last of the *Untimely Meditations, Richard Wagner in Bayreuth* published.

1878 *Human, All Too Human* (volume I) published.

1879 "Miscellaneous Maxims and Opinions" (later to be incorporated into *Human, All Too Human*, volume II) written and published as an appendix to *Human, All Too Human* (volume I).

1880 "The Wanderer and His Shadow" published as second appendix to *Human, All Too Human* (volume I).

1881 *Daybreak* published.

1882 *The Gay Science* published.

1883 Parts I and II of *Thus Spoke Zarathustra* published (separately).

1884 Part III of *Thus Spoke Zarathustra* published.

1885 Part IV of *Thus Spoke Zarathustra* published and circulated among a few of Nietzsche's friends.

1886 *Beyond Good and Evil* published. The second edition of *The Birth of Tragedy* is published with a new preface. A second edition of *Human, All Too Human* is published. "Miscellaneous

Maxims and Opinions" and "The Wanderer and His Shadow" are incorporated into *Human, All Too Human*, volume II.

1887 *On the Genealogy of Morals* published. The second edition of *The Gay Science*, including a new fifth book and an appendix of poems, is published.

1888 *The Case of Wagner* published. *Twilight of the Idols, The Antichrist, Nietzsche Contra Wagner*, and *Ecce Homo* are written.

1889 Nietzsche becomes insane (January). *Twilight of the Idols* published.

1892 Part IV of *Thus Spoke Zarathustra* published.

1895 *The Antichrist* and *Nietzsche Contra Wagner* published.

1900 Nietzsche dies (August 25).

1901 First version of *The Will to Power* (collected from Nietzsche's notes) published. (Additional versions, with more material incorporated, appear in 1904 and 1910–11.)

1908 *Ecce Homo* published.

Reading Nietzsche

Introduction: Reading Nietzsche

ROBERT C. SOLOMON

Nietzsche has always been a favorite philosopher of undergraduate students. He attacks authority with relish and sarcasm. He is rude. He states his mind without academic pomp. He calls a spade a spade. He defends individual differences. He stresses the new. He is prophetic without being preachy. He writes short, easy-to-read paragraphs—and mercifully short books. He is exciting, inflammatory. He is, they would like to believe, so much like them, so tempestuous, so "timely."

And yet, when Walter Kaufmann published the first edition of his *Nietzsche* back in 1950, Friedrich Nietzsche was still a philosophical outlaw, read by students perhaps but excluded altogether from the legitimate philosophy curriculum. And it was just over twenty years ago, when Arthur Danto published his book *Nietzsche as Philosopher*, that Nietzsche could be treated not only as a legitimate philosopher but as teachable too, with deep theses that could challenge the assumptions of the great philosophers and provide topics for thought for contemporary analysts as well as provoke young Leopolds and Loebs. Nietzsche became a standard figure in courses on ethics—no longer lampooned as the elitist inventor of the "superman" but taught as a serious philosopher who called into question the very basis of the morality that Kant and others merely took for granted and analyzed. He became not only mentionable but an essential figure in the history of philosophy, the iconoclast who heralded some of the most important philosophical movements of the twentieth century.

But Nietzsche's profound importance extends far beyond the narrow confines of the history of philosophy. It may or may not be the case, as Allan Bloom has argued recently in his book, *The Closing of the American Mind*, that Nietzsche is the unnamed dark force behind contemporary student nihilism and relativism in America, but it is certainly

3

true that Nietzsche continues to attract and inspire thoughtful students from every corner and at every level of the curriculum. It is to them that this book is directed. After teaching Nietzsche for twenty years, it is easy to forget—but not hard to remember—that a first encounter with Nietzsche is, intellectually, as shattering and as self-revelatory as virtually any other adolescent or college experience. Nietzsche speaks not so much to the mind of the scholar and the sophisticate, nor to the heart (an overrated cognitive organ in any case), but rather to the viscera, the place where doubts and rebellion grow, the parts of the body not easily tamed by merely valid arguments or the authority of professors. These are organs not readily persuaded by the gesticulations of scholarship and the weight of tradition, and they are even less touched by the latest fashions in Reader Response theory, neural network hypotheses, deconstruction, or analytic philology. Nietzsche is the vivisectionist who twists our fashions, our theories, our ideas, and our organs out of shape and back again, but with him the discomfort seems like exhilaration.

Reading Nietzsche is a rare and intoxicating experience. It is one of those few times one feels in immediate, intimate contact with an author. One rarely meets an enthusiastic student who does not consider Nietzsche in some sense *his* (less frequently *her*) author. He is our students' perverse and dangerous private tutor with whom (book in hand) they might cautiously approach some recognized authority on Nietzsche, but most likely just to confirm their suspicions, or clarify an intuition, or to make sure that they are not completely crazy. Usually, it seems, they talk to us just to confirm that we, after all, had not really understood Nietzsche either, that they were indeed the unique possessors of rare and dangerous knowledge. This is our audience, and the danger of writing with authority about reading Nietzsche is that we are so often preaching to the disciples rather than just the converted.

This is a book about reading Nietzsche, but it is by no means a "how to" book nor a dogmatic introduction to the one "correct" way of approaching or understanding Nietzsche. To be sure, we have not tried to capture the entire range of Nietzsche interpretation and enthusiasm. We have included only a sample of the important recent work among literary critics and theorists, and virtually none of the radical readings of Nietzsche among religious and theological thinkers. We have only touched upon some of the interpretations that have been designated "the new Nietzsche" and "the postmodern Nietzsche." What we have tried to do is to provide a variety of readings by a number of different scholars, but this could not possibly be enough, for every reader of Nietzsche tends to find or make him his or her own. More than any other philosopher of modern times, Nietzsche is not so much an object of scholarship as a mirror of self-reflection and probe for self-identity.

Nietzsche is an author whose power has not been undermined by decades of the wrong kind of readers, the wrong kind of enthusiasts, the wrong kind of interpretations, and the wrong kind of criticism. For decades, scholars who understood the categorical imperative without asking about Kant's drinking habits insisted on knowing about Nietzsche's insanity (was it syphilis?) Philosophers who would never have ignored Frege for his anti-Semitism rejected Nietzsche because of his (posthumous) influence on the Kaiser and—through his twisted sister—on Hitler. Nietzsche's notorious views on women are taken to be the refutation of his entire philosophy (are his comments any less nasty about Goethe or Socrates—his avowed heroes?) And then, of course, there is Nietzsche's—shall we say it—virginity! Has anything ever served better to refute a philosopher—unless, of course, he is Kant?

Nietzsche himself is not without blame, of course. Hyperbole, sarcasm, and the rave were his standard rhetorical devices, and so he has made himself a court of appeal for cranks of all kinds. Embittered professors use the concepts of the *übermensch* and "higher" men, to prove that—the quality of their own publications aside—there really is a superior breed—guess who? There are fumbled dictators calling Nietzsche to their side, citing his warrior imagery and justifications of cruelty. Literary critics have recently summoned Nietzsche to kill *Moby Dick*, using the "gay science" as grounds for the murder of great texts and the denial of masterpieces as well as a frontal assault on philosophy. Focusing on Nietzsche's early writings on the inscrutability of language and ignoring his personal commitment and passion, too many modern commentators make him appear to be a mere progenitor of contemporary literary criticism, perhaps an intellectual trickster and not an impassioned and dedicated moralist.

It is ironic that Nietzsche, the clearest and most belligerent of writers, has today become the darling of the obscurantists, depersonalized, anaesthetized and defanged. As Arthur Danto points out in his remarks on the *Genealogy*, scholars have taken Nietzsche and tried to "cage him into a system of repressive categories, put his toxin on ice, slip the manacles of asceticism onto his wrists," and, perhaps worst of all, "locate him in the history of thought." They deny that he may be "dangerous and even terrible." And Nietzsche, who had the most outrageous am-

bition for philosophy since Plato, who often announced with great an-
ticipation the arrival of "new philosophers," and who wrote the
"prelude" to the future of philosophy, has been hailed as the end of
philosophy. The ruthless critic of metaphysics has been called, notably
by Heidegger, "the last metaphysician." In Nietzsche's name, the politics of univerity departments have been elevated to a cosmic principle,
and in the hands of the scholars, whom Nietzsche so lampooned,
Nietzsche has become one more text, or nontext, from which the most
exotic bits of elitism are announced in the most inaccessible journals.

In reaction to these various glosses and abuses of Nietzsche, we want
to get back down to the basics—reading Nietzsche. There is no hidden
agenda or new interpretation of Nietzsche hidden in these pages, no
"new" or "new improved" Nietzsche who will emerge. The idea is to
recapture the thrill of reading through Nietzsche himself, without other
axes to grind, without any attempt to say, in one voice, what Nietzsche
was or was not trying to do. This is not to say that this volume is without
bias or free of interpretation (as if that were even possible), but it is to
insist that it does not represent a polemic or a test of scholarly wills or
a fancy presentation of interpretations for their own sake, theories of
interpretation and theories about theories of theories of interpretation.
The idea of the book is to be just about Nietzsche, about *Reading
Nietzsche*, and trying to say something helpful and interesting to real
readers about the most exciting intellectual and personal experiences
that many young philosophers will ever have.

The problems and pitfalls in reading Nietzsche are well-enough known.
One conservative philosophical stylist—Brand Blandshard of Yale, com-
mented that he always wanted to throw Nietzsche, or at least one of his
books, across the room. Even when he is not infuriating, Nietzsche is
often perplexing, and it is such confusion that comes of excessive style
and exuberance that the essays that follow address.

First and foremost, there are Nietzsche's adolescent pronouncements
and his often embarrassing militarized language. From snatches of prose,
one might well conclude that Nietzsche wants nothing more fervently
than the life of Conan the Barbarian, a role for which he, in particular,
was notoriously ill-suited. "Live dangerously" he tells us, from the
posher resorts in Southern Europe. But the warrior imagery may be
misleading. Alexander Nehamas has done a piece of empirical research:
out of the hundred plus names that appear in *Beyond Good and Evil*,
for example, a full ninety percent are writers and artists, not führers
and Homeric heroes. So what are we to make of that warrior imagery,

and of the multitude of belligerent and even cruel images that populate Nietzsche's writings? In general, to what extent should we ignore or dismiss Nietzsche's hyperbole and outrageousness—for instance his infamous comments about women such as "better to fall into the hands of a murderer than into the dreams of a woman in heat"? To what extent should such comments cast doubt on his whole philosophy? How seriously should we take his venomous personal attacks on Christians and moralists? Does the allegedly vicious and pathetic motivation of Christianity and morality undermine their validity, or is the whole idea of "genealogy" a grand genetic fallacy, or, perhaps, a collective *ad hominem* argument? Is Nietzsche's vitriolic indignation a reason not to take him seriously, as so many critics in the past have suggested?

And then there are the notorious problems of interpretation. What do "will to power" and "eternal recurrence" mean? How literally are we to take such categories such as "master and slave"? Does Nietzsche really reject morality as such, or does he just reject one particular version of moral thinking? What is *ressentiment* and how does it differ, if at all, from resentment? Does he really reject free will, or is he only attacking certain abuses of the Will in Kant and Schopenhauer? Does Nietzsche really reject pessimism, nihilism, or does he emerge, despite himself, a pessimist and a nihilist? Who is Zarathustra? For that matter, who is Friedrich Nietzsche, *"ecce homo"*? It must be said that Nietzsche does not make such matters easy for us, but neither can such questions be avoided. Are Nietzsche's many metaphors mere metaphors or should they be taken literally—or is this just the sort of question that Nietzsche would have us leave behind?

How should one read aphorisms, those darts that Nietzsche keeps flinging at our metaphysical balloons? Consider such epistemological teasers as "All truth is simple; is that not doubly a lie?" or such tantalizing falsehoods as "What does not destroy me makes me stronger," or such tactless summations as "The Christian principle of love: in the end it wants to be PAID well." Karl Kraus once wrote that every aphorism is either a half-truth or a truth and a half. Which are which in Nietzsche? Furthermore, that Nietzsche wrote in aphorisms is such an idée fixe that it is often assumed he wrote all of his works in aphoristic style. But most of the time he did *not* write in aphorisms. His paragraphs are often short and not infrequently disjointed, but that is not the same thing, and some of his seemingly aphoristic sentences are nevertheless an intrinsic and inseparable part of some larger argument or structure. The *variety* of styles is what is most striking about Nietzsche's writings, and the aphoristic style is just one of these. How are we to understand his strategy (or strategies)? How does the style reveal the philosophy, and why does the philosophy require the style?

Should we look for an overall system? Nietzsche at one point writes, "the will to a system is a lack of integrity": does that mean that we shouldn't look for coherence, that contradictions are intentional rather than the result of a change of mind or a slip of confusion? What sorts of links should we look for between texts? What thematic ideas? What pervasive concerns? Nietzsche refers back to his own works quite frequently, but often with a kind of delighted surprise rather than by way of tying his ideas together.

And finally, in what order should one read these books and what is their relation to one another? Nietzsche is not, for example, like Kant, who had and gives us a clear plan for his works. Did Nietzsche have any plans at all, and, if he did, did he ever follow them? How does *Zarathustra* fit in?—as the centerpiece, as Nietzsche sometimes claims, or as a literary diversion of only derivative philosophical importance? Is there a single book that should serve as a syntopticon, as a guide or a summary, as the cornerstone of the entire corpus? It is one of the unexpected charms of the essays that follow that almost every contributor suggests that, in some sense, the book that he or she has chosen is Nietzsche's seminal or central work, but that of course makes the question all the more difficult, for each choice represents a quite different perspective and interpretation of Nietzsche's philosophy.

The problem one faces when reading Nietzsche is not the presence of formidable technical formulations or difficult jargon or a particularly convoluted style of writing. Nietzsche writes with admirable clarity, if more than occasional hyperbole. His brilliant style does not hide or cloud issues but dramatizes them. And yet, it is also surely false to say that Nietzsche has no philosophy, or constantly contradicts himself, or is incapable of sustained philosophical argument. *On the Genealogy of Morals* is as much of a philosophical essay as one would expect from John Stuart Mill, and *Twilight of the Idols* is only slightly less well organized than the earlier (not to mention the later) works of Wittgenstein.

The problem is what to do with the bewildering richness of these texts, how to take them and how to understand their author. The topics most often celebrated—the *übermensch*, the will to power, eternal recurrence—in fact play an almost negligible role in the published philosophical works. (The *übermensch* is confined to *Zarathustra*; the will to power and eternal recurrence, apart from a few pregnant paragraphs, are found mainly in Nietzsche's unpublished notes, not to be neglected perhaps but not to be taken—as Hiedegger perversely suggested—as the key to his thought either.) The real topics that Nietzsche developed—his perspectivism, his attacks on (and attempts at) metaphysics and morality, his romantic worries about "nature" and "life" and the nature of the self—are scattered through his texts and often treated differently. It is no small task to bring them together into a single coherent set of theses. But this still is not the real problem, the problem that got glimpsed even by those older students reading the outlawed Nietzsche. The real problem was and remains Nietzsche himself, and what he was trying to do. Was he trying to tell us how to live, give us prescriptions and recommendations, and, if so, did he follow them himself? And if he did not intend to give us prescriptions and recommendations, but just tell us, in so many different words, to "become ourselves" and "find our own way," then what is all the fuss about?

Central to Nietzsche's middle works is the idea, and the style, of "perspectivism." Unlike most philosophers, who argue directly for the truth of a single idea or system, Nietzsche argues for a plurality of perspectives, a plurality of "truths" if you like, with none of them the "true" one. The problem is how to defend this thesis without falling into self-referential contradiction or relativism (which he calls "childish"). So too, where most philosophers write in an abstract, third-person "omniscient" voice, Nietzsche writes often in the first person—usually singular, occasionally plural—and there is no question whose opinion he is stating. His style draws attention to the author, and unlike most philosophers—who rarely employ a first person (much less singular) pronoun—Nietzsche's writings abound in self-reference and self-glorification, reminding us that *his* judgments, *his* insights, *his* perspectives, all are very much his own. But how is this apparent egomania to be understood? It is among the most popular undergraduate theses that "everyone is entitled to his or her own opinion," but it is brandished as a way of dismissing serious thought rather than provoking it. In Nietzsche, perspectivism seems instead to underscore and force us to pay more attention to his opinions even while, in some sense, undermining them. He hits us with uncompromising judgments and statements of the facts that are often brutal, disruptive, and anything but "just his opinion," but after giving us a framework within which "there are no facts, only interpretations." Does Nietzsche really accept the perspectivism he advocates so forcefully in such works as *Daybreak* and *Gay*

Science? And even if he does accept it in these middle works, does he continue to do so later, in the pointed polemics that define such works as the *Genealogy* and the *Antichrist*? How does Nietzsche escape the paradox in which one asserts but at the same time undermines the truth of the claim that "there is no truth"? Is he really a skeptic, even a nihilist, despite his denials? What does he really have to say to his neorelativist, subjectivist, business and law-school-bound junior readers? Is philosophy and morality really just a matter of personal opinion and prejudice, or are there much larger and more objective issues that validate some positions and invalidate others?

Like so many philosophers before him, Nietzsche defends the ideal of self-reflection, but unlike the contemplation encouraged by Aristotle or by Socrates' classic appeal to the Delphic oracle, "Know thyself," Nietzsche teaches self-*creation*, ethics as aesthetics, which is not, however, to exaggerate our freedom to be creative or overemphasize a dubious notion of individual uniqueness. Like the later existentialists, Nietzsche stresses self-transformation and personal resolution, but unlike Sartre in particular, he is wary of all talk of "freedom" and "self-hood." He does not talk about "responsibility" or "authenticity," but his philosophy nevertheless displays that personal, passionate, "engaged" (if not at all political) sensibility that Kierkegaard, Jaspers, Heidegger, and Sartre all shared. But with this emphasis on the personal, Nietzsche can argue that perspectivism is not the view that every opinion is as good as every other but rather that an opinion is only as good as its author, as meaningful as the thought that goes into it and the energy and sincerity that motivate it. Nietzsche's own writing is itself a lifelong and totally absorbing exercise in self-creation and self-validation. Nietzsche, like Sartre's Proust, is no one other than the net effect of his writings.

Who was Friedrich Nietzsche? He was born on October 15, 1844, in Rocken, a small village in Prussian Saxony. His father died when he was only four, and he was raised in his family household of five pious women. He attended a Protestant boarding school, studied classics, and moved on to the University of Bonn. There he studied theology and classical philosophy, composed music, and fought with his professors until he transferred to the University of Leipzig in 1865. He worked for his doctorate (received later, in 1869), won an important prize, and began military service in an artillery regiment in which he was soon injured, mounting a horse. He resumed his studies, discovered the philosophy of Schopenhauer and the music of Richard Wagner, the two most powerful creative influences in his life.

In 1868 he became a professor of classical philology in Basel, one of the youngest men ever to do so. Despite a long history of illness and frailty, he volunteered as a medical orderly in the Franco-Prussian War of 1870, but be became seriously ill while transporting wounded soldiers. He never regained good health and took leave from the university. In 1872, he published his first book—in part a product of his admiration and fateful friendship with Wagner—*The Birth of Tragedy*. A series of "untimely" essays followed, and his first full book of aphoristic philosophy, *Human, All Too Human*, appeared in 1878. About this time, he resigned from the university once and for all, and was to live the rest of his life on a small pension.

Nietzsche's mock-biblical literary masterpiece, *Thus Spoke Zarathustra*, appeared in four parts, between 1883 and 1885. *Beyond Good and Evil* and *On the Genealogy of Morals* were published in 1886 and 1887. The last productive year of his life, 1888, saw the appearance of *The Case of Wagner, Twilight of the Idols, The Antichrist, Nietzsche Contra Wagner* and *Ecce Homo* (not published until 1908). Nietzsche collapsed in Turin in January of 1889, according to most sources, weeping and hugging a horse in the street to protect it from a beating. He never again regained his mental faculties. He died in 1900, right at the beginning of the century whose chaos he had so thoroughly anticipated.

Like many great philosophers, Nietzsche saw himself as a new beginning. But whether it is better to read him as part of the Western philosophical tradition, or rather as its greatest antagonist, is one of the interpretive questions that emerges again and again in the essays that follow. Perhaps it is better to view Nietzsche, as both Bergmann and Schacht do in their essays, as a kind of philosophical anthropologist, perhaps a kind of antiphilosopher, or at any rate a problem for philosophy (Danto, Magnus, Shapiro), certainly at least in part a literary innovator (Higgins, Nehamas) or a psychologist (Soll). But whatever categories we try to force him into, Nietzsche and his work resist and mock our efforts. He is that rare figure in the history of philosophy, a true individual, defining himself and inviting his readers to a very special, very private experience. It is not the least of Nietzsche's charms that he manages, in books that are read by millions, to present his advice as if it were a private confidence, "for the few", and by so doing prompts personal reflection far more effectively than the routine pedagogical search for counterexamples to Kant's first formulation of the Categorical Imperative or Mill's principle of utility. Nietzsche is, more than any other philosopher, the mirror of his readers' concerns, reflecting their deepest prejudices, refracting their thoughts with his own brilliant style and insights. The essays that follow are one small sample of the variety of perspectives and reflections that reading Nietzsche invites. Some are more scholarly, some more playful, some more celebratory, some more critical. Together, they are intended to introduce, once again, the works of one of the truly great philosophers of modern times, whose reputation has too often been rooted in misreadings, misconceptions, neglect, and ignorance and whose fate has too often been manipulated by authoritative rather than sympathetic readings.

Portions of this introduction appeared in *Teaching Philosophy* 10 (June 1987).

Some Remarks on
The Genealogy of Morals

ARTHUR C. DANTO

Zarathustra's animals:

Step out of your cave. The world awaits you like a garden. The
wind is playing with heavy fragrances that want to get to you, and
all the brooks would run after you . . . Step out of your cave. All
things would be your physicians.   Z III 13

The third essay of the three which compose *The Genealogy of Morals*
is, according to Nietzsche's preface to the work, a gloss on its prefixed
aphorism, which reads: "Unconcerned, mocking, violent—thus wisdom
wants *us*: She is a woman, and always loves only a warrior." What sort
of warrior is unconcerned? One, I suppose, for whom the means is an
end, for whom warmaking is not so much what you do but what you
are, so that it is not a matter of warring for, but as, an end. There is,
he tell us in the first essay "no being behind doing . . . the 'doer' is merely
a fiction added to the deed." So the unconcerned warrior is perhaps
best exemplified by the great archer Arjuna, in the *Bhagavad Gita*,
instructed by Krishna that unconcern for consequences, hence disinter-
ested participation in the battle, is the path to follow if release is sought
from karma: it is not desisting from action, which is in any case impossible as much for the *Gita* as for Nietzsche, but a certain enlightened
view of the metaphysics of action, which wisdom loves. If this is the
recommended morality, what does the warrior mock? Clearly those still
locked in the world of goals and purposes, who subscribe to hypothetical
imperatives, who fight for causes, rather than those who are categorical
fighters, for whom warring is for its own sake. So violence too is not

13

instrumental but the moral essence of the warrior, not something he especially uses to terrorize, but a secondary effect of the martial art. Why should wisdom then love only the anticonsequentialist? The author of the *Gita* would answer this out of a moral metaphysics in which karmic transmigration is a form of hell, a view finally negativistic and, as we shall see, predicated on a kind of *ressentiment*, since we blame our suffering on karmic pollutions we ourselves are responsible for. These considerations scarcely would have daunted the discoverer of eternal recurrences, hence of the certitude of unending repeated Mahabaratas, in each of which Arjuna fufills himself by drawing bowstrings and steering chariots; nor would they faze the prophet of *amor fati* for whom the evil to be avoided consists in trying to be something other than one is. Kant, the other dominant anticonsequentialist, has a metaphysics of morals, in which it is true that an effort is made to derive our duties from our being *except* that it construes derivation itself to be our characteristic form of action and our essence itself to be reason, and so entraps an opponent as a confirmer, since denial too exemplifies rationality. So, if you are Nietzsche, you don't deny, you *reject*. And that is what is to be expected from a warrior whose campaigns happen to be philosophical and who philosophizes with a hammer; who does not so much love wisdom as he is, like a warrior, loved by wisdom. So not Nietzsche as a philosopher but Nietzsche as *sophiaphiler*, and whose weapons are words, sometimes used as hammers. (Erase the human-all-too-human fraudulence of "the old artilleryman" as he referred to himself on occasion with an affected gruffness.) As one does not argue with an idealist if one does not want to be enmeshed in his web—one instead kicks a rock; or, to cite the practice of one of our most influential contemporary philosophic critics, one does not refute the thinkers one opposes, but instead sneers at them. One puts metaphysics *on ice*, as Nietzsche says in another place: one *mocks*. Mockery is the violence of the metaphysician as warrior. And if one's writings are to be mocking and violent, hence meant to *hurt*, the aphorism is a natural, obvious form to use, for piercing like a dart the defenses of reason, it lodges inextricably in the mind, where it sticks as a perpetual invasion: like a barbed arrow, it cannot be extricated without tearing its host.

This aphorism has a complex pragmatics, since it is as once used *and* used to demonstrate what it means to use language in this way; and the commentary, while it does not quite mitigate the pain to philosophical susceptibilities the aphorism may cause—wisdom does not love those who love wisdom—at least reduces the chance of such suffering as it may cause being smothered in *ressentiment* it is also the task of that commentary to dissolve. In some way its use is meant to have an effect quite opposite to the instillation of an ascetic ideal, as he generalizes upon that concept in the third essay, and so is not meant to transform one into a philosopher, since philosophers are the first to be discussed in that essay as falling under the balefulness of asceticism. The aphorism is a special use of language it is also *about*, and it is the second time in two books that he has drawn a joke from the grammar of gender, feminizing wisdom and truth, both times in order to emphasize a difference between the way he uses language and the ways "philosophers" use it. In *Beyond Good and Evil* he observes that if truth has the attributes of femininity, then she is unlikely to yield her favors to the cloddish and clumsy idiom of philosophers who do not know how to seduce, as he, Nietzsche, does. But, in the same way, the aphorism is the way to approach wisdom, epitomized as female in *this* aphorism: wisdom does not bestow herself upon writers who write as philosophers write, hence not from books that are read as philosophical books are read. Rather language must *implant* itself in the reader, and wisdom comes from an experience which is literary only in the sense that it is caused by a book. So it is language used in a way meant to bypass the faculties ordinarily used in reading. "An aphorism," he writes aphoristically, "when properly stamped and molded, has not been 'deciphered' when it has simply been read." In my address to the American Philosophical Association, *"Philosophy as/and/of Literature,"* I argued that by treating philosophy in general as the sort of thing that can be expressed in articles of the sort we define ourselves professionally through as readers and writers, we misperceive that vast diversity of literary forms the historical bibliography of our discipline displays. Each kind of book has to be read in its own way, and just possibly each kind of reader is to be transformed into a different kind of person—the sort of person the philosopher requires the reader to be if the philosophy is to reach him. So we have to realize that in reading Nietzsche we are being attacked; we need some kind of shield or the aphorism will *land* and we lose to the words. One way of fighting back *is* of course to treat him as a philosopher himself: the net, too, is a gladiatorial weapon in the skilled left hand of the *retarius*. So to cage him in a system of repressive categories, to put *his* toxin on ice, to slip the manacles of asceticism onto his wrists, to locate him in the history of thought, is like driving a stake through Nero's heart in order to keep his ghost stable. There is a tendency to divide commentators on Nietzsche into those who portray a hard Nietzsche and those who portray a soft Nietzsche. But it is possible to acknowledge him as hard by treating him as though he were soft. When Philippa Foot reviewed my book on him with a certain appreciation for the originality of treating him as a kind of linguistic epistemologist, and then raised the question of why, if this was what he was *au fond*, anyone would be especially interested in him any longer, I felt I had won a kind of victory: as though I had transformed him into a minotaur by devising a maze. But certainly there is a Nietzsche who genuinely stands against philosophy rather than illustrating it, and who is dangerous and even terrible: and in this paper I would like to acknowledge the virulent Nietzsche, not this time examining his views on language but his use of language: to see what he must have intended by this use and what his beliefs may have been for such intentions to have been coherent. This approach too is a way of standing aside and at a distance.

The psychology of metaphorical address is, since metaphor is a rhetorician's device, that the audience will itself supply the connection withheld by the metaphor, so that the rhetorician opens a kind of gap with the intention that the logical energies of his audience will arc it, with the consequence that having participated in the progression of argument, that audience convinces itself. There is another but comparable psychology for the aphorism, namely that once heard it is unlikely to pass from recollection, so its pointed terseness is a means of ensouling the message it carries, and to counteract the predictable deteriorations of memory. So it is a natural instrument for the moralist. The whole great second essay of the *Genealogy* is precisely addressed to the role of pain in the forging of a moral memory. *Forgetting* is a dimension of animal health, a requisite of mental hygiene—"no mere *vis inertiae* as the superficial imagine," Nietzsche writes, "It is rather an active and in the strictest sense positive faculty of repression." *Consciousness*, in which attention and memory or memorability coincide, is contrary to animal nature and possibly even a sort of disease—one of the discontents of civilization—a disturbance against which forgetfulness is a preserver of psychic order and peace: "It will be immediately obvious how there could be no happiness, no cheerfulness, no hope, no pride, no present, without forgetfulness." Nietzsche is speaking of what we might call deep forgetfulness here, a complete metabolization of experience rather than the repressive forgetfulness that Freud's later concept of the unconscious introduces into mental economy, where what is put there clamors to be made conscious and so is not *deeply* forgotten. In order, then, that this sustaining mental entropy should be arrested or reversed, some mnemonotechnic is required: as he puts it, "If something is to stay in the memory it must be burned in; only that which never ceases hurting stays in the memory." This, he continues, "is a main cause of the oldest (unhappily also the most enduring psychology on earth)." And, a moment later, "Man could never do without blood, torture, and sacrifices when he felt a need to create a memory for himself." Then, after a catalogue of medieval cruelties, he concludes, "All this has its origin in the instinct that realizes that pain is the most powerful aid to mnemonics." We still talk of teaching someone a lesson as a synonym for administrating a beating, we still say "this will learn you" as we land a punch. And we all admire Kafka's brilliant image in *The Penal Colony* where the inscription of the crime is the crime's punishment, since in the medium of the victim's agony. And, when one comes to it—as we shall in more detail—the entire office of religion has consisted in teaching us that our suffering has meaning, so that the chosen people spontaneously turn to its prophets to explain what lesson they are being taught through the suffering they have come to accept as the avenues of communication.

Nietzsche was too much the classicist not to know that aphorism and remembering are pragmatically co-implicated, or to be ignorant that the earliest collection of aphorisms was attributed to Hippocrates, and constituted a kind of *vade mecum* of medical praxeology, a body of maxims pointed and polished in order to stick in the intern's mind. Since aphoristic form is prophylactic against forgetfulness, and since pain is the prime reenforcer of retention, aphorism and pain are internally related, and so this form spontaneously presents itself to a writer whose warrior violence must be turned against those he appears to admire: the healthy forgetters, the innocent brutes. So when, in the second essay's discussion of the mnemonics of hurt, he writes, "in a certain sense the whole of asceticism lies here," he is being disingenuous when he inveighs against asceticism while using language specifically framed to scourge. Someone who uses ascetic practices to kill asceticism is engaged in a very complex communication, supposing he is coherent at all, and he would be right that we are missing what is taking place when we merely *read the words*. An apologist for paganism, for the happy instinctive unconscious life of the spontaneously unremembering beast, has no business creating a moral memory in the course of such apologetics, leaving a scar of consciousness against the easy viscosities of the mental life he celebrates: so the apology for paganism must itself be a moral stab, and self-conscious paganism is logically unlivable. So the remarks on paganism are *meant to hurt* in a way in which the memory of happiness becomes, in Dante's scale, the *maggiore dolore* in a general context of torment:

it is as though the entirety of the the *Genealogy* is a cell of inflictions and an instrument of asectic transformation—and a very rough book. "Even those who suppose, erroneously, that *Beyond Good and Evil* is a collection of aphorisms that may be read in any order whatever," Walter Kauffman wrote (meaning specifically me) "generally recognize that the *Genealogy* comprises three essays." This in his view brings the book closest to what we Anglo-American philosophers expect philosophical writing to be, all the more so in that "Nietzsche's manner is much more sober and single-minded than usual." But the manner of the essayist is a marvelous camouflage for the sort of moral terrorist Nietzsche really was, as the essay itself is a kind of literary camouflage for the sharpened stakes of aphorism he has concealed for the unwary, making this in a deep sense the most treacherous book he ever compiled, one almost impossible to read without being cut to ribbons ("flaying alive"). ("Cutting straps" is itemized in his inventory of ghastly interventions which at last instill "the kind of meaning by the aid of which one comes at last "to reason.") For how precisely is one to forget what he writes about Jews, slaves, justice, seriousness; about barbarism, morality itself, sensuality, torture, cruelty; about war, women, and will— even if the book also seems to provide passages of modulating analgesis, enabling him to say, soothingly, that he did not exactly mean what he said, enabling his commentators to reassure us that those who took him at his word had taken him out of context—as though he was after all just to be read. It is like saying the lace handkerchief is the context for the stiletto it hides, or the wine the context for the powdered glass, or the rose an extenuation of the thorn. A man cannot write this way and then stand back in mock innocence and point to the fine print, to the footnote, to the subtle conciliatory phrase written in all but invisible ink, or say that we were expected to be subtle enough to read between the lines: This book was not written for Nietzsche scholars, capable of handling even deadly poison with the long forceps of *Wissenschaft*. And often Nietzsche tells us as much. At the very beginning, for example, he talks about the English moral psychologists, whose interest for us in part lies in their having written uninteresting books, the question being what were they *doing* by writing such books—"What do they really want?—hoping we will be clever enough to ask that of this book, take the hint, raise the query why he wipes away with his left hand the blood he has drawn with his right: and not pretend that we are not bleeding or that it is our fault if we are. Just by printing on the package the warning against the contents, you have not provided prophylaxis. There is a passage in Wittgenstein in which he explains certain confusions about language as being due to "the uniform appearance of words when we hear them spoken or meet them in script or print." "It is like looking into the cabin of the locomotive," he goes on to say, "We see handles all looking more or less alike." But what shows a greater uniformity of appearance than *books*? *The Genealogy of Morals* is of about the shape and heft of *Utilitarianisms* or *Foundations of a Metaphysics of Morals*— or for that matter the *Imitation Christi*. But that does not mean that they are all to be treated the same say, or that reading is a uniform matter—"especially," as Wittgenstein writes, "when we are doing philosophy." To treat the *Genealogy* as though it were precocious analytical philosophy is to have swallowed the bait without having yet felt the hook. After all the subtitle is "Eine Streitschrifft." So *à la guerre comme à la guerre*: one had better study one's defenses!

In fact the *Geneaology* is in some ways the least analytical of Nietzsche's books, for all that it contains one of the subtlest discussions of moral predicates I know. For the question must be raised who the readers were to be, what was to bring them to this book, and what particularly were they to get from it? And this returns me to the Hippocratic model of the aphoristic collection. Such collections, our resources claim, were regarded as suitable for dealing with subjects to which no scientific or methodical treatment had been as yet successfully applied, such as, in particular, medicine. I want to claim that the *Genealogy* is in this respect a medical book: etiological, diagnostic, therapeutic, prognostic. I want to underscore *therapeutic* here, for the book is not so much for other practitioners of the caring art (and who would they be?) so much as it is for those who suffer from the diseases it addresses. So the assumption must be that the intended reader is sick, if typically in ways unrecognized by him: one learns the nature of one's illness as one reads the book. Part of the reason the aphorism is so suitable a form is that it has to get past the defenses we bring to the book, since the defenses are in a way part of the disease, as, in neurosis, according to the classic analysis, the repression of the pathogen is part of the pathogen. As in analysis, the therapist must bring to consciousness the mechanisms of disassociation and, if there is such a word, of disconsciation. So the reader is, as it were, being treated as he reads, and a condition of therapeutic success is that he be kept continuously conscious of the disorder the book means to drive out: as Hippocrates says, the practitioner is to be "seconded by the patient." And in a way the patient, or reader here, must be helped by the practitioner to cure himself. In a way, I suppose, there is an analogy to Socratic maieutic, here the point being that only the sufferer can solve the problem of his suffering, the doctor's role being simply to show him that he is sick. So the book has to be painful. And arguably the cure is more painful than the disease, with which, after all, we have grown comfortable.

It scarcely can pass notice how frequently and characteristically Nietzsche here employs the vocabularies of pathology (it would be an interesting scholarly enterprise to see the degree to which the same vocabularies occur in all the main books, or whether each book has its paradigm lexicon, from which the mode of literary address can then be inferred). The period of Nietzsche's great productivity was the great age of German physiology— Johannes Müller, Justus vön Leibig, Karl Ludwig, had made Germany the center for physiological investigation in the form it has had ever since, and though in no sense myself an historian of medicine, I am certain that a suitable scholarship would discover among their procedures certain ones which Nietzsche adapted, transforming them of course through his own special genius. It is still difficult, and it must in Nietzsche's time have been all but impossible, to draw a careful distinction between physiological and physiognomic differences, and not to suppose that a certain blue-eyed blondness might connote a physiological distinctiveness of some importance: or that shortness of stature might be a physiological defect. The physiologization of moral concepts, the proposal that in the end moral differences must be physiological differences, or that a certain physiognomic paradigm must be a paradigm of health, all other variants being sick, are among his most reckless and dangerous conjectures. But the shock of Darwinism was still being felt, and he was not immune to the moralization of natural selection that almost defines nineteenth century thought, which can lead to the view, as we know, that those with different moral beliefs may be contagious, ought to be segregated at least, and at worst may have to be eliminated in the interests of moral sepsis. And it can lead, in the other direction, to the view that those who are physiologically distinctive must fall under a different moral order and need not be treated the way we treat one another. I imagine that the great movements towards equal rights, equal no matter what one's age, sex, color, competence, or creed, constitute an effort to make physiological differences irrelevant to moral consideration. And while we must not be dismissive since, as Horace says, "art is long, life is short," and there will always be more to find out than we possibly can hope—no one knows whether criminality is chromosomal, or for that matter generosity genetic—it remains unclear how such discoveries should be responded to morally. It is also doubtful that reading a book of *this* sort could be regarded as a significant intervention if it turned out that a certain moral difference *were* a physiological one in that way. But neither would Nietzsche have supposed it were—so the question is what sort of disease could it have been for which he might have thought the book *was* significantly interventive? And here I can say perhaps most of what I have to say about this work.

I think the answer must lie in a distinction between what I shall term extensional suffering and intensional suffering, where the latter consists in an interpretation of the former. As I see Nietzsche's thesis, it is this: the main suffering human beings have throughout history been subject to is due to certain interpretive responses to the fact of extensional suffering. It is not clear that Nietzsche believes he can deal with extensional suffering. But he can deal with intensional suffering, thus helping reduce, often by a significant factor, the total suffering in the world. For while extensional suffering is bad enough, often it is many times compounded by our interpretations of it, which are often far worse than the disorder itself. Consider the example of impotence in the human male, which is in certain cases a physiological symptom of an underlying sickness with no clinical identity of its own: diabetes, prostate disorder, and the like. For most impotent men, and doubtless for most women sexually involved with them, it is a pretty appalling symptom. But to explain why it is refers us to the complex of ideas connected with the male's self-image of adequacy and power, and the extreme vulnerability sexual incapacity opens up. It can lead, it has led, to suicide, depression, despair, divorce. So if we subtracted all this suffering from the sum total of suffering, the actual symptom might not amount to very much in the scale of human agony. Compare it to the other symptoms of diabetes— polyuria, polydipsia, retinopathy, renal malfunction, circulatory problems, propensity to gangrene, susceptibility to fungus, to heart disease, acidosis, coma—and a flaccid penis seems pretty minor. But knowing the male temperament I am certain that this morally overcharged symptom would be singled out as the most intolerable effect of this disorder. Very few, I think, attach mush significance to the mere fact of hypoglycemia, or would commit suicide over that, or regard themselves as flawed—or sick. It is a good example of moralized physiology, but in any case the disorders addressed by Nietzsche in this book, and which it is his enterprise to help us cure ourselves of, are interpretations of suffering which themselves generate suffering.

They are due, one and all, to bad philosophy, bad psychology, religion—in Nietzsche's scheme "bad religion" would be redundant—and of course bad moral systems, such as the one which takes as its primary value-opposition the distinction between good and evil. All of these are in a way modalities of *schlechtes Gewissen*, as I shall persist in translating "bad consciousness." Bad *conscience*—in English usage at least—is more or less the same as guilty conscience, but guilt is only one of the modalities of badness. Bad consciousness is consciousness of badness, which of course may be illusory, as when someone good seems to himself, falsely, to be bad. Any suffering due to false moral beliefs about ourselves is due to bad consciousness, when there is nothing really bad about us *except* our consciousness of being bad. And the book might then in part be addressed specifically to curing this sort of suffering. Though at times Nietzsche speaks as though only the extensionally strong and healthy are subject to bad consciousness, in truth it is difficult to see how anyone in our civilization can have altogether escaped it: and even those who in his view really do suffer, really are in his sense "bad"—that is, bad specimens of the species *human*—typically also suffer from misinterpretations of his disorder, and no less than the good may for this reason be subject to bad consciousness. It is possible, of course, that Nietzsche's psychohistorical account is correct, and the particular form bad consciousness takes may be traced back to the pathogens of what he terms *ressentiment*, to which the extensionally bad are subject; even so they themselves suffer from the epidemics of bad consciousness which define the subsequent history of our civilization, i.e., not to be coy about it, from Chiristianity if he is right. So even the bad might profit from the reduction of this sort of intensional suffering, leaving extensional suffering to be treated by those whose specialty it is. After all identification of the real disease is the first step in medicine.

Let us attend, for a moment, to the concept of *ressentiment*. Nietzsche more or less assumed that anyone in a state of *ressentiment* must also be in some state or other, in his scheme, of actual physiological suffering. For what *ressentiment*—which is only distantly connected to the English word *resentment*—amounts to is a certain sort of interpretive explanation of suffering in the mind of the sufferer. In actual fact it would not matter if the suffering in question were real, i.e. physiological, or only believed to be real, as in cases of what used to be called hysteria. Nietzsche's point is put into what one might term an *a priori* of suffering: "Every sufferer instinctively seeks a cause for his suffering, more exactly an agent . . . some living thing upon which he can, on some pretext or other, vent his affects, actually or in effigy. For the venting of his affects represents the greatest attempt on the part of the sufferer to win relief—anesthesia—the narcotic he cannot help desiring to deaden pain of every kind." (127) This, which Nietzsche glosses as "the actual physiological cause of ressentiment, vengefulness, and the like," could easily have formed a section in the Hippocratic collection. The implication is clear: sufferers tend to *moralize* suffering by holding someone or something responsible for it: as though mere suffering, undeserved only in the sense that it makes no sense to speak of it as deserved, is simply unintelligible. "Why me, Lord?" is the spontaneous response to being stricken, "What did I do to deserve this?"—as though there were no unearned suffering, as it were, as though suffering were in every instance a *sentence* of some sort. "Someone or other must be to blame for my feeling ill," Nietzsche puts in the mind of the sufferer, a kind of reasoning "held the more firmly the more the real cause of their feeling ill, the physiological cause, remains hidden." And Nietzsche adds at this point a parade of medical opinion that reflects the state of knowledge of the time, or his state of knowledge, as well as the intention of the text:

> It may perhaps lie in some disease of the *nervous sympathicus*, or in an excessive secretion of bile, or in a deficiency of potassium sulfate and phosphate in the blood, or in an obstruction of the abdomen which impedes blood circulation, or in degeneration of the ovaries, and the like.

Readers of Nietzsche's letters appreciate the degree to which he was a dietary crank, but in any case, amateur diagnostics notwithstanding, it is perfectly plain that the disease he was addressing was not of the sort itemized here, but a metadisease which requires of the sufferer that his illness be, as Susan Sontag has phrased it, metaphorical. In any case, *ressentiment* consists in refeeling suffering as the *effect* of a *moral* cause one may also *resent* if one feels it is undeserved, as did Job, whose classic posture is exactly that of resentment in this form, since he can see no *reason* why God should be causing him to suffer. But even if he did feel he deserved the boils and losses, it would still be a case of *ressentiment* because he moralized his suffering.

Religion, save in the rather rare case of Job, abolishes all possibility of resentment, but it scarcely abolishes all possibility of *ressentiment*, since in fact it depends upon it for its existence: for what does religion do except to teach us that the suffering we endure we also deserve: religion redirects ressentiment, as Nietzsche puts it, by making the patient the very agent he seeks, informing us that we have brought it on ourselves. Consider the Black Death which swept Florence and Siena in the fourteenth century. Of course it was physiological, but men alive at that time had no way of knowing how: *b. plagus* was not an available concept. But they immediately assumed they were at fault (as they doubtless were in matters of elementary hygiene), chiefly through the arrogance displayed toward God in the treatment of human subjects in painting after Giotto! So the most rational thing, under prevailing theory, was to change the styles of representation, which have been traced for us by Millard Miess. I don't say this was wholly silly, and the consequence could be benign, as when an outbreak of some epidemic in Venice moved the governing body to commission a church from Palladio. True, this did not help any sufferers, but nothing they knew how to do would have done that anyway, and *Il Redentore* still stands. Religion, then, makes suffering intelligible—but only in the framework of a scheme which makes the search after its true causes unintelligible. And this is true even in those cases where we ourselves *have* brought on our own suffering, as in the case of gout or obesity, or venereal disease or cirrhosis of the liver or chronic drug addiction, for though these disorders are the consequences of, they are not *punishments* for, the excesses that led to them.

Interestingly, Nietzsche observes (73) "This plant blooms best today among the anarchists and the Antisemites." That is, blaming the Jews, or blaming the bourgeoisie, for all social ills, rather than looking more deeply into the social structure for etiology, parallels the classic forms of the *a priori* of affect. Admittedly, we may know as much about what affects society as Florentines knew in the *cinquecento* about what affects the human body, and often in our ignorance we attack as cause what may be only another effect. I tend to think that certain feminist accounts, in which men (*qua* men) are blamed for the suffering of women (*qua* women), must ultimately yield to a finer analysis in which what is considered the cause is itself a symptom of the same sickness. I have often *also* thought no better specimen of *schlechtes Gewissen* can be found than the sort of self-castigation shown by men, say in the weekly column "For Men" in the *New York Times Magazine*, where men boast of their degree of feminization. I have no criticism of this, and nothing but criticism of its opposite, where men vaunt the paraphernalia of *machismo*: but it is a good illustration of self-despising, as Nietzsche uses the term in his moral psychology. Nietzsche condenses his general insight in one of his profoundest aphorisms: "What really arouses indignation against suffering is not suffering as such but the senselessness of suffering." And if there is any single moral/metaphysical teaching I would ascribe to him, it would be this: suffering really is meaningless, there is no point to it, and the amount of suffering caused by *giving* it a meaning chills the blood to contemplate.

I of course am not talking about suffering we cause under the name of punishment, where some complex balance must be struck between the suffering caused by the culprit and the suffering the culprit must undergo in order to restore equilibrium. That is a model of justice that must be debated on grounds other than any I want to advance here. What Nietzsche objects to is not so much this model but its total generalization, making *all* suffering punitive and the entire *world* a court of justice with a penitentiary annex. If I am right that this is his view, the final aphorism of the *Genealogy*, "Man would rather will nothing than not will," does not so much heroize mankind, after all: what it does is restate the instinct of *ressentiment*: man would rather his suffering be meaningful, hence would rather will meaning into it, than acquiesce in the meaninglessness of it. It goes against this instinct to believe, what is essentially the most liberating thought imaginable, that life is without meaning. In a way, the deep affliction from which he seeks to relieve us is what today we think of as hermeneutics: the method of interpretation primarily of suffering. And when he says, in so many places and in so many ways "there are no facts, only interpretation," he is, I believe, finally addressing the deep, perhaps ineradicable propensity for *ressentiment*. Meaning, si je puis aphoriser moi-même, is demeaning.

There is an obverse, which is that to accept the consolations of religion, the dubious gift of meaning, as it were, one must accept the anthropology which alone makes religion applicable in the first place, namely that we are weak, defective, and almost defined through our propensity to suffer. The limits of man are such that we are unable to release ourselves save through the mediation of a being whose power is adequate to the salvation. Of course, with religions in general, salvation is often revealed through suffering. Who would know we were contaminated by original sin, for instance, that we needed to be saved from it, and that this might be achieved if God took on a form whereby he might purge our suffering through his? Leaving life as it was, since the suffering we were told was ours was not felt, and the redemption we have been given does not release us from any felt suffering. And the limits are finally limits only relative to the scheme of suffering and relief erected alongside the actual human agonies and joys the scheme itself does not penetrate. Whatever the case, the picture of man as limited and weak goes hand in hand with exactly *schlechtes Gewissen* if believed. And to release us from that is to release us from the picture: and that is the therapeutic task of the *Genealogy*, and of Nietzsche's philosophical work as such.

Let me return to hermeneutics. I would concede to the continental theorists that it is the fundamental fact of human being, and hence must be the final datum for the human sciences, that men cannot experience without interpreting, and that we live in a world of intersignification. I am far from certain that the human sciences must themselves reflect the structure of their subject, that science itself is only a form of interpretation, of a piece with the interpretations it is supposed to study: hence I am far from certain that there is a hermeneutical circle which somehow invalidates such a science: for there may be ways of representing interpretations which are not at all of a piece with the interpretations represented. Even so, we may accept the hermeneutical picture that our *esse est interpretare*. But then the contrast must be perfect between ourselves and the *Bestie*, and it is less their cheerful innocent savagery that Nietzsche applauds in the blond beasts than their absolute freedom from meaning. They live, as he says in his early book on history, as beasts do, "in a happy blindness between the walls of the past and the future." Human existence, by deep contrast, is "an imperfect tense that never becomes a present." It is not so much history as the philosophy of history that robs life of happiness, since the latter seeks perennially the significance of events it would be happiness instead merely to forget or, next best, to take as they came, at a kind of absolute magnitude, without forming a kind of text. Nietzsche's doctrine of eternal recurrence, itself the topic of so much speculation and scholarship, must be perceived by everyone, however otherwise divided on its cognitive status, as deeply contrary to any philosophy of history: iteration dissolves meaning, and infinite iteration erases it totally. It is a rock against which history as significance must shatter, and in particular religious history, the history of fall, covenant, sin, redemption, trial, judgment, and hell, where it is an unrelieved anxiety about where we stand and what we can hope.

When Zarathustra announces the death of God, he goes on to say he died of pity. The implication is that what he pitied us for was him: pitied us for the hopeless disporportion between a being of infinite value and his creatures who must in comparison to him be incalculably worthless. By disappearing, the ratio is broken and the disvalue which depended upon the disporportion itself vanishes. It is a beautiful gift, that of disappearance: which of the parents among us is capable of it? By comparison, sacrificing even only begotten sons is easy: our world is full of gold star mothers and fathers, proud of their distinction. With the death of God we are returned to what Kundera speaks of, alas as unbearable, a certain lightness of being.

It is plain that God did not die that something else should take His place: rather, He meant for the place to die with the occupant. The genius of the third essay of the *Genealogy* lies in its inventory of the disguises the ascetic ideal takes, so that often positions which define themselves as contrary to asceticism only exemplify it. As a class, these occupants of the position vacated by God impose on their subscribers a network of interpretation of suffering and project a kind of utopian redemption: science, politics, art, and certainly much that passes for psychological therapy, only change the name of the game. There are even ways of understanding the notorious concept of the superman which vest the same demeaning armature that Christianity did, another disguise of asceticism. But this could not be Nietzsche's superman if he has the least consistency. The superman does not reside in a kind of *beyond* since it is precisely that *kind* of 'Beyond' Nietzsche is bent on stultifying. The man of the future, he writes as the end of the second essay is "this bell-stroke of man and the great decision that liberates the will again and restores its goal to earth and his hope to man."

I return to the aphorism I began by interpreting. The *unconcern* that wisdom is supposed to love clearly is associated with the will. It is an unconcern with goals that impose a program of choices on life, which depend on schemes of meaning it is the goal of Nietzsche's philosophy to demolish. It is not so much the extirpation of the will as its re-education and redirection: its return to the goals of simply normal life. Nietzsche's philosophical mood is one of lightness, cheer, sunniness, which was also his personal mood, heroic in view of his familiar sufferings. He complains of terrible headaches, nausea, stomachache: he was afflicted by the cold, the damp, bad food, and of course a sense of isolation and unrecognition. He sought like a cat a comfortable corner of Europe, and his preposterous exultation at discovering the alleged salubrities of Turin are an index to his discomforts. He did not suffer, however, in the way in which, on his view, the bulk of mankind suffers: from meanings which truncate the lives they are supposed to redeem. When we contemplate the sufferings human beings have endured in the century since God made the supreme sacrifice, we wonder at the wisdom of that evacuation. If we were to subtract all the intensional suffering from the history of our century, we would subtract the history of the century.

But that is what he would like to have achieved: to subtract all those schemes of disvaluation of the present by reference to an inflated valuation of a future: to make the world the place we live rather than pass through to some higher state: to restore the present to the present: to replace a morality of means with a morality of principle: to act in such a way as to be consistent with acting that way eternally: to stultify the instinct for significance. This is the posture of unconcern, and while it is unclear that it would make us altogether happy, it is perfectly plain that it erases most of what has made for human unhappiness through history: the martyrdoms, the crucifixions, the eggs cracked in the name of political omelettes, man as a means. Not surprisingly it is the only view consistent with human dignity: of man as an end.

An earlier version of this essay appeared in *International Studies in Philosophy* 18 (Summer 1986).

Nietzsche's Critique of Morality

FRITHJOF BERGMANN

Nietzsche's most brilliant and sustained critique of morality is contained in his long essay describing the origin of two juxtaposed types: the master and the slave moralities. In that essay Nietzsche raises a question, not mildly, or in quietly bemused philosophical wonder, but in outrage, and consternation, in an effort to ring a storm-bell and to wake us up. He asks: how was it ever possible for meekness, humility and self-denial, modesty, pity and compassion to become *values*? What happened? For it is weird and monstrous and dumbfounding, and precisely the kind of unnatural untowardness that cries out for an explanation.

The question is not: why do so many feign modesty to hide their arrogance, or make a show of pity while they gloat with malice? Pretense and hypocrisy are not the issue. That query would be mild and common and would still reconfirm and bow before these values. And exactly that is what Nietzsche wants to undercut and to deny. The question, rather, is: how can one fathom or imagine the process through which these qualities were elevated into values? How were they placed upon this pedestal—since on the face of it they so clearly have no claim to this status?

In effect Nietzsche responds with a story. He, himself, provides much evidence for it and insists on its truth, but it also has a mythic quality, and we might begin by reading it in this fashion. Very early, in primordial times, the prevailing morality was created by those whom Nietzsche provocatively calls the "masters." Their morality could not have been more direct and straightforward: Human beings were evaluated very naturally like all other things. There were desirable attributes: health, strength, physical or sexual attractiveness, but also talents and gifts of every sort: wit, imagination, as well as cunning, the capacity to sustain passion, and beyond this toughness and endurance, and much more. In

29

the beginning the word "good" simply stood for these traits; it was no more than a generic summary, or a spontaneous exclamation. For those who possessed these qualities the word "good" signified the joy and pride and happiness of their possession; it reflected back to them the qualities in which they took delight. And the word "bad"—the initial antipode—was also no more than the naturally expected other half, or even less: a lame afterthought. "Bad" expressed the lack, the absence of these excellencies. It therefore was always mixed with a sense of regret, of deprivation, of everybody being poorer on account of that deficiency.

With this in place, Nietzsche envisions the story of a protracted struggle. Nietzsche's "slaves"—he again uses the word provocatively and in his own way—are not the members of a lower disenfranchised class, nor are they in any obvious way an oppressed group or people. Instead they are the collectivity of the untalented and ungifted—poor in stamina and health, poor in energy, vitality and spirit, poor in physical or sexual attractiveness—the wretched, the dregs, those who are weary because they are a constant burden to themselves. They, who, imprisoned in their inferiority, raged for a long time against the dullness and joyless-ness of their lives, eventually made war against the fortunate, against those blessed by nature. The match was of course hopeless, and nothing availed. Finally, when all the strategies and last devices of the slaves had been exhausted, then—and this is the crux of Nietzsche's story—the slaves at last had recourse to their final weapon: they inverted the up-till-then existing values: in a mad gamble they poisoned "the very springs of life." They made a sudden turn against their own envy and performed an act of exorcism: what they had thus far desperately craved, they now pronounced to be "evil." This is how the concept of evil was conceived. It is not parallel to, but instead juxtaposed to the original "bad," for it designates the very attributes that had so far been "good." (Pride that had been "good" now becomes "evil.") It is also different in connotation: gone is the sense of loss—and in its place stands what Nietzsche associates with the fantasy of "extirpation." Similarly with "good." The concept "good" is also the result of a crossing-over, or of a turning upside down: it was created when the slaves made peace with their own failures and inadequacies, when they sanctified them and pronounced them "good."

In the story lies Nietzsche's answer to his starting question. This is how meekness, and humility, and modesty, and the denial of the flesh were first made into virtues: it was through a great act of deception, through a Trojan horse trick of the disadvantaged!

The account we have just given could be a paraphrase of a typical surface reading of this famous passage. That reading makes it small wonder that many are swept off their feet by Nietzsche but then after a week or a semester seem to collect themselves, and then grow calm and cynical and even sad. For a brief span a door seems to open into another much more brightly lit room, but soon, disillusioned, they slip back again into the grey reality of ordinary life.

The ease with which Nietzsche's attack on morality can be dodged, or parried, if one reads him only to this depth, throws light on how and why this disappointment happens. Consider, as a sampling, the force of three rejoinders: first, and only on the side: is the account of the primordial morality at all convincing? Do the moralities we find in early cultures, with their endlessly complex and particular restrictions, at all resemble the morality of Nietzsche's masters? And if not, does this not deprive Nietzsche's slave rebellion of both its object and its motive? Must we not first believe in the rule of Nietzsche's masters—i.e. in the rule of the favored and the gifted—before the plausibility of his moral *coup d'état* can be accepted?

This could be followed up with the objection that the origin of all cultural phenomena has no bearing whatsoever on their eventual function, use, or value—a consideration that Nietzsche himself reiterated and underscored in a spate of different contexts. But even apart from that, does Nietzsche really go beyond turning the old proposition that Thrasymachus already advanced upside down; for did not Thrasymachus insist that morality was "the invention of the strong," designed to make the weak more pliable and more obedient to their will? And is not Nietzsche's claim only that it was the other way around: that morality was the creation of the inferior and the weak? Granted, Nietzsche's version is more tantalizing and intriguing; still it is surely inconclusive. But even more important, is it not in any case only one more tale of our early history, that leaves the much more serious and urgent task undone: namely that of assessment and ajudication? For even if a set of moral precepts had been invented by the slaves, this tells us nothing about their truth or their legitimacy. To suppose that it does clearly perpetrates the genetic fallacy.

This prepares the third and probably most powerful retort: if morality was indeed conceived by those who are more frail and weak—then honor and congratulations to them! Is it not precisely the essential purpose of morality to provide some safeguard and protection for the disadvantaged, and did the so-called slaves in this case not undertake exactly what was needed: precisely what one would wish and recommend they do?

This brings us back to the reaction that many have to Nietzsche after the first overwhelming rush has passed. Is this not why they grow disillusioned and resigned after a brief fling with hope? To believe in the sheer delight of spirited vitality would of course be splendid. Who would not be tempted and seduced by it? But not, unfortunately, in this harsh and struggling world: here we need a moral code that restrains the powerful, and imposes justice and control. The fantasy of Nietzsche's early master-values becomes, therefore, no more than a brief delicious sigh. Regardless of who conceived the invention, traditional values are the values which we in the end require, and we and Nietzsche must therefore part.

It might be best to think of what we have so far said as no more than a curtain-raiser, as a grotesque and clownish Punch and Judy opening diversion, and therefore to begin once more with a quite different new approach.

What if in much of our thinking we made a truly massive and at the same time crude mistake? What if our blithe presumption that all cultures do have *some* morality, and perhaps even a morality similar to our own, was palpably mistaken? And what if this were so, not mainly because the surface of the codes of other cultures is vastly more variegated than we currently assume, but for much more serious and deeply weighing reasons? What if the understructure of the codes of other cultures was radically different from the foundations that support morality, and what if that difference was so great that these other codes were not other versions of morality, but fell outside of that domain and were not moralities at all?

One suggestive indication that this may be the case is that in a great span of various cultures (including, for instance, the Balinese) even the most appalling and serious transgressions—the violation of the incest taboo, for example—provoke a reaction and a judgment that is radically different in its *quality* from anything to which we are accustomed. Even such outrageous violations are interpreted as what we might call "stupidities." This has nothing at all to do with the greater mildness or permissiveness, or with the sweeter temper, of these cultures. Transgressions are categorized as "stupidities" because the understructure of the presupposed conceptions is astonishingly different from the one we take for granted.

The idea of freedom, for instance, in anything resembling the form to which we are accustomed, simply is not known, and not just in deeply different, or much less developed cultures, but even in very highly advanced and by some measures relatively closely related cultures, for example, in the Chinese culture or in that of Japan.

As a correlate to that we also find that anything like our conception of responsibility is missing, the idea of guilt in our sense is also absent. Yet it cuts deeper still: for it seems reasonable to suppose that the cluster of concepts mentioned so far could have a common root, or an underlying set of shared presumptions. It also seems plausible that this would be a very basic preconception, so the idea of a self that is independent, and circumscribed, and marked off against nature seems a likely candidate.

However, even this idea does not yet capture the deepest and most crucial root, for still more fundamental is the sense of agency, of being capable of initiating and generating genuine actions. And, indeed, there seems to be overwhelming evidence that this deep-rooted premise is either absent, or at least very different, in the host of cultures that we are discussing.

It should be upsetting to us that on this very deep-seated level our standard accepted view of the self is not at all obviously defensible or rational. On the contrary, the general posture that a human being is not an anomaly in nature but is an integral part of it seems more secular and up to date than our view. This is so in part because this assumption accompanies the conviction that the flow of causally linked events runs *through* a human being, as it does through all other things, while the notion that causality is somehow brought to a standstill at the moat surrounding a human being, so that inside that individual a truly autonomous action can be generated, surely does not seem self-evident.

The iceberg tip that betrays the presence of the underlying conceptualizations we are suggesting is the fact that even heinous transgressions are interpreted as mere "stupidities." Further proof of this is that what appears to us as "punishment" is very differently comprehended in the categories of these other cultures. Since the human being is not delimited from or juxtaposed to nature, but is regarded in these cultures as engulfed by it, a misdeed or transgression is understood as an act that disrupts *nature*. An offense, even an offense like incest, is thus analogous to a violation of the natural order—much more serious, but in principle a "stupidity," like forgetting to drain the pipes before the temperature falls below zero or getting all one's wedges stuck in the piece of wood one wants to split. True, a rectifying action is required in both cases after the transgression has occurred, but the demanded actions have radically different meanings: In one system the performances brought on by the transgression are meant to punish, or to equalize the moral balance that has been upset; in most early cultures they are meant to restore again the natural harmony, or the natural lawfulness that has been disturbed. (Cf. *even* Oedipus Rex.)

The transgressing act itself is also understood in two quite different and parallel ways: in many early cultures it is very much less "*a deed*" decided upon by a perpetrator, than an event brought into the world by an agency almost divine. It is thought that once a certain configuration of circumstances has taken shape, the occurrence of the act has become next to inevitable. It is as if the act from then on circled high above the village, like a large black bird searching for the agent on whose hut it will alight. The perpetrator thus is seen as suffering almost a mishap. It was he that was chosen by the act, and thereby became its instrument. We abbreviate this and translate it into our system in the idea of "fate."

One way of bringing this part of the discussion to summation would be to introduce, as a main distinction, the division between the "content" and the "modality" of a certain code. One could then say that the apparatus of agency, selfhood, freedom, responsibility, blame, and guilt furnished the accouterments for the modality to which we are accustomed, while the codes of other cultures present themselves in a modality that is fundamentally distinct. In these terms the pratfall error we have much of the time committed is to have mistaken the superficial sameness in two radically different kinds of codes for a complete identity. True, the same actions are proscribed in both situations. But this may be no more than the most cursory of resemblances. If anything, the terms "content" and "modality" may still *understate* the thinness of this similarity and downplay the disparity involved. Perhaps one should say that it is only a sameness of the sign: A land-surveyor and a priest can both make a cross, but the difference between the modalities is as large and deep as the difference between the two meanings that these crosses would convey.

The articulation of this distinction leads to quite a different perception of the larger landscape in which we have lived. For it now seems plausible to propose that morality, in a more specific and serious sense, should be identified with the presence of the configuration which on the surface includes notions like freedom, responsibility, blame, and guilt and, on a deeper level, selfhood and agency. And, on the other hand, it is to suggest that there are a great diversity of other action-guiding or person-judging codes which are *not* moralities in that stricter sense.

A further corollary—and one indispensable for Nietzsche—is the explicit acknowledgment that one certainly can have values, and assess and rank and discriminate with them, without having a morality: To have a morality one must have a code in the one quite particular modality we have described.

I want to emphasize that this, from one angle, is a stipulation, but that from another it merely sharpens an understanding we already have. For example, when A. S. Neill, in his much discussed book *Summerhill*, wrote that he will "never use morality on a child," he invokes the same distinction that we have just drawn. And his book throws light on Nietzsche—perhaps all the more because Neill was not influenced by him. Neill explains that it is far better to confront a child with one's own will and individual person and to say: "I will not let you pound nails into this piano, because it is my piano, and because I love it" rather than: "This is *wrong*; this is something that a child *ought* not to do," for that in effect puts the entire normal and obedient world on one side, and the solitary child on the other, and it overwhelms the child with a disproportionately great authority. Again, in therapy—especially marriage counseling—the therapist might easily say that nothing hopeful can begin until the two partners together abandon the moral tug-of-war over who is responsible and who should bear the guilt, and that both must begin to think in terms of what they want and need to do. In the framework that we have begun to describe, this would be equivalent to leaving morality—i.e., the code couched in that modality—behind.

If morality is now indeed only one very specialized and peculiar modality in which codes can be cast, and if, in fact, it is a modality that may be relatively rare and idiosyncratic, then on the crudest but nonetheless most important level this means that the alternative to it is neither chaos, nor nihilism, nor the complete abandonment of values. Far from it. One may decide that other ways of holding values are less problematic, or less mystifying, or less apt to lead to self-deception, and then choose those. The fear that morality alone stands between us and apocalypse, which for many is the final thunderous word that sends them back into the moral fold, is thus quite unjustified.

It should go without saying that Nietzsche himself did not use the terminology of "content" and "modality" and that he did not even, in so many words, draw the distinction we have just articulated. But at the same time it is a fact that he pronounced all *moral* facts to be fantasies and hallucinations, and that he was far from doing this just once, or in rare and isolated places. Also, he did designate himself an *immoralist*, and there are moreover a great many different passages in which he writes, for instance, that the "thou shalt" should be abolished in favor of the "I will," or that one should not say either "wrong" or "evil" but should instead confine oneself to words like "weak," "ill," or "foolish."

This, and a great deal more, indicates that the distinction is actually present in Nietzsche's writings, though it stays just below the fully stated surface. Cutting through the skin and bringing it out into the open seems terribly important, for even the most basic outlines of Nietzsche's intellectual enterprise cannot be seen unless that demarcation is first firmly in place. On one side, it establishes that Nietzsche did not only attack Christian morality but all morality "as such." But very much more important is the other side: namely, that other values, or ways of encoding values, are vigorously split off from the modality that makes them "moral."

That is central, for without it one could suppose that Nietzsche meant that *all* values are fantasies, or unreal, or unfounded. This is not only what Nietzsche flagrantly did *not* think—it literally inverts the basic thrust of his work until it points in the exact opposite direction from what he intended. To undermine, or erode, or otherwise derogate the reality of values was not his purpose. It was the other way around: he believed that the moral way of holding values was losing its credibility and foundation (that is part of the significance of "the death of God"), and he felt horror at the thought that many would confuse this decay with a decline of the totality of values. For that disintegration and dissolution Nietzsche used the word "nihilism." And to warn against it, to stave off its arrival, and to ring the alarm for those who were still sleeping was probably his most all-consuming and all-demanding mission. He attacked morality because it threatened to pull the rest of values down with it. More than anything, morality needed to be severed and pushed aside, so that one could redeem and salvage the other values (or the ways of holding values) that it had overlain and nearly killed.

The overall picture of the isolatedness and downright strangeness of morality makes it natural to ask how its surprising appearance is to be explained. If we emphasize sufficiently that the crucial understructure on which morality depends is indeed absent in most other cultures, and that the surface markings of guilt and freedom and responsibility are also missing, and that this is maybe even truer for the most radical and indispensable precondition, namely the idea of a segregated and autonomously acting self—then the proposition that the belief not just in monotheism, but in a very special monotheism in which the divinity lays down ultimate and personal commands and jealously supervises obedience to them, was the decisive cause has considerable plausibility and force. It appears that the two do seem to complement each other: if anything could produce the unobvious and even counterintuitive notion that the individual person is autonomous and isolated, then it would be the image—or the nightmare—that the creature which made the galaxies would focus its whole glance solely and entirely on us. Could anything *less* than the fantasy of this isolation—where the storm of that glance would strip us naked, and we would stand totally alone and be confronted—have this effect?

This now places us in the position to take the evident next step. For even the vaguest popular thinking affirms that there is some relationship between morality and the belief in God. And it is certainly not debatable that Nietzsche felt strongly that this connection did exist—for in fact, this is presupposed by Nietzsche's single most widely publicized conviction, namely that the still occurring "death of God" would erode and undermine morality. But we can now clarify the seriousness of that link. Popularly one imagines that the sudden disappearance of the threat of punishment and of the lure of reward will endanger the force and guiding-power of morality. In contrast to this we can now say that the dependency is a great deal deeper and more intimate. In effect, one can now maintain that the entire coterie of concepts that articulate morality are in the same position as that in which common agreement places the idea of "sin." A sin is not just an injudicious or otherwise mistaken action—strictly speaking, it is by definition nothing other than the transgression of a commandment pronounced by God. It follows that one's belief in "sins" therefore has to be abandoned together with one's faith in God. Naturally, an act can still be a transgression in numerous other ways, but it cannot be a "sin." One can suggest that the same is true for "guilt," and moreover that this is by no means merely a matter of degree. The point is not that a very similar but milder or toned down condemnation can still be pronounced. The guilt that followed the violation of one of God's commandments was not merely a few notches worse than the guilt resulting from the violation of either a Roman civic or ritual law or the codes of early cultures. The guilt that ensued if one offended God was not on the same continuum. It was highly defined and specific, and it was possible only in the web of quite particular stories and ideas. One could pursue this further and insist that the same is true for the ideas of "freedom" and "responsibility."

One major component of the moral modality that so far we have not mentioned is the powerful egalitarian element. Part of what makes a code moral, in our eyes, is the fact that it judges us *equally* as *equal* human persons. This quality, too, is much more extraordinary and problematic then we customarily suppose. One could say that it involves, on one side, the leaving behind of codes that address merely one demarcated segment of a human being—that judge him, for example, only as a fisherman, or a hunter, or a warrior—but that it, on the other side, also requires that one has relinquished the conception that all human beings remain encompassed and enwebbed in the flow of merely natural events. Again one could propose that this idea of equality, which was foreign even to the Greeks, in which we are not just a member of this or that tribe, but are instead a member of the "family of humankind," is directly tied to the conception of a single and moral God: one could suggest that the conception of equality which morality presupposes originated only in the conviction that we are all equal in His eyes and are all equally His children. (This last idea, that a code in the modality of the moral judges us as *persons*, and that this is anything but innocuous and marginal, but on the contrary rare, and that it is also highly problematic, I developed in much more detail in "The Modality of Moral Codes," unpublished.)

This points to one of the more critical implications which this train of thought has for contemporary philosophic ethics. For the contention is not merely that the belief in monotheism was instrumental in the genesis and development of the family of concepts forming the understructure of the modality of the moral. The claim is that the connection is *conceptual*, that the full meaning of any of these terms—of "guilt", but also of "responsible" (in the moral sense), but also of "morally wrong" or "evil" and all the rest—cannot be captured or restated if one separates them off the belief in God. Strictly speaking they are part of a *theological* language which cannot be secularized!

Though in this essay I cannot develop this argument in the detail that is required, one first step towards a clarification would be to assert that all kinds of reasons for either the laudibility or the inadvisability of an action can be given, but it is far from evident why being either a Kantian or a Utilitarian—or holding any other *secular* position—would entitle one to use words like "guilty" or "immoral" or justify their use. A further articulation of this—which seems relatively uncontroversial— would be the idea that the secular re-embodiments of this originally divinely ordained code have no claim to the reverence, or *"weight,"* or *force* of reprobation that attached to that earlier code. But the claim is actually stronger, for what is in question is the entire context, and not just one of degree, as I indicated before. The transplantation of phrases like "morally wrong" or "morally guilty" from their deep theological ground into the enlightened greenhouse soil of the eighteenth century creates an unworkable ambivalence: one invokes the biblical terror and power of these conceptions without being prepared to pay the price in theological commitments that alone would justify it.

This last point raises an issue that is something of a philosophical scandal: the disproportion between the formidable precision with which extended and derivative questions in ethics are now discussed, and our embarrassment and innocence about the arguably more elementary and decisive question, namely, how does one distinguish the entire domain of the moral from its surroundings? Neither the Kantian nor the Utilitarian tradition has significantly advanced towards specifying the types of actions to which the respective criteria are to be applied. Instead we flounder and slide with an astonishing nonchalance: Sometimes we speak of ethics as teaching us "how to live," which gives the impression of a very large, almost borderless domain, but at other times we presume that full-fledged and genuinely *moral* decisions are called for only on very distinctive and quite rare occasions.

That equivocation is of the greatest possible importance if one is to grasp even the main outlines of Nietzsche's thinking. One way to bring this to light is to focus on an area in our culture, the sexual realm, which for many is still the very paradigm of the realm of the moral, whereas to others it is clearly not, as the use of expressions like "sexual *preference*" implies. Similarly, to some the use of certain words is still *morally* offensive, while others would shake their heads in amazement at the thought that such old-fashioned prudery could still exist. And of course there are circumstances in which many people would not consider a lie an immoral offense; even in cases of murder, there is disagreement. The fact that there are conflicts here is undeniable, which rules out an appeal to shared intuitions as a way out of this dilemma. But how then is it be settled?

For Nietzsche this unclarity assumes a fearful significance, for it portends the nemesis, nihilism. Why should nihilism announce its arrival with theatrical aplomb? Why should it not make its appearance in a drab or genteel costume? And could not the appearance of nihilism in that guise be hastened by shifting the *level* of the disagreement so that whole areas of experience are simply peremptorily exempted from the realm of the moral? From Nietzsche's point of view, it is most tempting to have the best of both worlds cheaply: one decorates oneself with the accoutrements of a severe and still intact morality, but one picks and chooses opportunistically the contexts in which one allows these moral values to apply. What Nietzsche foresees is the possibility of continuing to be engaged with the formalities of morality—still passing the beads of the rosary through one's hands—while one in fact by gradual degrees has exempted successively all areas to which it was applicable—till *none* are left! The relic of morality will still be in place, while in practice "everything will be permitted."

In more narrowly philosophic terms one could observe that the theoretical difficulty which we experience in delineating this distinction at least partially confirms the larger claim we were suggesting. For if the demarcation of the domain of the moral from the areas to which morality does not apply was originally accomplished by God in the list of His commandments, then the difficulty we now have with fixing and justifying that distinction has, at any rate, an explanation. (The same could be suggested for the "universalizing" of the moral: if it represents an attempt to translate equality before God into secular terms, then the nagging dissatisfactions with its various formulations are not surprising.)

If we narrow the focus more specifically to the interpretation of Nietzsche, we could stress that Nietzsche's works contain an extraordinarily diverse and ramified critique of the separate concepts which together form (in our terms) the understructure of the moral code. One randomly picked example would be Nietzsche's dissections of the ideas of "blaming" and of "someone's *deserving* punishment" and, in conjunction with this, his exposure of the sophistries which surround the ideas of "free will" and of "responsibility." Here Nietzsche frequently suggests that behind these disguises often hides a sadism that wants to cling to its own innocence. Our conception of the single modality of the moral subsumes and integrates these widely dispersed fragments into the coherent intellectual enterprise of the critique of that modality. Among other things this means that the desecration of the master into the slave morality involves the transposition of not just the content but of the modality into the moral mode (as indicated by the arrival of the idea of "evil").

But perhaps more important for one's general view of Nietzsche, introducing the conception of the modality of the moral makes it possible to refute the oft-repeated notion that Nietzsche urged the "naturalization of the ethical," a seriously misleading understatement. It would be more correct to say that Nietzsche wanted to abolish the strictly moral, and that he wanted to put a set of purely natural codes into its place. To put this another way: Nietzsche did not think that the privileged status—together with the greater dignity and weight—that we still assign (from earlier religious habit) to the moral could be rationally justified. In his view such excessive significance required the manipulation of figments and imaginings (in many different contexts he wrote that there are no *moral* facts), for not only God, but the entire tribe of concepts that buttress the modality of the moral are in his judgment made of delusional and treacherous stuff. The additional claim which they support should therefore be surrendered, and all values should be treated on one and the same natural plane. So the distinction between the moral and the rest is rejected, but the "reality" or "viability" or "seriousness" of other values is not just asserted; it is extolled and celebrated.

Of course, Nietzsche's allegation was not just that rational reconstructions of morality are philosophically unjustified. He believed that the last-ditch defense of that modality, after its life-giving center (namely the belief in God) had lost its hold, represented a cultural peril and calamity. Not that the modality of the moral had not at some point served important purposes. The overweening force which it attached to some few principles no doubt imposed the kind of discipline and uniformity, and maybe the kind of "leveling," that helped to bring us out of an earlier, more inchoate state. (Recall the many passages in which Nietzsche describes the harsh and age-long cultural pedagogy that finally brought us to the point where we had learned to predict our own behavior well enough that we could meaningfully make a promise.) But not precisely that disproportionate and unequalled force adds to the threat and the danger which it now embodies—and in several distinctive ways.

To begin with there is the "complementary *de*-evaluation." The force of morality was so great that by contrast all other values became unreal and flimsy and "subjective." (Possibly this is when "taste" for the first time became *only* taste.) But one could also say that the glare of morality produced a "snowblindness." Those who grew accustomed to its fire now cannot see the subtler and more nuanced values that lie outside its sphere. But worse: formerly the belief in God fixed both the content *and* the domain of the moral, while—as we just saw—without that anchor this domain now shifts and floats. From Nietzsche's perspective this means that a cultural instrument of enormous weight hangs from the ceiling like a wrecking-ball—and the path it will swing and the place it will strike cannot be controlled.

Proof of this precariousness, for instance, is the fact that many regard nearly all of politics as a matter of morality, while others have resigned themselves to the impracticality of doing so, or dismiss it with weariness and cynicism. Many again exempt business conduct from moral standards in the same way. (Try arguing with an executive that a new labor policy would clearly be more "moral," even though it would reduce his profits by one third!)

Without a firm agreement on the areas to which morality applies vituperative accusations are flung back and forth to no avail. One danger of this, in Nietzsche's mind, is that many will be offended by the clumsy and pathetic spectacle and will *mistakenly* assume that the disputes surrounding the other modalities of value operate on the same low plane, and in this way they too will slip slowly down into the slime of nihilism which Nietzsche so intensely dreaded.

We cannot grasp the import of this critique of the moral unless we have a fuller and more vivid sense of what nonmoral codes are like. Here it is extraordinarily important to understand that these are not exotic or unusual or strange—and that they are emphatically not peculiar to cultures which are "early," let alone "primitive." On the contrary, these codes are common and mundane, and indefinitely numerous. That few things are more common in our culture than opting out and withdrawing from morality exemplifies this. Typically, many scientists, who are understandably much lampooned, throw up their hands when they are asked to take "responsibility" for the consequences their research might produce. In the context we have established it is possible to respond to this not just with righteous censoriousness, but to see in it a reflection of the problematic nature of the concept of "*moral* responsibility," and by extension of the modality of moral codes. (Could one suggest that in this instance something approaching divine omniscience would be required to accept "responsibility" in earnest—and that this is how the theological origin of this concept here betrays itself?) Scientists, so confronted, frequently claim that they are done with the lofty flights and hellish pitfalls of morality in this part of their lives, and that their aim is only to be good *as* scientists. The conception of judging oneself *as* a human being—as one equal member of God's flock of children—is here explicitly set aside in favor of the separate identity of scientist, and at the same time all or most of the concepts that make up the modal understructure undergo a noticeable shift.

This shift is perhaps more pronounced if we substitute the artist for the scientist. The general disavowal of moral standards on the part of artists (and I do not mean in their "bohemian" private lives) is more flamboyant. It is seen as a credo on which one rises upwards into higher realms. The this-worldly consequences, the political effects, everything mundane, is left behind, and one submits oneself only to the standards of "art—for its own sake." For our purposes it is especially illuminating to note that included in the ballast which one throws overboard are the concepts which make up the understructure of the moral mode: the idea of "automomy," of deliberately acting, with one's ego-self in hermetically sealed-off and dominant control, is ludicrous when it comes to art.

One does *not* know where one's best ideas come from—which chance encounter, which fragment of an overheard conversation, which whiff of passing air, may have triggered or inspired them—and it seems therefore picaresque to receive praise or blame for them, or even just to claim them as one's own.

The same is naturally true for many more professions. Captains, at least until recently, were expected to go down with their ship—even if the disaster was *not* their responsibility or fault. And something similar obtained for soldiers generally, and military officers in particular. Here the sheer indefensibility, the blindingly obvious truth that the consequences of one's actions are *of course* incalculable, and that one of course is not autonomous or responsible, but on the contrary "under orders," is part of the force that brings about the imposition of borderlines, till one no longer sees and judges oneself "as a person," but "as an officer."

This avoidance is of course exactly the sort of behavior that to many demonstrates the superiority and the indispensability of a moral code. But in Nietzsche's perspective, one begins to appreciate the other side. Perhaps the fact that abdicating morality is so tempting and so common—and so understandable—raises questions about the nature of the code? (One can appreciate this argument by considering one of Hegel's stunningly simple observations: in the most peasantlike of spirits, he said that it is very possible for ethical principles to be *too* high and *too* demanding, and that this is not a coy advantage but a genuine defect. He suggested that there was no reason not to draw the analogy to laws: laws that cannot be enforced are bad because they weaken the entire institution. Likewise with moral rules, and perhaps with the entire modality of the moral: If the standards invoked by the concepts of its understructure cannot possibly be met, then this weakens the general force of *values*.)

One could go on to sports (where part of being "a pro" or "good"— say in boxing or in mountain-climbing—is "that there are *no* excuses"), or again to crafts, where the dismissal of everything but the perfection with which one can wield a tool is often even stronger then in art. Or one could turn to the kinds of codes that govern families, or regions, or that differentiate classes, or to the very general cultural rules that govern how people arrange themselves in space (in China you sit down *next* to the only other person on a bus, while in our culture we try to evenly distribute ourselves), or again to the rules that govern how one goes through the ritual of a conversation (see Goffman) or of an exchange of glances, or smiles, or winks (see Clifford Geertz). Finally, at the opposite extreme, very individual, solitary, private rules (Heming-way's "grace under pressure," for example) often represent the last foothold someone has against disgust or despair (W. C. Fields: "There still is—style".)

These illustrations should suffice to conjure up a general *Gestalt* that has some bearing on how contemporary philosophers write about mo-rality: Often the impression is conveyed that there are perhaps no more than three codes or valuational perspectives: say, the moral, the pru-dential, and etiquette. That picture is nothing short of silly. To be "good" as an artist, or a scientist, or a boxer is not a matter of manners (Emily Post does not preside) and it is even less prudential. In a quick, off-handed way anthropologists say that "all of culture is made up out of nests of codes," which, I believe, suggests something closer to the truth. The reality about which we are trying to theorize is very much more complicated, and differentiated, and subtle and complex then we much of the time admit. It should be understood as a starting premise that there are an indefinite number of different kinds of codes, and that they conceivably all have their own separate logic, which governs how judgments are passed and adjudicated. Which means, among many other things, that we should never—not even in introductory courses—an-nounce that ethics or morality teaches us "how we should live." Ethics does a great deal *less*—it describes only the mechanism of one quite special code.

It is sickening and dismaying, but many still imagine that Nietzsche's central message was a sermon in praise of ruthlessness. (And this thirty-three years after the publication of Kaufmann's translation!) That dis-tortion of Nietzsche may give some adolescent emotions a quick flaring rush, yet it may also be a devious tactic, for nothing makes it easier to dismiss Nietzsche than to first transform him into a crude boor. All the same, it is a travesty.

The thrust of the distinction between the moralities engendered by masters and those engendered by slaves is not that the slaves tricked us into consideration for others, which it is now time to drop. Nothing like it! The bifurcation which runs like a spine through the body of Nietzsche's writings is the division between what debilitates and maims *life*, versus everything that strengthens and invigorates it. He reiterates this again and again and with as few circumlocutions and qualifications as one could wish.

Even standing by itself, this fact should tourniquet some of the modish postmodernist talk about the relativistic and perspectivalistic Nietzsche, whom a host of writers now want to make into the pope of their nihilism. On the contrary, he often wields the most cutting and "objective" standard: for in all fields he separates that which is dying from that which will live.

Nietzsche's objection to the morality promulgated by slaves can be condensed into the assertion that it is "hostile to life." Among other things this means that it is destructive to *both* sides. It is *not* an intelligent strategy—that would underestimate the venomous irrationality Nietzsche built into his idea of the slave's resentment. The slave moralities debilitate both the slave and the master.

The different distinction between content and modality, which we have drawn, has beyond this a very specific relevance to the current academic philosophical enterprise. For a considerable period of time the endeavor of Ethics has been to find the formulation that would fit the right content into the moral mode. (Slowly this enterprise has devolved down to the rival claims that either some form of utilitarianism or some form of Kantianism will give us the more specific valuations we want.) Underlying this has been the assumption that the modality of the moral (or the moral point of view) is so precious and crucial, and possibly even indispensable, that it should override all other possible modes. This is now subject to serious question. Now the supporting modality, and not just the surface content, is under attack, for according to Nietzsche it "as such" is destructive and crippling.

This means that not only the conceptual apparatus of guilt is "a mistake"; that much many philosophers would by now concede. The objection is that the entire machinery which constitutes the moral perspective—i.e. the apparatus of "responsibility," of isolated and autonomous "freedom," as well as the authoritative and terrorizing power of the moral "ought," and the substantivized and reified "ego" which undergirds all of this—are all (contrary to our usual views) weakening and destructive, and therefore to be cast off and rejected.

The upshot of Nietzsche's critique of morality is ultimately a very bright and hopeful perspective: if even some of our supposedly highest conceptual achievements have so far been self-destructive, then it is no great wonder that we have been problematic and dubious creatures. But we can do better than invent new content for the wineskins of the old modes. We can devise wholly new modes in which the values of the future will be encoded. These much deeper changes promise a cure, and that could realize the hopes which Nietzsche (at times) has for the more vigorous and cheerful humanity that is yet to come.

Who Are "The Philosophers of the Future"?: A Reading of *Beyond Good and Evil*

ALEXANDER NEHAMAS

Though it is one of Nietzsche's most popular and most widely read books, *Beyond Good and Evil* remains, in structure and content (if we can provisionally distinguish between them), a work of dazzling obscurity. Two reasons make this oxymoron appropriate.

In a very elementary sense, we still do not know how to read this book. We simply do not understand its structure, its narrative line. Indeed, we do not even know whether it has any narrative line at all. And the reason why, which is also precisely the reason why the structure of *Beyond Good and Evil* still remains obscure, is the sheer brilliance, the dazzle, of many of the two hundred and ninety-six sections of which (along with its preface and "Aftersong") the work consists. In their perfection, such passages stand out against the rest of the text. In their brilliance, they have blinded us to the sometimes less brilliant passages that surround them. Singled out and discussed in their own right, they have therefore also blinded us to questions concerning the relationship they bear to the sections that appear simply to frame them, the order in which they are presented, and the principles, if any, that may govern their seemingly horizontal, sometimes even random and haphazard juxtaposition.

The tendency to avoid these questions has been reinforced by the general view that all of Nietzsche's writings, including the individual sections of *Beyond Good and Evil*, are aphoristic.[1] Taking these passages as aphorisms, and recalling Zarathustra's view that "in the mountains the shortest way is from peak to peak: but for that one must have long legs. Aphorisms should be peaks" (Z I 7), we have often read *Beyond Good and Evil* only for its peaks. We have therefore overlooked, or skipped over, the valleys without which the peaks could not exist. But not all short prose passages are aphorisms.[2] And, in any case, there is much more to *Beyond Good and Evil* than, for example, its biting description of previous philosophers as "wily spokesmen of their prejudices which they baptize 'truths' " (5), its grand characterization of the free spirits as "at home, or at least having been guests, in many countries of the spirit" (44), its declaration that "genuine philosophers ... are commanders and legislators" (211), and, of course, so much more. The question how, or at least whether, the work is to be read as a whole should not be avoided.

An obvious answer to this question is that *Beyond Good and Evil* is, despite its many differences from other such works, a philosophic treatise. Perhaps, then, it should be read as a long, sustained argument (or set of arguments) concerning a particular philosophic thesis (or set of theses). This suggestion is supported by the fact that *Beyond Good and Evil* does indeed contain a number of recognizable arguments.

In section 15, for example, we find what seems like a clear *reductio ad absurdum*, characterized as such by Nietzsche himself, of an idealist view according to which the external world is "the work of our organs." If that were true, Nietzsche argues, then our body, which is itself part of the external world as defined by idealism, would also be the work of our organs. But in that case, our organs, which are in turn parts of our body, would be themselves their own work, which is absurd, given the reasonable assumption that nothing can be its own cause.

But Nietzsche's purpose here is not to refute idealism, as we shall see in a moment when we discuss the final sentence of this section. Nor does the section, as we shall also see, fit into a continuous argument with those that precede and follow it. Though *Beyond Good and Evil* contains a number of arguments, some of which may even be good, its primary goal still is not to establish specific philosophic positions. Read as a series of arguments aimed at such positions, too much of the work seems not to argue well, or at all, our text becomes a very poor philosophic work—in fact, a failure. It becomes actually unreadable. This point is reinforced by the nature of part IV, "Epigrams and Interludes," which *does* consist of aphorisms, and which breaks in a radical way whatever narrative coherence the work may have displayed in its first three parts. That part IV has this disruptive effect has been both my personal experience and the experience of most of the students to whom I have taught *Beyond Good and Evil*. The intrusiveness of this section forces one to stop and ask what it is supposed to be doing there, how it is to be taken, how, in short, the work is to be read.

Faced with the conclusion that *Beyond Good and Evil* cannot be read as a philosophical treatise, a number of readers have assumed instead that the work is just a collection of short independent aphorisms or essays, with no overarching purpose or structure. This assumption is reflected in the common practice of using individual passages, or groups of passages, to illustrate some particular view that Nietzsche holds. I do not plan to claim that this practice is wrong. But I do want to say that this approach makes *Beyond Good and Evil* equally unreadable. If we try to find purely argumentative connections between its various sections, or if, frustrated by the failure of this effort, we take each section by itself, then it becomes impossible, with the exception of a few particularly striking passages, to remember what any section is about almost as soon as we have finished reading it. That, at least, has been my own experience on a number of different occasions. Most of *Beyond Good and Evil* seems to disappear from consciousness, and memory, as soon as it has been read—consumed but undigested.

And yet its various sections are not unconnected. Consider, once again, section 15, where Nietzsche attacks the view that the external world is the work of our sensory organs. Instead of ending with this conclusion, however, he ends with a question: "Consequently, the external world is *not* the world of our organs?—." But why ask a question here at all? Why does Nietzsche make this apparent effort to introduce doubt at the conclusion of this seemingly rigorous proof?

The reason, I think, may well be that Nietzsche does not want his readers to infer from his "refutation" of idealism that some version of realism, of the idea that the character of the world is determined in total independence of all experience, is therefore correct. The point of his *reductio* is not that a particular view regarding the nature of our knowledge of the world is or is not correct, but, rather, that a question must be raised about the idea that since the world is often thought to be our "creation," it is something that can be known with absolute certainty.

It is precisely this question regarding certainty that explains why, in section 16, Nietzsche turns to the Cartesian view that consciousness, at least, can be known with certainty since, in contrast to our awareness of the external world, our awareness of it is direct and immediate. Mentioning as an aside, and without in any way developing or justifying his point, that Schopenhauer's view of the will is part of this Cartesian tradition, he now claims (without much argument) that this tradition is deeply mistaken. The assertion "I think," he writes, is extremely complex, and so is thinking itself: it is an activity (*if* it is an activity) which we can come to recognize, and to distinguish from others, only through an intricate process of inference and interpretation. Thinking not only fails to yield certainty: it also raises a number of additional questions regarding the various concepts involved in the assertion "I think," especially regarding the concept of the ego. The Cartesian view, he claims, supposes that the ego is given in the same act of awareness in which we become conscious of our thinking. But if there is no such act, where does our very concept of the ego come from?

This is just the question taken up in the next section. The indivisible subject which is prior to its thoughts, and which is presupposed by Cartesianism, is, according to Nietzsche, the product of our taking too seriously the grammatical form of our sentences. Because every verb requires a subject, we infer that every activity presupposes an independent agent. He does not in any way elaborate on this claim—which was radically novel and startling at the time—but proceeds to the even more startling assertion that the very same grammatical error has generated the concept of the atom in natural science. The same misinterpretation of our language has led us to suppose that both the inner and the outer world consist of independent, self-sufficient units, whose features are in many respects parallel to one another. Nietzsche thus establishes another kind of continuity between these two worlds: sections 15 and 16 together suggested that neither the external nor the inner world can be known with certainty; section 17 suggests that the parallel structure that has been attributed to them is the result of the same wrong assumption. And just as "more rigorous minds [have] learned at last to get along without this 'earth-residuum'," the atom, so he hopes, one day nothing will be left of the ego, either.

Nietzsche has nothing to say about the considerations that have led the unnamed "rigorous minds" of this section to abandon the idea of the atom nor about how that idea has been refuted. But the very idea of refutation raises, in a way that is reasonable though not strictly speaking logical, the idea of refutability. And Nietzsche opens the next section, 18, by writing, "It is certainly not the least charm of a theory that it is refutable; it is precisely thereby that it attracts subtler minds." This statement echoes the view of section 51 of *The Gay Science*:

> *Truthfulness.*—I favor any *skepsis* to which I may reply: "Let us try it!".
> But I no longer wish to hear anything of all those things and questions

that do not permit any experiment. This is the limit of "truthfulness"; for there courage has lost its right.[3]

The issue of "experimentalism" is picked up again in the discussion of the "new philosophers" (who have already been mentioned only to be immediately dropped in section 2) in sections 42–43 of *Beyond Good and Evil*, as well as in section 210 later on. At this point, however, instead of pursuing his ideas about refutability in general, Nietzsche remarks, casually and as an aside, that the doctrine of the freedom of the will, which has already been refuted a "hundred times . . . owes its persistence to this charm alone."

Prompted by this incidental reference to this doctrine, Nietzsche now engages, in section 19, in a general discussion of the notion of the will. In this way, he is able also to pick up again his earlier allusion to Schopenhauer, to whom he refers explicitly here, connecting his present discussion, which claims that willing is itself at least as complicated as thinking, with his previous attack on Cartesianism. He follows this with some suggestive though inconclusive remarks on the "illusion" that the will is free, and he once again breaks down the indivisible agent into a conglomeratgion of semi-independent drives, a collection of "underwills or under-souls."

Nietzsche's view that the person, the subject, is internally complex and multiple strains language, which seems to refer to a unitary "I," to a considerable extent. And this, along with his point that the concept of the will is tied not only to metaphysical but also to practical and moral considerations and needs, prompts him to change directions once again. He drops until section 21 his discussion of freedom and turns instead, in section 20, to the issue of the dependence of philosophical views in general on one another and, even more important, on grammatical and linguistic factors. Our traditional concepts, he claims, are deeply influenced by our language (or, as I would prefer to put it, by our assumption that the structure of our language has to reflect the structure of the world). In this way, he provides some support for his attack against the view that the self and the atom are indivisible in section 17, and he suggests that the strain his own view of the multiple self places upon language is not in itself a reason for rejecting it.

Even in regard to these very few passages my discussion has been sketchy and incomplete. But I hope that it has given a hint of the complicated connections that tie the various sections of *Beyond Good and Evil* to one another. These connections, as I have already said, are not in a strict sense logical; that is, the sections cannot easily be considered as steps in a long argument. Nietzsche, as we have seen, introduces topics only to drop them and pick them up later; what is in one place alluded to in an aside becomes a central issue elsewhere; discussions are interrupted in order to examine in detail some casually introduced tangential point. Such connections are dialectical in the most original sense of the term; they are, that is, conversational. They replicate the way in which someone who was engaged in a long and sustained monologue— which is a species of conversation—would naturally and inevitably have to proceed.

My suggestion, now, is that we must read *Beyond Good and Evil* as a long, sustained, sometimes rambling and disorganized but ultimately coherent, monologue. Its major parts, and its individual sections, are related to one another as stages in such a monologue. Sometimes they are sparked by what precedes them, sometimes by what is anticipated to follow them; sometimes they are concerned to pick up again a question earlier left aside because, perhaps, of a lateral change of subject prompted by some particular association or by an imagined objection; sometimes they set the stage so that an important idea can be introduced later on when it becomes appropriate, with some of its connections to other topics already established. Nietzsche often moves from one subject to another not because he has offered a satisfactory solution to his problem, but because a monologue is, or can reasonably be expected to be, such an inconclusive mode of communication. Connections are developed as we go along; subjects are left open until later; continuities are established between questions that in turn generate their own questions, which are then pursued instead of the questions that prompted them in the first place.

A monologue may, of course, answer all sorts of questions. But, considered as a literary genre, it finds the principle of its coherence not so much in the questions it does answer, but in the coherence of the narrator who must be supposed to engaged in it. This narrator is, in a way, constructed out of the monologue with which we are faced. The narrator, then, reflects Nietzsche's view that the subject of an activity is not given antecedently of the activity in question; and the monologue's various interconnected but also semi-independent parts reflect Nietzsche's view of the person as a conglomeration of "under-souls," which may or may not be in harmony with one another.

If we are to understand *Beyond Good and Evil* as a whole, then, it becomes crucial to understand the character who engages or who is manifested, in the monologue which the text constitutes. Far from being always agreeable, likable, or right, this character is nevertheless one who, if he engages us at all, engages us as a whole. *Beyond Good and Evil* is the monologue of a character who is, not only implicitly, projecting himself as someone worth listening to and perhaps, in at least one sense of that term, also being. The question is whether this character, despite those of his views that are wrong, silly, or obnoxious, despite his errors and his faults, is still a character worth taking seriously. And this, of course, raises the further question of what it would be like to take seriously the particular character implicit in this work. Read in this way, *Beyond Good and Evil* acquires an urgency which it did not and could not have as long as it was considered simply as a mine for a number of Nietzsche's ideas, however valuable, or as a failed effort to establish a single and coherent philosophical position.

To do any of this, we must first determine, in an elementary way, who the narrator of *Beyond Good and Evil* is. And this now brings me to my second reason for characterizing this work, as I did at the very beginning of this essay, by means of an oxymoron. An oxymoron is a kind of paradox, even though it is not usually vicious. And our search for the character generated by *Beyond Good and Evil* will itself generate a paradox—even though, I hope, it will be no more vicious than the statement that Nietzsche's book is dazzlingly obscure. This new paradox arises when we try to say exactly how the narrator of *Beyond Good and Evil* thinks of himself.

Beyond Good and Evil bears the subtitle "Prelude to a Philosophy of the Future" ("Vorspiel einer Philosophie der Zukunft"). The direction of the whole book seems to be forward-looking, announcing the emergence of a new way of philosophizing and of a new kind of philosopher, neither of which seems to have existed, if they ever did, since the time of Heracleitus, Plato, and Empedocles (204). As early as his preface, Nietzsche writes that the long fight against Platonism and Christianity, that is, the fight against dogmatism (to which we shall have to return) "has created in Europe a magnificent tension of the spirit . . . : with so tense a bow we can now shoot for the most distant goals." Despite various attempts to "unbend this bow," he continues, "we who are neither Jesuits nor democrats, nor even German enough, we *good Europeans* and free, *very* free spirits—we still feel it, the whole need of the spirit and the whole tension of its bow. And perhaps also the arrow, the task, and—who knows?—the goal—."

This goal is the philosophy of the future, to be practiced by the "philosophers of the dangerous 'maybe.' . . . And in all seriousness," the narrator claims, "I see such new philosophers coming up" (2). Yet these "philosophers of the future" (42–44), these "new" (203) or "genuine" philosophers who are "commanders and legislators" (211) are, at least as the book says, creatures of tomorrow and the day after tomorrow. The narrator speaks about, but not for them. The group for which he *does* speak, though small and select, exists today: it consists of "good Europeans" (preface), "free spirits" (part II), even "scholars" (part VI), from all of whom the genuine philosophers are at least apparently distinguished. Nietzsche, therefore, or at least the narrator of *Beyond Good and Evil*, puts himself in the position of a sort of prophet announcing the expected coming of these genuine philosophers.

Part V of *Beyond Good and Evil*, "Natural History of Morals," ends with a vicious attack against "herd morality," and against democracy and socialism conceived as efforts to apply that morality to politics. What is it that Nietzsche finds so repulsive in this morality? The common answer is that he detests the specific values it promotes: pity and love, altruism and self-sacrifice—all of which, he believes, are different methods of ensuring mediocrity. This is certainly, but only partly, true. Nietzsche despises herd morality not only for its values, but also for its attitude toward them, for its claim that they are the only values that can, and that therefore must, be accepted:

> Morality in Europe today is herd animal morality—in other words, as we understand it, merely *one* type of human morality beside which, before which, and after which many other types, above all *higher* moralities, are, or ought to be possible. But his morality resists such a "possibility," such an "ought" with all its power: it says stubbornly and inexorably: "I am morality itself and nothing besides is morality." (202, cf. *WP* 285)

This last claim is a special case of the claim made by all dogmatic approaches—approaches, that is, that will not countenance the possibility of alternatives to them. It is a claim which it is necessary for the herd morality to make, since its aim, according to Nietzsche, is precisely to regulate human conduct so that all differences between individuals are eliminated as much as possible. By being presented as the only possible morality, herd morality is enabled to regulate the lives not only of those many people who need its code and cannot live without it but also those few rare individuals who actually do not need it and cannot live, or at least thrive, with it (cf. *GM* III 14). The herd can be preserved, Nietzsche writes, only through the *total* "degeneration and diminution of human beings into the perfect herd animal" (202, cf. 201). But "we," he continues,

> have a different faith . . . where must *we* reach with our hopes? Toward *new* philosophers; there is no choice; toward spirits strong and original

enough to provide the stimuli for opposite valuations and to revalue and invert 'eternal values' . . . .It is the image of such leaders that *we* envisage: may I say this out loud, you free spirits? (203)

And with the introduction of these new philosophers, part V ends and part VI begins, and develops a contrast between such philosophers on the one hand and those who pass for philosophers today as well as with "those of us who are scholars" ("wir Gelehrten"), among whom the narrator seems to include himself.

Part VI may be the most carefully constructed stretch of *Beyond Good and Evil*. It consists of ten sections. The first five (204–208) examine the current decadence of philosophy, the reasons for it, the nature of scholarship and objectivity which are valued today, and the skepticism to which those lead: this is a skepticism which results in an inability to make choices. The second five sections (209–213) begin by introducing another kind of skepticism, a suspiciousness of established values and practices, which can be combined with criticism, the willingness and ability to refute those values and practices. These two are then presented as ingredients of genuine philosophy, "commanding and legislating," the "bad conscience" of its time (cf. Z I 1). This is not the sort of philosophy that can be taught: "What a philosopher is, that is hard to learn because it cannot be taught: one must 'know' it, from experience— or one should have the pride *not* to know it" (213).

Now what of the narrator of *Beyond Good and Evil*? Does he know what a philosopher is, or does he have the pride not to know it? One might easily think the latter, since the narrator often describes himself as merely the herald of the new philosophers. And yet this herald does not simply announce their imminent arrival—he also describes them in considerable detail. Does he then know what a philosopher is, after all? Or shall we resort to the easy distinction between knowing what a philosopher is in general terms and knowing it from experience—between just knowing what a philosopher is and being a philosopher oneself?

What does this narrator, both free spirit and scholar, say about the new philosophers? One of their most important features is that in contrast to those who remain tied to old values the philosophers "create" new ones (211). This is their "secret: to know of a *new* greatness for human beings, of a new untrodden way to their enhancement" (212). Genuine philosophers

first determine the Whither and For What of humanity . . . .With a creative hand they reach for the future, and all that is and has been becomes a means for them, an instrument, a hammer. Their "knowing" is *creating*, their creating is a legislation, their will to truth is—*will to power*. (211)

Statements of this sort have suggested that Nietzsche urges that we think of philosophy as aiming toward a normative ethical theory of some sort or another, though he did not consider himself as having developed such a theory.[4] This view has recently been given clear expression by Richard Schacht:

> Nietzsche's concern . . . was above all to work out a new theory of value which would at once provide an interpretation [the philosopher as skeptic] and decisive reassessment [the philosopher as critic] of existing moral and evaluative schemes, and also fill the normative void which their mere "devaluation" under critical scrutiny would otherwise leave.[5]

And taking the subtitle of *Beyond Good and Evil* seriously (that is, literally), Schacht writes, in agreement with many other recent authors, that Nietzsche's

> mature thought generally may be considered to constitute such a "prelude," rather than anything approaching (or intended to stand as) the full development of such a philosophy.[6]

Schacht admits that in Nietzsche's view it is perhaps impossible for any philosophical system ever to be complete. But the important point is that he takes Nietzsche to be offering such a system, however incomplete. Schacht supports his "positive" reading of sections 210–211 of *Beyond Good and Evil* by referring to section 972 of *The Will to Power*, where Nietzsche writes: "There are two kinds of philosopher: (1) Those who want to ascertain a complex fact of evaluations (logical or moral); (2) Those who are legislators of such evaluations." The second sort, of course, are the genuine philosophers of *Beyond Good and Evil*.

Some other readers of this work, however, cannot convince themselves that Nietzsche is only the herald of a new philosophy. These are readers who tend to consider *Thus Spoke Zarathustra* as Nietzsche's major work, embodying his own real positive views. Harold Alderman, for example, writes that "the very subtitle of *Beyond Good and Evil* . . . indicates its character as an overture and it is obvious that Nietzsche meant *Zarathustra* to represent the philosopher of the future."[7] And Laurence Lampert, in his detailed study of *Zarathustra*, believes that in *Beyond Good and Evil* Nietzsche is hiding his own philosophical ambition and achievement behind a mask:

> In a book that assigns the greatest responsibility to the philosopher as the one who knows what religions are good for, who knows how to order the

politics of fatherlands, who commands and legislates how the world ought
to be, and who has the whole future of mankind on his conscience, the
philosopher Nietzsche must conceal himself behind the mask of a free
spirit.[8]

The difference between those two approaches to Nietzsche's attitude
toward philosophy concern the question whether Neitzsche did or did
not think of himself as a genuine philosopher of the sort described in
Beyond Good and Evil. They both agree on what genuine philosophy
is: it is a body of positive doctrine, continuous with the greatest philosophies of the past though much more aware than they ever were of
its own creative status.

But let us take a further look at the unpublished passage Schacht
quotes in order to support his attribution to Nietzsche of a philosophy
of this sort (*WP* 972). In what is clearly an early version of section 211
of *Beyond Good and Evil*, Nietzsche writes:

> This second kind of philosopher rarely prospers; and their situation and
> danger are indeed fearful. How often they have deliberately blinded them-
> selves simply so as not to have to behold the narrow ledge that separates
> them from a plunge into the abyss; e.g., Plato, when he convinced himself
> that the "good" as *he* desired it was not the good of Plato but the "good
> in itself," the eternal treasure that some man, named Plato, had chanced
> to discover on his way!

It is at least striking, if this sort of philosopher is to include the
philosophers of the future of *Beyond Good and Evil*, that Plato is said
to be part of it (it is even more striking that *BGE* 212 seems to count
Socrates as a genuine philosopher). But we should notice the difficult
problem with which this second sort of philosopher is faced. What they
come to realize, according to Nietzsche, is what they themselves are
like, what is good for them, through what values they can live and flouish.
But they do not stop there (that would be to take "a plunge into the
abyss"): they project what is good for them onto the world and onto
every human being. It is precisely by thinking of what is good for them
as what is good in itself (that is, good for everyone) that they become

> wily spokesmen for their prejudices which they baptize "truths"—and
> [are] *very* far from having the courage of the conscience that admits this,
> precisely this, to itself; very far from having the good taste of the courage
> which also lets this be known, whether to warn an enemy or friend, or,
> from exuberance, to mock itself. (5)

Nietzsche makes a very similar point at *WP* 446:

What, then, is regressive in philosophers?—That they teach that *their* qualities are and necessary and sole qualities for the attainment of the "highest good" (e.g., dialectic, as with Plato). That they order people of all kinds *gradatim* up to *their* type as the highest . . . .The typical philosopher is here an absolute dogmatist.

It is in my opinion clear that such passages make it extremely difficult to accept the common and most intuitive interpretation of the nature of Nietzsche's genuine philosophers. Even when he describes them as "commanders and legislators," it is difficult to believe that what he has in mind, and what the narrator of *Beyond Good and Evil* is the herald of, are people who in some way will *replace* the Platonic, Christian, or Kantian scheme of values (if Nietzsche thinks that Kant does have a value scheme of his own) with alternative values. When Nietzsche writes that genuine philosophers "create" values, we must ask, before we try to determine precisely what values they are, *for whom* they are being created. When he writes that his philosophers will find new ways for the "enhancement" of human beings, we must ask *who* it is who will be thereby enhanced.

We must always remember that the approach Nietzsche attributes to Plato is the essence of dogmatism, of taking what is good for one or good for some as good for all, as *the* good. By contrast, his own "coming philosophers," like Plato, will "love" their truths since "all philosophers so far have loved their truths:"

But they will certainly not be dogmatists. It must offend their pride, also their taste, if their truth is supposed to be a truth for everyone— which has so far been the secret wish and hidden meaning of all dogmatic aspirations. "My judgment is *my* judgment": no one else is easily entitled to it. (43)

This, of course, is just another way of putting Zarathustra's point when he says:

He, however, has discovered himself who says, "This is *my* good and evil"; with that he has reduced to silence the mole and dwarf who say, "Good for all, evil for all" (*Z* III 11)

The philosophers of the future, therefore, cannot engage in the creation of a new table of values that will hold for all people and that will "enhance" everyone. They can only create values by which they themselves can live and flourish—they and perhaps a few others like them (recall that the coming philosophers say that no one else is *easily* entitled to their judgment, not that no one ever is). Whom do they therefore "enhance"? Only themselves, and perhaps a few others like them, if there are any.

Now this may seem difficult to make consistent with Nietzsche's view that the new philosophers devise "a new greatness for human beings . . . a new untrodden way to their enhancement" (212) and that they therefore benefit humanity as a whole. But this is a difficulty only if we assume that to benefit humanity as a whole is to benefit all human beings. It is not a difficulty if one believes, as Nietzsche believes, that "the goal of humanity cannot lie in its ends but only in its highest exemplars" (*SE* 9) and if one claims, as Nietzsche claims, that his "idea" is that "goals are lacking and these must be individuals" (*WP* 269). Nietzsche can believe in perfect consistency that humanity as a whole will be "enhanced" if a few great individual human beings are somehow made possible.

A crucial point to consider here is that the expressions "philosophy of the future" and "philosopher of the future" need not necessarily be interpreted in the obvious chronological sense in which they have been taken by Nietzsche's readers. A philosophy of the future need not be a philosophy *that is composed in the future*. It can also well be a philosophy *that concerns the future*. Once we see that this reading is possible, we will also see that it is plausible.

Consider the "philosophical laborers" described in section 211. Their task is

> to determine and press into formulas . . . some great data of valuations— that is former *positings* of values, creations of value that have become dominant and are for a time called "truths." It is for these investigators to make everything that has happened and been esteemed so far easy to look over, easy to think over, intelligible and manageable, to abbreviate everything long, even "time," and to *overcome* the entire past.

Philosophical laborers, then, can fairly be considered philosophers of the past not because they have already existed but because the past has been the primary concern of their thought. Their usefulness is that they make its overcoming possible for the "genuine philosophers . . . [who] are commanders and legislators [and] say 'thus it shall be!'." The future, therefore, is the time with which genuine philosophers are concerned, not the time when they exist.

This reading is supported by the beginning of section 212:

> Philosophers, being *of necessity* people of tomorrow and the day after tomorrow, have always found themselves, and *had* to find themselves, in contradiction to their today: their enemy was ever the ideal of today.

The narrator continues and makes it very clear that such philosophers have existed in the past, though they have far more often appeared as "disagreeable fools and question marks" instead of possessors of wisdom. Their task, he writes, has always been to be "the bad conscience of their time." By "vivisecting" the virtues of their time they have always pointed the way, as we have seen, to "a *new* greatness for humanity." Once again, the future is the *content*, not the time-frame, of genuine philosophy. And it is just this adversarial and forward-looking position that allows Nietzsche to describe Socrates, his greatest enemy, as a philosopher after all.

Consider now the very end of section 211, in which philosophical laborers are distinguished from genuine philosophers. It ends with three questions: "Are there such philosophers today? Have there been such philosophers yet? *Must* there not be such philosophers?—[Muss es nicht solche Philosophen geben?...]." R. J. Hollingdale, commenting on this passage, claims that Nietzsche asks these questions precisely "in case it should be thought that he is here describing himself."[9] But I am not at all sure that this is the correct interpretation. After all, as we have just seen, Socrates seems to be considered as a genuine philosopher in section 212. So the answer to the second question, "Have there been such philosophers yet?," may well be affirmative. If this is so, then we can also give an affirmative answer to the last question as well: There *must* be such philosophers, not only in the sense that they are necessary or needed, but in the sense that they are actual, that they really exist. And so the first question, "Are there such philosophers today?," also finally receives an affirmative answer.

But why *must* there exist such philosophers? What sort of necessity is involved here? Nietzsche certainly does not believe that history makes their emergence inevitable, that the fact that they are needed (if this is indeed a fact) will bring them into being. This is a different sort of "must" altogether. And—this is the central claim I am making in this essay—this question is intended to make the reader ask "Why?," as we have, and answer, as we do, "There *must* be such philosophers because I am in the process of engaging with one right now, as I am reading this work." *Beyond Good and Evil* itself *is* a philosophy of the future; its narrator (and its author as well) is a genuine philosopher. The work is a "prelude" to such a philosophy not because it simply heralds its arrival, but because—like Wagner's preludes to his artworks of the future (which themselves existed in what was for them the present)—it sounds the major themes and motifs of one philosophy of that kind.

Four difficult questions now present themselves. First, on what

grounds can we read *Beyond Good and Evil* self-referentially in the way
I have suggested? What justifies our taking its narrator to be implicitly
presenting himself as a genuine philosopher? Second, on what basis can
we describe this work as a prelude, introducing themes and motifs to
be fully developed later on? Third, what distinguishes *this* genuine philosopher from others who have already existed? What enables him, and
not them, to belong to "a new species of philosophers" (*eine neue
Gattung von Philosophen*, 42)? And, finally, why does the narrator
present himself as a philosopher in this implicit, oblique manner? Why,
in the way that is so often characteristic of Nietzsche, is he not the first
to proclaim and flaunt his role, his position, and his importance?

The reason for reading *Beyond Good and Evil* self-referentially is
that so many of the features of the philosopher mentioned in section
212 characterize both the narrator of this work and, more generally,
Nietzsche himself (that is, the author of the other works that bear his
name). Philosophers, for example,

> exposed how much hypocrisy, comfortableness, letting oneself go and
> letting oneself drop, how many lies lay hidden under the best honored
> type of their contemporary morality, how much virtue was outlived.

But this is one of Nietzsche's most central and most persistent themes.
The exposure mentioned here has already been made explicit in section
202:

> That which here believes it knows [what is good and evil], that which
> glorifies itself with its praises and reproaches, calling itself good, that is
> the instinct of the herd animal, man, which has scored a breakthrough
> and attained prevalence and predominance over other instincts.

And the view that Christianity and its morality have outlived their usefulness runs through the whole of Nietzsche's later work, including part
III of *Beyond Good and Evil*, "What is Religious."

Faced with the modern preference for specialization, we read in section 212, a philosopher "would be compelled to find the greatness
of human beings, the concept of 'greatness,' precisely in their range
and multiplicity, in their wholeness in manifoldness." According to
such a philosopher, "precisely this shall be called *greatness*: being
capable of being as manifold as whole, as ample as full." This classical
ideal is clearly Nietzsche's own (*TI* V 3, IX 38; *WP* 464, 847, 928,
967). It appears explicitly in part VI, "Our Virtues," where "we
Europeans of the day after tomorrow . . . we modern men" are said
to be "determined . . . by *different* moralities" (215). And the narrator
continues:

> The past of every form and way of life, of cultures that formerly lay right next to each other or one of top of the other, now flows into us 'modern souls,' thanks to this mixture; our instincts now run back everywhere; we ourselves are a kind of chaos. Finally . . . "the spirit" sees its advantage in this. (224)

What is this advantage? The answer is given, in terms connected to the wholeness in multiplicity we have already seen praised, in section 842 of *The Will to Power*: here the "grand style" is described as the effort "to become master of the chaos one is; to compel one's chaos to become form: to become logical, simple, unambiguous, mathematics, *law*."

The notion that in contrast to "the taste of the time and the virtue of the times [which] weakens and thins down the will" the genuine philosopher's concept of greatness includes "precisely strength of will, hardness, and the capacity for long-range decisions" (212) is developed at length and in detail in part VI. And finally, the requirement that the philosopher today "would determine value and rank in accordance with how much and how many things one could bear and take upon himself, how *far* one could extend his responsibility" (212) is satisfied in

> the ideal of the most high-spirited, alive, and world-affirming human being who has not only come to terms and learned to get along with whatever was and is, but who wants to have *what was and is* repeated into all eternity, shouting insatiably *da capo*—not only to himself but to the whole play and spectacle. (56)

This ideal, of course, is embodied in the thought of the eternal recurrence. The thought is this, Every single aspect of an individual life is equally essential to that life being what it is; also, since Nietzsche believes that everything in the world consists simply of its interconnections to everything else, every single aspect of the whole world is equally essential to that life being what it is. To want, therefore, even a single moment of one's life to recur is to want the whole world, exactly as it has been, to recur again. But this is to take on responsibility for absolutely everything, since it is to realize that absolutely everything has determined who one is, and to want everything, including oneself, to be just what it already has been—and to want this to the extent of wanting one's life and the whole world to recur just as they already have.[10]

Our second question, concerning the manner in which *Beyond Good and Evil* is a prelude, is not difficult to answer. Section 260, for example, quickly introduces the contrast between master and slave morality. This contrast is developed in detail in the first essay of *The Genealogy of Morals*, which also discusses at length the origins and functions of Christian morality, sketchily touched upon in parts III and VII of *Beyond Good and Evil*. The casual comments on interpretation we find throughout this work (e.g., 22, 192) are made the central topics of *The Genealogy of Morals*, Book Five of *The Gay Science*, and *The Antichrist*. It is in this way that *Beyond Good and Evil*, in its casual, conversational, often paratactic manner, introduces many of the themes that were to occupy Nietzsche centrally in the little time that was left to him as an author.

But why is this philosophy, assuming that it is genuine, different from its predecessors? How does our philosopher differ, say, from Socrates? Is it only in that his specific views are different from Socrates', as section 212 may suggest? Or is the difference more profound, as Nietzsche's immense animosity toward him would rather lead us to believe? These questions cannot be answered independent of the fourth problem we listed above, that is, why it is that the narrator of *Beyond Good and Evil* does not present himself as a philosopher directly and prefers to refer to himself as a "free spirit" and as the philosopher's herald.

The answer to these interconnected sets of questions is that though genuine philosophers so far have all been dogmatists, the narrator of *Beyond Good and Evil* is an avowed perspectivist. The new philosophers of *Beyond Good and Evil* will differ from philosophers like Plato and Socrates, even if they were in fact "genuine," because they will never consider that what is good for them is, or can be, good for all. And just for this reason the work's narrator has to be confined to presenting himself as a philosopher obliquely.

Nietzsche's notion of what constitutes dogmatism is very broad. It includes every approach that does not admit, as we have seen, "whether to warn an enemy or friend, or, from exuberance, to mock itself" (5), that it is only one approach among many. The problem with this (and the paradox to which I referred above) is that it is very difficult, if not impossible, to make such an admission with consistency and still remain credible.[11]

To set a view out in detail and then to add, "But this is only an interpretation," disposes one's audience either to disregard the view in question altogether or, if they are independently attracted to it, to disregard the qualification. The perspectivist, therefore, is faced with a dilemma between simply not being believed on the one hand and being accepted dogmatically on the other. And, I think, it is no comfort to perspectivists to know that they have made their warning and that the responsibility for their dogmatic reception lies with their audience. For the perspectivist's most important message is, *necessarily*, perspectivism itself. Since, according to the view, many views and values are possible and, indeed, appropriate for different people, the important point that needs to be communicated is precisely that—not some particular set of views and values which may or, more probably, may not be appropriate for any individual member of one's audience.

If the repetition of the phrase "But this is only an interpretation" is self-defeating in this way, its omission obviously can only make matters worse. The central problem facing perspectivism, therefore, is how the view can be effectively communicated in the first place.

One method, in my opinion, is to try to present one's views not so much through describing, supporting, and articulating them—though this will be to a great extent both necessary and inevitable—but, most centrally, by exemplifying them. Exemplification displays views and values without thereby asserting that they are views and values that *must* be accepted. It displays them (if their display is coherent) as views and values that *can* be accepted, and it leaves the decision whether to accept them or not—a decision as to what kind of person one wants to be—to each member of the audience.

This, I think, is the main reason why *Beyond Good and Evil*, like so many of Nietzsche's works, is so short on argument. Nietzsche does not shun argument because, as is so often thought, he is a "merely negative" thinker; he does not shun it because he is feeble-minded, finding reason and argument beyond his abilities; and he does not shun it because he is an "irrationalist," finding reason and argument repugnant, atavistic remnants of an age that has come to an end. Rather, argument is often absent from his works as the result of a consistent and shrewd policy which allows him to alert his readers to the features of his writing and of his attitudes toward life for which he wants them to look in his work, and to be able to embody those features in the work itself. By embodying them, as we have seen, he makes no claim that his readers *should* accept them: he offers them (commending them, of course, simply in virtue of his having chosen them to offer) for his audience's inspection, but he leaves the decision whether to accept them or not, the decision what sorts of persons the member of his audience want to be, to them.

The narrator of *Beyond Good and Evil* claims that, among many other things, genuine philosophers are always suspicious of the ideals of their time. He himself exhibits this suspiciousness—in regard, for example, to equality, to democracy, to Christianity, to scientific detachment, to the absolute distinction between good and evil. One might disagree about whether these are ideas and institutions one should be suspicious about or even about whether one should be so suspicious of the ideas of one's time in the first place. But this suspiciousness does in fact characterize the work's narrator, as it is supposed to characterize the philosophers of the future, and is at least partly responsible for his belonging among them. One, of course, might also doubt whether advocating this sort of philosopher is in any respect a good idea. But such a doubt cannot be articulated and defended simply by reacting to the summary description of the features of these philosophers in part VI. The doubt becomes serious only after one engages with the work as a whole; one needs to react to the specific details of the narrator's character, approach, ideas, and values.

This character can prompt at least three different reactions. We might think, first, that he is right both in his perspectivism and in the specific ideas he opposes and supports. This reaction, in fact, is a *decision* to accept him as a whole, and to be like him, because in so far as we also accept his perspectivism we cannot believe that there is any objective reason, that is, a reason good for all individuals, for accepting it. Alternatively, we might accept his perspectivism, but reject some or all of the specific views he presents. This, too, would be a decision of the same sort. Or, finally, we may think that perspectivism is a bad idea in principle. In that case, we will have to argue with this character and with Nietzsche himself over the virtues and vices of perspectivism. Nietzsche cannot believe that he can convince all his readers of the correctness of his views. Perspectivism is the sort of view in connection with which it cannot possibly be proved that one is obliged to accept it; it is noncoercive in the sense which Robert Nozick has discussed in his *Philosophical Explanations*[12] But Nietzsche does have a view, presented in many of his late works, about why it is that dogmatism is appealing to some, perhaps most, people. Nietzsche, in other words, cannot show that one *should* be a perspectivist without contradicting himself. But he can give an account in psychological terms (terms which may or may not be plausible) of why some people choose (or, in their own terms, are convinced) not to be perspectivists. One's attitude toward perspectivism will be to a great extent determined by one's reaction to this account.

In *Crime and Punishment*, Dostoevsky makes it clear that one crucial reason why Raskolnikov is both pathetic and repugnant is that he be-lieves that the decision that one is a superior person, allowed to perform unusual actions, can be made independently of the performance of those actions. He reasons that if one is such a choice person, then one can do what one wants. He only realizes later on, when he is already in Siberia for his stupid and pointless murder, that these are not inde-pendent facts but two aspects of the same realization (though Dostoev-sky himself makes it obvious he does not think that this realization was penance enough). If all illegal acts, Raskolnikov claims, were imme-diately punished, then

> many benefactors of mankind who did not inherit power but seized it for themselves, should have been punished at their very first steps. But their first steps were successfully carried out, and therefore *they were right*, while mine failed, which means I had no right to permit myself that step.

To proclaim that one is "a genuine philosopher," I now want to suggest, is precisely to claim that one has the right to think unusual thoughts and promote uncommon values because one already thinks of oneself as a person of a certain rare sort. But, once again, these two go indivisibly together. One is a genuine philosopher only to the extent that one produces a coherent and livable picture of life—coherent and livable at least for oneself. And in this context, the mere description of such a picture is not only insufficient but misleading. What is also nec-essary is to embody these thoughts and values into a coherent self, a coherent character, and, in our case, a coherent narrator. Nietzsche is obliged to remain silent about the status of the character engaged in the long monologue which *Beyond Good and Evil* constitutes. Nietzsche's narrator does not want to separate the two aspects Raskolnikov severs from one another. He refuses thereby to encourage his readers to do the same, first to declare themselves, that is, to be genuine philosophers and then to give themselves the right to "command and legislate." The question whether one is or is not a genuine philosopher is just the question whether one can indeed command and legislate, whether one can fashion a life of one's own. Nietzsche's communication is bound to be, in this sense, indirect.

Beyond Good and Evil, then, is a prelude, but it is a prelude to a philosophy which it contains, in outline, within itself. Much more needs to be said about the details of this philosophy, and this we cannot do here. The reading of *Beyond Good and Evil* is far from over. What I have attempted here is the least preliminary to a read-ing which will try to articulate in detail the various interconnections of its parts. But, so long as we address the dazzling obscurity of this work, we will be engaged both with its narrator and with its author. Therefore, even when they prompt us to try to refute them and to replace their views and values with values and views of our own, they will themselves remain the commanders and legislators they know themselves to be—a knowledge they express precisely by remaining silent.[13]

Notes

1. I have argued, in general terms, against such an approach to Nietzsche in *Nietzsche: Life as Literature* (Cambridge, Mass.: Harvard University Press, 1985), chap. 1.1.

2. A relatively ambivalent attitude toward the nature of the individual sections of *Beyond Good and Evil* is expressed by Peter Bergmann, *Nietzsche: "The Last Antipolitical German"* (Bloomington: Indiana University Press, 1987), pp. 160–161: "In *Beyond Good and Evil* . . . , Nietzsche did achieve some success by lengthening his aphorisms and arranging them more cohesively in the manner of an essay. His focus was less scattered, his points more consistently pursued." Bergmann, however, does not himself pursue this idea any further.

3. A discussion of Nietzsche's "experimentalism" can be found in Walter Kaufmann, *Nietzsche: Philosopher, Psychologist, Antichrist*, 4th ed. (Princeton, N.J.: Princeton University Press, 1974), pp. 85–95. I express some doubts about the conclusions Kaufmann reaches through his discussion in *Nietzsche: Life as Literature*, pp. 14–15, 20–21.

4. See, for example, Kaufmann's n. 34 to his translation of *Beyond Good and Evil*, in *Basic Writings of Nietzsche* (New York: Random House, 1968), p. 326, as well as his *Nietzsche*, p. 108. Kaufmann thinks it clear that Nietzsche did not consider himself such a philosopher, pp. 87, 403–404. In this he is followed by R. J. Hollingdale, *Nietzsche* (London: Routledge and Kegan Paul, 1973), p. 173; Allan Megill, *Prophets of Extremity: Nietzsche, Heidegger, Foucault, Derrida* (Berkeley: University of California Press, 1985), p. 92; Ofelia Schutte, *Beyond Nihilism: Nietzsche Without Masks* (Chicago: University of Chicago Press, 1984), p. 10; and J. P. Stern, *A Study of Nietzsche* (Cambridge: Cambridge University Press, 1979), pp. 66–68.

5. Richard Schacht, *Nietzsche* (London: Routledge and Kegan Paul, 1983), p. 344.

6. Schacht, p. 534.

7. Harold Alderman, *Nietzsche's Gift* (Athens: Ohio University Press, 1977), p. 152.

8. Laurence Lampert, *Nietzsche's Teaching: An Interpretation of "Thus Spake Zarathustra"* (New Haven: Yale University Press, 1986), p. 247.

9. Hollingdale, p. 173.

10. A detailed discussion of this version of the eternal recurrence can be found in *Nietzsche: Life as Literature*, chap. 5.

11. A detailed argument for this view can be found in *Nietzsche: Life as Literature*, chaps. 1–2.

12. Robert Nozick, *Philosophical Explanations* (Cambridge, Mass.: Harvard University Press, 1981), pp. 1–24. It should be made clear, however, that Nozick would not accept a perspectivism as radical as Nietzsche's: see pp. 20–21.

13. Paul Guyer was kind enough to discuss some aspects of this essay with me.

Nietzsche's *Gay Science*, Or, How to Naturalize Cheerfully

RICHARD SCHACHT

> When will all these shadows of God cease to darken our minds? When will we complete our de-deification of nature? When may we begin to *"naturalize"* humanity in terms of a pure, newly discovered, newly redeemed nature? GS 109

For one interested in Nietzsche as philosopher, *Die Fröhliche Wissenschaft (The Gay Science)* is without question one of his finest, most illuminating, and most important published works. In the four "books" in which this work originally consisted, and the fifth added five years later, continuing the project begun in the first four, we have much more than the disjointed collection of reflections and aphorisms which it may at first glance appear to be. In this work Nietzsche the philosopher emerges with greater clarity than in any of his previous works, revealing a great deal about the issues in which he was interested, and how and what he thought about them. In style and format it is similar to the series of volumes of such collections preceding it, to which he stated in the original edition that it belongs.[1] Yet it goes well beyond the other volumes in this series, in both coherence and content. Indeed, I shall argue that it constitutes a sustained attempt to sketch the outlines of the kind of reinterpretation of nature and humanity he calls for in the passage cited above, and to indicate how they are to be filled in.

The Gay Science is Nietzsche's first and perhaps his most complete attempt to take seriously the proposition he states in the preceding section—"God is dead"—and to reckon with its many consequences: "And we—we still have to vanquish his shadow, too." (108) The "death of God"—the demise of the God-hypothesis as an idea worthy of acceptance— is the theme with which he explicitly begins both the third and the fifth books of the volume, and which hovers over the others. It implicitly sets the context of the opening of the first book, and again the fourth; and it animates the second, as well as the rhymes and songs with which the volume is framed. The pathos of the "madman" section (125) is a pathos Nietzsche may have experienced; but it is one which—like the "nihilistic rebound" he suggests elsewhere is "pathologically" linked to it[2]—he himself has overcome and left behind.

In tone and in content, the volume deserves its title. After having struggled through a period of some years of intellectual crisis, its author has attained a new philosophical and spiritual health, of the sort he describes at the fifth book's end. (382) He has become profoundly and joyfully affirmative of life and the world, and has discovered that "all the daring of the lover of knowledge is permitted again." (343) He is in love with knowledge and with life and the world, and with the humanity emerging out of them; for, having earlier become hard and disillusioned by them, he has now become newly appreciative of them. Thus he cheerfully and confidently sets out to explore them as they stand revealed in the "new dawn" that has broken in the aftermath of "the news that 'the old god is dead'." (343) While he recognizes that there is more to life and living than knowledge and its pursuit, he goes so far as to say that with the idea of *"Life as a means to knowledge"* in one's heart, "one can live not only boldly but even gaily, and laugh gaily, too." (324) He is intent upon attaining a new and better knowledge of our world and ourselves; and he also is fascinated by the human and philosophical problem he calls "*incorporating* knowledge and making it instinctive." (11) What he calls "the ultimate question about the conditions of life" has come to have a new and great interest for him: "To what extent can truth endure incorporation? That is the question; that is the experiment." (110)

To be sure, the truth and knowledge of which Nietzsche here speaks—the possibility of which he evidently is persuaded—must be squared with his contention that "How far the perspective character of existence extends or indeed whether existence has any other character than this" is a question which "cannot be decided," and that we therefore "cannot reject the possibility" that the world may admit of "infinite interpretations," or limitless "possibilities of interpretation." (374) The force of the entire volume, however, is that this reflection does not doom the "lover of knowledge" to despair, but rather should serve to redirect his quest: away from the impossible dream of absolute knowledge, and toward the comprehension of our own human reality and possibility in the world with which we find ourselves confronted.

Here, as so often elsewhere, Nietzsche deals with many large problems and issues in succession, usually relatively briefly. Near the end of the fifth book, he confronts and rejects the idea that his brevity is ill-suited to the treatment of such problems in an insightful way:

> For I approach deep problems like cold baths: quickly into them and quickly out again. That one does not get to the depths that way, not deep enough down, is the superstition of those afraid of the water, enemies of cold water. . . .
>
> does a matter necessarily remain ununderstood and unfathomed merely because it has been touched only in flight, glanced at, at a flash? . . . At least there are truths that are singularly shy and ticklish and cannot be caught except suddenly—that must be *surprised* or left alone. (381)

It is Nietzsche's clear aim in the five books of this volume to touch upon, surprise, fathom, and understand many of the matters which require being considered anew in the aftermath of the collapse of the "God-hypothesis" and associated modes of interpretation. To cover as much ground as he attempts to cover, brevity was in any event a necessity; and his manner of covering it also has the advantage of enabling one to discern more readily the general shape of the comprehensive interpretation he is working out, and the connections between its various particular features.

Nietzsche moreover is far from being altogether unfaithful to the association of the term *Wissenschaft* he employs in his title with the idea of a systematic cognitive endeavor. The surface disorderliness of the volume only lightly masks the rather remarkable thoroughness of his reexamination of the philosophical and intellectual landscape, and the fundamental coherence of his treatment of its various features. This coherence is all the more noteworthy in view of the passage of the time between the publication of the first four books (in 1882) and the addition of the fifth (in the "New Edition" of 1887).

The continuation of the task begun in the first four books in the fifth also entitles one to considerable confidence in taking them to be indicative of the contours of Nietzsche's thought during the period they span, and in all likelihood beyond it into the final year of his productive life. It therefore is something of a mystery to me why this volume does not receive more attention and figure more centrally in interpretations of his philosophical concerns and thought. If there is any one of his published works in which "the essential philosophical Nietzsche" is to be found, it would seem to me to be this one. And Nietzsche the philosopher is nowhere more accessible, persuasive, and impressive in any single thing he wrote, in my opinion, than he is in the fifth book in particular (the date of which further warrants regarding it as an expression of his mature thought). Indeed, I would suggest that the cause of understanding and appreciating Nietzsche's philosophical thought would be markedly advanced if the rest of his writings were read in relation to it, and construed in the light of what he does and says in it.

Very broadly speaking, what Nietzsche undertakes to do in *The Gay Science* is to show how he proposes to carry out the task of "naturalizing" our conception of humanity and redirecting our thinking about human possibility. This is held to involve first reading humanity back into a post-Christian and postmetaphysical, "newly discovered and newly redeemed" nature—and then reading it out again, as something no longer *merely* natural in consequence of its transformation. Through a variety of sorts of reflections, all of which shed light on these matters in different but important complementary ways, he seeks to arrive at an understanding and appreciation of the kind of creature we fundamentally are, the basic features of our existence, our all-too-human tendencies and the kinds of development of which they admit, and the ways in which human life may be enhanced.

One of Nietzsche's main themes here is thus *what we are*; and another, equally important to him, is *what we may become*. These twin themes—of the generally human, naturalistically reconsidered, and of the genuinely or more-than-merely-human, reconceived accordingly—are the point and counterpoint which give the volume its underlying structure and unity, with the "death of God" as pedal-tone. Along the way, Nietzsche finds it needful and appropriate to say something about nearly every major domain of philosophical inquiry, in order both to shed further light upon our nature and possibilities and to suggest what light his emerging view of the latter sheds upon the former. His concern with what we are and may become, however, is accorded centrality in relation to his thinking with respect to other philosophical and related matters, at once drawing upon them and providing inquiry into them with a new organizational and interpretive orientation.

Rather like Marx, but (it seems to me) with greater sophistication and power, Nietzsche thus advocates and exemplifies what might be called an *anthropological shift* in philosophy. By this I mean a general reorientation of philosophical thinking, involving the attainment of what might be called an *anthropological optic* whereby to carry out the program of a de-deification and reinterpretation of ourselves and our world.

It thus in effect involves the replacement of epistomology and metaphysics by a kind of *philosophical anthropology* as the fundamental and central philosophical endeavor. Philosophy for Nietzsche does not reduce to philosophical anthropology in *The Gay Science*; but it revolves around and finds its way by means of the project of comprehending our nature and possibilities.

His "gay science," as this volume shows, is a comprehensive philosophical enterprise which extends to the consideration of truth and knowledge, science and logic, religion and art, social and cultural phenomena, morality and value, and even life and the world more generally. Its point of departure and constant return, however, is *human life and possibility*. To come to know ourselves—our fundamental nature, what we have become, and what we may have it in us to be—is for the author of this volume something at once difficult and possible, and of the greatest importance. And he is further convinced that in the course of coming to do so, a great many other matters with which philosophers have long concerned themselves may be better comprehended and more appropriately dealt with as well.

These, for Nietzsche, are philosophical tasks, even if the kind of thinking required to pursue them departs in various ways from those favored by most philosophers before and since. He calls it "gay science" as well as "philosophy," as he understands and practices it; and its manner reflects what he takes to be the basic requirements of pursuing these tasks as unproblematically and successfully as is humanly possible. It is avowedly experimental, multiperspectival, and interpretive; but it also is without question cognitive in intent. It has the attainment of sound and penetrating comprehension as a central aim (even if not its only one); and it has as its primary focus a domain in which Nietzsche considers this attainment to be a genuine possibility—both because there is something there to be known, and because it is within our power to come to know it.

That domain, once again, is the domain of the human. He does reject the notion of "man" as a being possessed of some sort of immutable metaphysical essence; but he is very differently disposed toward the notion of "man" reconceived along the lines of the " 'naturalized' humanity" to which he seeks to direct our attention in *The Gay Science*. It is his main topic in this work; and the elaboration of a philosophical anthropology, in the sense of a comprehensive understanding of the nature and prospects of this remarkable and peculiar creature that is at once animal and no longer merely animal, is his general task. Indeed, with this volume Nietzsche may be said to have launched the project of such a philosophical anthropology, the importance of which has yet to be adequately appreciated, and the example of which has all too rarely been followed.

This lamentable situation may at long last be changing; and I venture to hope that it will soon come to have the high place on the agenda of philosophical inquiry it deserves. I doubt, however, that we are likely to see anyone surpass Nietzsche's wealth of contributions to it. Wrong or unsatisfactory though some of his conjectures and analyses may have been, the richness and suggestiveness of his reflections along these lines in *The Gay Science* and subsequent writings render them an invaluable and virtually inexhaustible source and stimulus for anyone who chooses to work in this area. And anyone who does so should come to terms with him.

While I shall for the most part focus on the fifth book of the volume, the structure and content of the first four books warrant some comment. The point and counterpoint mentioned above are sounded at the very outset, in the opening sections of the first book. In the first section we are immediately confronted with an example of how Nietzsche would have us go about reading man back into nature, and thinking about man as a piece of nature in whom fundamental natural principles are powerfully at work, even in dispositions which might seem to be of a loftier nature. In the next two sections, he shifts his attention abruptly to a consideration of certain marks of a higher humanity which set some human beings above and apart from the common run of mankind. Then, in the fourth, he just as abruptly returns to another reflection of the former sort.

This point and counterpoint continues throughout the first book, with many variations. Nietzsche considers a wide variety of human phenomena, reflecting upon basic human traits and their common manifestations, and also upon the more uncommon and exceptional transformations and developments of which they admit. He is at pains both to show how the latter are linked to the former and to stress how they differ from them, thereby to counter our tendency to become so preoccupied with the one that we lose sight of the other, and thus fail to attain a due appreciation of each. It is through such reflections, he appears to think, and only through many of them, that one can make significant headway with the project he describes in the passage from the beginning of the third book cited at the outset (in which he has been engaged all along, and continues to pursue throughout the volume). Our affects, morality, science, knowledge more generally, art, and religion are among the many matters which come under consideration in the first book, and to which he return subsequently—at greatest length in the third book, and again in the fifth. And the controlling perspective in which they are examined, interpreted, and assessed is what he else-where calls "the perspective of life."[3]

In the second book, and again toward the end of the third, one encounters a large number of reflections and aphorisms of several kinds which at first glance seem to have little relevance to this general project. Upon further consideration, however, they may be seen to have a good deal to do with it, and to be very instructive with respect to the way in which Nietzsche conceives of it and seeks to carry it out. Some are psychological and social-psychological; and their fundamental signifi-cance, beyond the astuteness and interest of the particular insights they often express, lies in their collective indication of how he proposes to understand the kinds of tendencies which inform most of what goes on in ordinary human life. In this way he seeks to take account of the commonplace surface features of our lives, in a manner enabling him to tie them in with the broader "naturalized" interpretation of our humanity he is developing, while at the same time attending to their fine texture and so demonstrating that his interpretation is not sim-plistically and objectionably oblivious to them.

Other sections in these books have a very different focus but serve the same general purpose. In them he deals with a broad range of social, cultural, artistic, and intellectual phenomena. On one level they can be taken and appreciated simply as the penetrating and often barbed ob-servations of a critic of this scene. On another, however, they too serve at once to marshal further evidence for the "naturalizing" account of human life he is advancing, and to show that such phenomena do not count against it, by revealing them to admit of inclusion in it. Remark-able though these phenomena may be, it is as remarkably wrought transformations and expressions of very human dispositions and fun-damental human capacities that they are so. On the other hand, Nietzsche would be the first to insist that the transmutation of our human animality into a spirituality that takes such forms is one of the most interesting and important features of our humanity, which is all the more deserving of appreciation once man has been translated back into nature.

With this observation, however, we are brought back to the coun-terpoint of Nietzsche's concern with the possibility of a higher humanity, repeatedly touched upon in the first books of the volume, heralded with considerable fanfare at the conclusion of the third, and made the main topic of the fourth. If, as Nietzsche announced in the original edition, his volume "marks the conclusion of a series . . . whose common goal is to erect *a new image and ideal of the free spirit*,"[4] this final book of the series is certainly the culmination of that endeavor. And in it, he shows very clearly how concerned he is to counter the nihilistic tendency to devalue our humanity, which he fears may all too readily be prompted by its "naturalization" and the broader "de-deification" of our thinking about ourselves and the world.

In one sense his efforts along these lines may be regarded as supplementary to his "naturalized" interpretation of our human nature. His investigation into our general human nature serves to prepare the ground for the development of a new approach to the question of human worth, constituting the centerpiece of a naturalistic theory of value complementing his philosophical anthropology. In another sense, however, what Nietzsche has to say along these lines may be understood as belonging importantly to his anthropology, which he would regard as incomplete without account being thus taken of the possibility of the sort of higher humanity he has in mind and of the significance of the enhancement of life it represents. Its exploration too is part of his "gay science"; for he considers it to require being extended in this way if justice is to be done to our human nature, the developmental potential of which is no less important to its comprehension and assessment than its basic character and commonplace manifestations.

Disillusioned inquiry into our fundamental nature and what we have come to be, for Nietzsche, must be accompanied by a consideration of what we have it in us further to become. Otherwise our understanding of our humanity will be incomplete and perhaps fatally short-sighted, leading to an underestimation of ourselves which may have lamentable consequences. Our human animality and past, and the varieties of the all-too-human and the general features of human life, may easily absorb the attention of philosophers who have made "de-deification" and "naturalization" their first orders of business. A preoccupation with them, however, is likely to result in an impoverished picture of ourselves, which leaves out something Nietzsche regards as essential. In his notion of "becoming those we are," which is one of his main themes in this fourth book, he underscores the point that *what we are* embraces not only what we *have* become but also what we *have it in us to* become. In this way, he seeks to establish a basis for deriving a kind of normative force from his philosophical anthropology, privileging the attainment of the higher humanity to which he directs attention in relation to more commonplace forms of human life.

To summarize my discussion to this point: the concerns and issues to which Nietzsche addresses himself in *The Gay Science*, and his manner of doing so, are indicative of the nature and tasks of the sort of thing philosophy is for him, which he considers it appropriate to characterize as *frohliche Wissenschaft*. His philosophical *Wissenschaft* aims at a comprehensive reinterpretation of a broad range of matters centering upon our nature and possibilities in the aftermath of the "death of God." Its intent is both cognitive and evocative; for it is animated by a hard-won confidence that it may at once issue in an enhancement of understanding, and also point the way to an enhancement of human life. And its point of departure for Nietzsche is "completing our de-deification of nature" and proceeding "to 'naturalize' humanity" accordingly.

I now shall turn to the fifth book of this volume. I consider it to be of particular significance because it confirms and continues the general project begun considerably earlier in the first four books; because it shows what kinds of questions and issues the mature Nietzsche took to require being dealt with in the course of carrying it out; and because it provides further indications of how he proposes to deal with them and what he is prepared to say about them. He is much more straightforward about these matters here than he frequently is in other writings. This book thus is also of considerable value as a guide to the interpretation of what he elsewhere does and says. More specifically, I would suggest that it is of particular value to the task of deciding what to make of the contents of his notebooks from the crucial period spanned by the writing and publication of the first and last books of the volume. Material from the notebooks that is consonant with things he shows himself here to be prepared to say may be taken with some confidence to likewise reflect his thinking with respect to the matters discussed.[5]

On the other hand, one feature of the fifth book, which virtually impels one to look at Nietzsche's notebooks as well as to other things he published, is that for the most part he here simply says what he thinks, stating his views on various issues without indicating at all clearly and completely what considerations may have led him to hold them. He sketches the outlines and main features of a rather comprehensive reinterpretation of human life and related matters; but he does relatively little in his book to elaborate his case for it. Here and there lines of argument and supporting considerations are suggested. On the whole, however, he is content merely to present it in quick and vivid strokes, as though concerned to ensure that the forest will not be lost sight of for the trees.

Consider now the structure and content of this remarkable set of forty sections and an epilogue. It begins (343) by "cheerfully" sounding the theme of the "death of God" and its consequences, and stressing the resulting liberation of "the lover of knowledge" for new ventures. It ends (382) with a celebration of the conception of a new "great health" and of a higher humanity, contrasting markedly with those of "present-day man," and superseding the transitional stage on the way to them described a few sections earlier (377). Immediately preceding this conclusion there is a retrospective section (381), noted above, in which Nietzsche remarks that he considers his reflections to be compromised neither by his style and brevity nor by the admitted limitations of his own knowledge of many matters with which scientists concern themselves. Thus, in the latter connection, he observes that "we need more, we also need less" than scientific inquiry, in dealing with "such questions as concern me."

The nature, limits, and value of science and scientific knowledge are among the issues with which he deals, beginning with his critical consideration of the "will to truth" in scientific inquiry in the second section (344), and continuing in a number of later sections.[6] In a related series of reflections he discusses the limitations of the kind of thinking characteristic of "scholarly" types;[7] and in others he extends his analysis and critique to the ways of thinking associated with religion.[8] As might be expected, he likewise subjects morality to scrutiny,[9] and art as well.[10]

The context in which he examines and assesses these various human types and phenomena, and in which these reflections take on their larger significance, is further set by what Nietzsche has to say in a number of other very important sections, in which he indicates his general view of the kind of world this is (346), the basic character of life (349), and certain salient features of our human nature (354–361). Our humanity— as it has come to be and as it may become—is Nietzsche's fundamental concern, here as in the four earlier books; and his way of bringing it into focus is by alternating between these complementary kinds of analysis, each of which is intended to illuminate the other.[11]

It is of no little importance to the understanding of Nietzsche's chosen task and thinking, at least as they are here to be seen, that his remarks about "the perspective character of existence" and "the possibility that it may contain infinite interpretations" (374) are offered as unanswerable questions, rather than as propositions he is prepared to assert. They certainly would not seem to be considerations he supposes to be fatal to the kind of knowledge he concedes to science. And he likewise does not appear to take them to preclude the more penetrating comprehension of ourselves and the world to which he suggests philosophical "lovers of knowledge" may newly aspire. He has a number of things to say about "the way of this world," for example, in one of the early sections of the fifth book which sets the stage for what follows; and they are said confidently, with no suggestion that they are subject to qualification along these lines. "We know it well," he says; "the world in which we live is ungodly, immoral, 'inhuman,'; we have interpreted it far too long in a false and mendacious way . . . , according to our *needs*." (346)

As these remarks suggest, Nietzsche supposes himself to be doing otherwise, and to be doing so more truthfully—notwithstanding the fact that, in the preceding section, he has cautioned against supposing the "will to truth" to be unproblematical with respect to both its underlying motivation and its value for life (345). A few sections later he further ventures to state what he takes "the really fundamental instinct of life" to be, saying that it "aims at *the expansion of power*" and asserting against the popular version of Darwinism:

> The struggle for existence is only an *exception*, a temporary restriction of the will to life. The great and small struggle always revolves around superiority, around growth and expansion, around power—in accordance with the will to power which is the will of life. (349)

This is not the manner of speaking of one who believes that our comprehension can extend no further than a recognition of the structure and contents of the world as we have arranged it for ourselves in a perspective determined by our needs. And even in the remainder of his discussion, most of which has to do with our human existence rather than with life and the world more generally, our existence is discussed from a standpoint Nietzsche considers himself to have attained which transcends ordinary human perspectives, and enables him to arrive at a more adequate and insightful interpretation and assessment of it. The attainment of such a standpoint, he grants, in a section near the end in which he is speaking specifically of morality, is difficult and cannot be supposed to yield knowledge that is absolute; but it is clear that he takes it to be possible. He writes:

> "Thoughts about moral prejudices," if they are not meant to be prejudices about prejudices, presuppose a position *outside* morality, some point beyond good and evil to which one has to rise, climb or fly. . . . That one *wants* to go precisely out there, up there, may be a minor madness, a peculiar and unreasonable "you must"—for we seekers for knowledge also have our idiosyncracies of "unfree will"—the question is whether one really *can* get up there.
> This may depend on manifold conditions. In the main the question is how light or heavy we are . . . . One has to be *very light* to drive one's will

to knowledge into such a distance and, as it were, beyond one's time, to create for oneself eyes to survey millennia and, moreover, clear skies in those eyes. (380)

This is something Nietzsche seeks to do not only in the case of morality, but with respect to the other human phenomena with which he specifically deals in the course of the book and to the broader contours of our humanity more generally. In his treatment of these matters too, he conceives of himself and proceeds as a "seeker for knowledge," impelled—perhaps "peculiarly and unreasonably" but nonetheless strongly—to "drive" his "will to knowledge" far enough to enable him to bring them into focus and achieve a just comprehension and assessment of them. So, for example, beyond what he has to say about the basic character of life and the world, he offers several sustained discussions relating directly and importantly to the understanding of human thought and action generally, and so to the comprehension of what he elsewhere frequently refers to as "the type 'man'." In one such section (354) he develops a general account of the fundamental relation between our consciousness (conscious thought and self-consciousness), language, and the need for communication associated with our social manner of existence. In another, he sketches what he takes to be one of his "most essential steps and advances" along these lines: learning "to distinguish the cause of acting"—which he characterizes as "a quantum of dammed-up energy that is waiting to be used up somehow"— "from the cause of acting in a particular way, in a particular direction, with a particular goal." (360)

Moreover, in many of the sections in which he directs his attention to such phenomena as art or morality, Nietzsche is concerned to draw upon his observations concerning them to shed light upon our nature, as well as to make particular points about them; for he considers them among the richest sources of insight into our nature.[12] In this respect Nietzsche shows himself to be an heir of Hegel, for whom "*Wesen ist was gewesen ist*," and the "phenomenology of spirit" is the path to the comprehension our fundamental and attained spiritual nature (in which connection such phenomena are taken to be particularly revealing). And one may even discern an echo of Kant here, for whom reflection upon the nature and conditions of the possibility of certain types of our experience can afford us otherwise unattainable insight into our fundamental mental constitution; although profound changes accompanied Nietzsche's naturalized and historicized revision of Kant's understanding of what we are.

Thus Nietzsche's strategy of looking at various forms of human experience and activity "in the perspective of life," while in some respects
importantly different from that of Kant as well as Hegel, in another is
interestingly similar. It is intended both to enhance our understanding
of these phenomena by bringing out their relation to our fundamental
nature and its modifications and to shed light upon the latter by reflecting
upon what they reveal about the kind of creature capable of them and
disposed to them. In some cases Nietzsche interprets such phenomena
as expressing and revealing something characteristic of particular types
of human beings. In others, he takes them to be indicative of something
more comprehensive—sometimes about "present-day man," and sometimes about our humanity more generally.

All of this, of course, is "interpretation," rather than argument of a
rigor that would yield conclusions of such certainty and finality that they
would preclude the possibility of error or improvement. Moreover, the
object of investigation is no fixed and immutable substance and has no
timeless essence, but rather is a form of life that has come to be what
it is, exhibits considerable diversity, and may be supposed to be capable
of further transformation. Thus the kind of knowledge of which this
object of inquiry admits must be recognized to be nothing absolute for
yet other reasons. But neither of these considerations serves to deter
Nietzsche. The fact that he did not complete his project, and indeed
that it cannot ever *be* completed, likewise does not tell against it. One
can get somewhere with it, just as one may go astray, and even though
one's attained understanding may always admit of being improved upon.

Nietzsche is prepared to allow, and indeed to insist, that the *value* of
the knowledge of ourselves which may thereby be attainable is prob-
lematical. He also holds that in any event there is more to the enhanced
sort of life he associates with the higher humanity he envisions than the
pursuit and attainment of such knowledge. Nonetheless, his conviction
of its possibility and his own commitment to its attainment are clear.
As he wrote in *Beyond Good and Evil*, a year earlier:

> To translate man back into nature; to become master over the many
> vain and overly enthusiastic interpretations and connotations that have so
> far been scrawled and painted over that eternal basic text of *homo natura*;
> to see to it that man henceforth stands before man even as today, hardened
> in the discipline of science, he stands before the *rest* of nature, with intrepid
> Oedipus eyes and sealed Odysseus ears . . . —that may be a strange and
> insane task, but it is a *task*—who would deny that?[13]

It is also significant that he goes on here to observe that, while one
may well ask "Why did we choose this insane task?", this question,

"put differently," is the question "Why have knowledge at all?" For this implies that, whatever the answer to these questions may turn out to be (and even if the last question should turn out to have no answer at all, or an answer cast ultimately in terms of the "will to power" rather than in terms of the intrinsic value of truth), Nietzsche is nonetheless persuaded that something deserving of the name of knowledge is possible and attainable here. It is to be distinguished from interpretations of the sort to which he refers, as the outcome of persisting in the "task" of which he speaks. And our nature is its central object.

In this connection, I would stress a point which comes through nicely and clearly in the fifth book of *The Gay Science*, as it also does in the earlier books, and elsewhere as well. The common view of Nietzsche's general conception of our nature, seemingly supported by passages of this sort, imputes to him strongly reductionist and biologistic tendencies. This view, however, is importantly distorted and misguided, misrepresenting his actual approach to it and understanding of it quite seriously. He may suggest, as he has Zarathustra say, that "the soul is only a word for something about the body,"[14] and that "perhaps the entire evolution of the spirit is a question of the body," as "the history of the development of a higher body that emerges into our sensibility."[15] But he also considers human life to have been fundamentally, pervasively and fatefully transformed—or rather, to have *become* human life in the first place—with the advent of *society*.

Nietzsche contends that this development "sundered" mankind from its "animal past." It is held to have established "new surroundings and conditions of existence" for the human animal, which resulted in its becoming "something so new, profound, unheard of, contradictory, *and pregnant with a future* that the aspect of the earth was essentially altered."[16] And the greater part of his philosophical-anthropological investigations—which in effect began in *The Birth of Tragedy*, and continued to the end of his productive life—proceed by way of reflections upon phenomena associated with human social and cultural life. As has been observed, he does insist upon the importance of bearing in mind that "the entire evolution of the spirit" along these lines is ultimately to be referred back to "the body" and our physiological constitution and interpreted accordingly. However, he considers it equally important to be instructed with respect to the way in which human life has come to be reconstituted and shaped in the course of its development by attending to the social and cultural phenomena in which its emergent nature is manifested, and through which the conditions of the possibility of its further enhancement have been established.

In his reflections upon these matters, therefore, far from setting his philosophical-anthropological concerns aside, Nietzsche actually is pursuing them in the manner he considers to be most illuminating and fruitful and indeed to be called for by the sort of thing our humanity has become. A kind of "higher body" our spirituality may fundamentally be; but it must be approached with eyes attentive to its attained features and subtleties if it is to afford us insight into the kind of creature we are, and if neither our emergent nature nor our potential higher humanity is to be too simplistically conceived and so misunderstood.

Nietzsche was ultimately more interested in what we as human beings have it in us to become—that "future" with which he says we are "pregnant"—than he is in what we already are. He was hard-headed enough to recognize, however, that any "new image and ideal" of a higher humanity that might be "erected," to be more than idle speculation and fantasy, must be grounded in and derived from a sober and clear-sighted assessment of our humanity as it is, taking account of both the general rule and exceptions to it. Moreover, he was astute enough to recognize that, to investigate and do anything approaching justice to something so complex, one must learn "how to employ a *variety* of perspectives" upon it "in the service of knowledge." For, as he goes on to observe, "the more eyes, different eyes, we can use to observe one thing, the more complete will our 'concept' of this thing, our 'objectivity,' be."[17] And what this means and implies for him, in the case of our own reality, is that one must approach it by attending to the many different phenomena which have emerged in the course of human events, in ways that are appropriate and sensitive to their emergent features as well as that lend themselves to a more comprehensive integration and interpretation.

In this light, good and important sense can be made of Nietzsche's excursion through many forms of human cultural and social life in the course of the fifth book of *The Gay Science*. It constitutes a kind of reckoning up of what humanity has made of itself in the course of its development to this point of a nature and "higher body" that is spiritual as well as physiological, and of the resources and capacities this schooling and transformation of the "basic text of *homo natura*" have placed at its disposal, to be drawn upon in effecting its further enhancement. So, when he in conclusion evokes "the ideal of a spirit" which, "from overflowing power and abundance," is able to "play" freely with "all that was hitherto called holy, good, untouchable, divine" (382), he has in mind a higher humanity that is heir to all that he has surveyed, while also overcoming the all-too-human limitations and defects upon which he remarks in doing so. These phenomena together flesh out the portrait of the sort of creature we have come to be, and in doing so also enable one to discern what we have to work with and build upon in becoming what we have it in us to be. Their examination is essential to the assembling of the materials required to elaborate the sort of philosophical anthropology Nietzsche has in mind and seeks to inaugurate, in this and subsequent works.

The Gay Science is thus a very revealing work. It exemplifies Nietzsche's philosophical "gay science," revealing both his conception of its main tasks and problems and his manner of approaching and dealing with them which he considers such inquiry to call for and involve. If one has some preconceived idea of what a philosophical anthropology would be and what it means to talk about human nature, it might well turn out that it would be inappropriate to characterize his concerns in such terms. But one may instead choose—as I do—to allow oneself to be instructed by what he does and says in this and related works in speaking of "man" and our "humanity" (as he so often does), and thus of the sort of nature he takes it to be appropriate to ascribe to ourselves. And one may further choose (as I do) to take what he does and says along these lines as constituting his version of a philosophical anthropology, conceived as philosophical inquiry into these matters.

There can be no doubt that Nietzsche does inquire into our nature so conceived, very extensively, here and elsewhere; and that his interest in it underlies and motivates many of his reflections on diverse particular human social, cultural, and psychological phenomena. It may seem that little is gained by calling all of this his version of a philosophical anthropology. My reason for doing so, however, is that I find it a very helpful way of bringing much of his discussion into focus. And I would further suggest that, when his efforts are viewed in this light, good and important sense can be made of them, not only piecemeal, but as a whole.

Nietzsche may have linked his proclamation of the "death of God" with an attack upon the "soul-hypothesis"; but he did not proceed to an announcement of what Foucault has called "the death of man"[18] as well, contrary to the efforts of Foucault and his kindred spirits to make Nietzsche out to be the herald of this sequel they themselves proclaim.[19] If one attends at all closely to what he says and undertakes to do in *The Gay Science* and subsequent writings, it should be clear that he instead supposes the "death of God" and the demise of the clutch of metaphysical hypotheses associated with the God-hypothesis (in particular the soul- and being-hypotheses) to serve rather to prepare the way for what might be called "the *birth* of man" as a newly significant philosophical notion.

Nietzsche did indeed repudiate the notion of "man" as a kind of "eternal truth," very early on.[20] But it is of no little significance that he did so very early—and that, having made this point, he then went on to *recast* this notion, devoting a great deal of effort to the investigation of our nature thus reconceived. He evidently was convinced that this notion can and should be rehabilitated—liberated from metaphysical and theological interpretations, and also from its status (made much of by Foucault[21]) as a conceptual correlate of certain disciplines originating earlier in his century—and made the focus of enlightened philosophical inquiry of the sort he commended to his "new philosophers" and sought himself to undertake.

For Nietzsche, such inquiry should serve not (as Foucault would have it) to bring to an end the "anthropological sleep" of the nineteenth century,[22] but rather to bring about what might be contrastingly termed a more sophisticated "anthropological awakening." Far from thinking that the end of metaphysics and the critique of the disciplines Foucault scrutinizes preclude anything like a philosophical anthropology,[23] Nietzsche writes as though they open the way for such inquiry to assume stage front and center in philosophy—along with the revaluation of values and the development of a new theory of value, the genealogy of morals, and the naturalization of morality.

Nietzsche did not think that the only questions which can meaningfully be asked and answered about our human nature are best handed over to the life sciences, and that beyond that level of discourse human nature dissolves into myriad forms of social and cultural life best left to cultural anthropologists, sociologists, and historians. He also did not think that conceptual, linguistic, and phenomenological analyses are the only available and proper alternatives to human-scientific inquiry to which a philosopher has recourse. And he did not suppose that the end of metaphysics spells the end of philosophy. He called for "*new* philosophers," convinced that philosophy has a future—and not merely as the handmaiden either of the sciences or of the literati. And the kind of philosophy he advocated and practiced had a reconsideration of our nature as one of its main items of business; for he was persuaded that it makes good and important sense to talk about "the type 'man'," and believed that the kind of thinking and inquiry in which he understood genuine philosophizing to consist has a crucial role to play in doing so.

In styling himself a psychologist, and in saying that from now on the other disciplines are to serve psychology which is the path to the resolution of the most fundamental problems,[24] Nietzsche is giving expression to these convictions and program—meaning a *philosophical* psychology and psychologically sensitive philosophy, rather than the particular behavioral-scientific discipline psychology has become in this century. So also when he calls for translating men back into nature—and then complements this call by directing attention to what our "disanimalization" has involved and accomplished—*our* "genealogy." And when he seeks to develop a "theory of affects," and reflects upon language, consciousness and self-consciousness, reason and knowledge as matters of *our* manner of existence.

It is thus no objection or fatal obstacle to the enterprise of a philosophical anthropology, for Nietzsche, that our humanity has a history and a genealogy, and that it remains capable of further transformation. In both cases, the moral he draws is not that the concept of humanity and notion of "the type 'man' " are ruled out, or that they are matters with which philosophy is incapable of dealing. Rather, it is that philosophy must and can adjust to the character of these objects of inquiry, in aspiration and method, as it proceeds to deal with them.

Why is this of interest? It is not merely because this is part of Nietzsche's thought, which has come to be of interest to growing numbers of us recently. More important, it is of interest because it should be instructive to us as philosophers, and relevant to a number of ongoing debates (about human nature and about philosophy itself, among others). It has significant implications for the setting of an agenda for philosophy today and tomorrow—the posing and framing of questions and issues with which we would do well to concern ourselves, and the decisions to be made about how we are to deal with them. And to my mind, it is further of interest because what Nietzsche had to say along these lines, when he got down to cases, warrants serious consideration, and richly rewards it.[25]

Notes

1. Not in the text itself, but on the back cover of this edition. See *GS*, p. 30.
2. *WP* 13.
3. *BT* preface, 2.
4. *GS,* p. 30.
5. In interpreting Nietzsche, it is undeniable that interpretive priority should

be given to what he actually published over the *Nachlass*. One should also be prepared to grant, however, that use of material from the *Nachlass* may be warranted by the appearance of comparable lines of thought in his published work.

6. E.g., secs. 355 and 373.

7. E.g., sec. 348, 349, 366.

8. E.g., secs. 347, 350, 351, 353, 358.

9. E.g., secs. 345, 352, 359, 380.

10. E.g., secs. 367, 368, 370.

11. Nietzsche thus anticipates Sartre's advocacy and practice of what Sartre calls the "progressive-regressive method" in his *Search for a Method* (New York: Vintage, 1968), in which he too is concerned to work out a way of arriving at an appropriate and fruitful way of conceiving and comprehending human existence and possibility.

12. In doing so, Nietzsche proceeds in a manner not unlike that of his near-contemporary Wilhelm Dilthey (with whose *Lebensphilosophie* his own enterprise is often associated). For Dilthey too took the key to the comprehension of human life to be its various expressions in the form of such social and cultural phenomena. See H. P. Rickman, ed., *Meaning in History: Dilthey's Thought on History and Society* (New York: Harper, 1962).

13. *BGE* 230.

14. *Z* I 4.

15. *WP* 676.

16. *GM* II 16.

17. *GM* III 12.

18. Michel Foucault, *The Order of Things* (New York: Vintage, 1973), p. 342.

19. Foucault, p. 385.

20. *HH* I 2.

21. Foucault, chap. 10.

22. Foucault, pp. 340–43.

23. As Foucault argues in chap. 10 of *The Order of Things* and indeed throughout the book.

24. *BGE* 23.

25. For a more extended discussion of Nietzsche's thinking with respect to human nature and related matters, see my *Nietzsche* (London: Routledge and Kegan Paul, 1983), chap. 5.

Nietzsche's Letters and a Poem

CHRISTOPHER MIDDLETON

Nietzsche's prose can captivate you with its dynamic linearity, its candor, its cleanness—until, impulsively, its polyphony carries you off into "the transcendent." Hence philosophers have tended to regard him as a writer, and writers as a philosopher: explicators are hard put to capture the magic of conjecture, the *superpositional* halo that his style gives off—like smoke rings rising from the far crest of his thought, signals decipherable to some other Euro-Indians on another crest, perhaps, in another age, even in ours. Faintly foreseeing that the Texas 1985 conference would generate spiky varieties of theoretical discourse with which to circumscribe the halo, I decided to contribute not another discourse on anything, but a series of downright phenomena, some of Nietzsche's letters, as a sort of blanket to cap off, then release, the halo-fumes. Wouldn't it, I thought, be valuable for these Nietzscheans to recognize how absent Nietzsche was from his friends? Shouldn't people appreciate the extent to which Nietzsche was, often enough, a dull stick as a letter-writer? After all, the letters hardly tell of any pleasant physical experiences before Nietzsche discovered ice-cream in Turin: he seems not to delight at all in anything commonplace. Shouldn't the woeful possibility at least be floated across our horizon, that, to judge by his letters, this most dynamic cultural psychologist never really warmed to a single individual human being wholeheartedly enough to confide in her or him (what he might have *said* to Lou we can only guess).

In contrast to Rilke, for instance, the hermetic Rilke, who wrote such inventive and stylish letters, Nietzsche seems not to have used letters as whetstones for his fabulous ideas. Compared to Mörike, whose letters rival in magic, concreteness, humor, eloquence and detail, those of Keats, Nietzsche is an owl. But when Nietzsche is walking about and making notes, or when he sits down and writes, what dash, what lucidity, what movement, what concertedness, what fertility—compared with the diffidence of his epistolary mode, its formulaic tightness. At all events, I thought there was a discrepancy that might be worth considering during the conference: between the afflicted and inhibited Nietzsche of the letters and Nietzsche the Neptune of tidal brainwaves, the sovereign colonist of the Inferno of Morality. The discrepancy had struck me twenty years before, while translating my selection of his letters: so now I would simply read a few of them, not to "cut Nietzsche down to size," not just to indicate how limited he was in his "affective" life—I realized that his letters shouldn't be generalized about, and that the French selection of 1937 (by Alexandre Vialatte) had deeply impressed Albert Camus. My aim was to suggest, and only to suggest, that we have here an enigma. Perhaps Nietzsche succeeded in transposing his entire neural apparatus of impulse into the play of his thought, objectifying it into his prose style. The enigma is that the farseeing clairvoyant of history and of the structures of consciousness, if we are to judge from his letters, seldom gave a thought to the singular harmonics of those feeling-tones which shape and color every individual's being, and in dialogue with others he could communicate, besides, precious little about profundities or even objects of feeling.

Before I was due to read some of the letters, right up to the last minute, I was scribbling away at a poem. The conference had been developing into a discussion of the *übermensch* concept, almost to the exclusion of other matters. This had vexed me. I have a reverse sympathy—for secret excellence in apparently everyday people. The heroics—of discourse or its referent—had been breaking against a will, on my part, to some kind of alternative action. Weeks before the conference I had tried to write a poem about a former neighbor of mine here in Central Texas. He had built the house I'd lived in. He'd always been amiably at hand to help when anything went wrong. He was a bricoleur, a working man, almost illiterate, but, for all that, a man who spoke interestingly about the world. Yet the poem hadn't worked out. I hadn't been able to hear the voice that might be right for what I guessed the poem might come to say. Then one evening during the days of the conference I did hear that voice. It wasn't quite mine, it was a bit like his voice, my old neighbor's. I started afresh and the poem was by now working out. I was finishing it during the last minutes before it was my turn to speak. It was anything but programmatic, the poem; I never meant it to be a critique of the *übermensch* or of his discussants. In fact the poem was still so strange to me that I asked, after I'd read it: "Well, can anyone tell me what that was all about?" Suspense. Then, touchingly enough, a student replied (it was Mark Toles): "A free man."

Some Gists from Nietzsche's Letters

June 11, 1865
I write this to you, dear Lisbeth, only in order to counter the most usual proofs of believing people, who invoke the evidence of their inner experiences and deduce from it the infallibility of their faith. Every true faith is indeed infallible; it performs what the believing person hopes to find in it, but it does not offer the least support for the establishing of an objective truth.

April 7, 1866
Yesterday a magnificent storm was in the sky, I hurried out to a nearby hilltop, called Leusch (perhaps you can tell me what that means), found a hut up there, a man who was slaughtering two kids, and his young son. The storm broke with immense force, with wind and hail. I felt an incomparable elation, and I knew for certain that we can rightly understand nature only when we have to run to her, away from our troubles and pressures. What to me were man and his unquiet will! What were the eternal "Thou shalt," "Thou shalt not"! How different the lightning, the wind, the hail, free powers, without ethics! How fortunate, how strong they are, pure will, without obscurings from the intellect!

January 16, 1867
Τί γάρ ἐστιν ἄνθρωπος; ἀσθηνείας ὑπόδειμα καιροῦ λάφυρον, τύχης παίγνιον, μεταπτώσεως εἰκών, φθόνου καὶ συμφορᾶς πλαστιγξ.

April 6, 1867
Should not the image of Sophocles put to shame the scholar who could dance so elegantly and knock a ball about and yet still showed some intellectual accomplishment? . . . Our egoism is not clever enough, our intellect not egoistic enough.

November 3, 1867
Suddenly you breathe the atmosphere of the stable. In the lanterns' half-light, figures loom up. Around you there are sounds of scraping,

whinnying, brushing, knocking. And in the midst of it all, in the garb
of a groom, making violent attempts to carry away in his bare hands
something unspeakable, unsightly, or to belabor the horse with a comb—
I shudder when I see his face—it is, by the Dog, none other than myself.

November 20, 1868
To see again from close at hand the seething brood of the philologists
of our time, and every day having to observe their moleish pullulating,
the baggy cheeks and the blind eyes, their joy at capturing worms and
their indifference to the true problems, the urgent problems of life—
not only the young ones doing it, but also the old, full-grown ones—all
this makes me see more and more clearly that the two of us, if this is
to be our only means of remaining true to the spirit in us, shall not go
our way in life without a variety of offenses and intrigues.

July 19, 1870
At this moment a terrible thunderclap: the Franco-German war is declared, and our whole threadbare culture plunges at the frightful demon's
breast . . . We may be already at the beginning of the end! What deso-
lations! We shall need monasteries again. And we shall be the first
fratres.

September 11, 1870
In Ars sur Moselle we took charge of casualties and returned with them
to Germany. These three days and nights spent together with the serious
casualties were the climax of our efforts. I had a miserable cattle truck
in which there were six bad cases; I tended them, bandaged them, nursed
them during the whole journey alone—moreover, I diagnosed in two
cases gangrene. That I survived those pestilential vapors, and could
even sleep and eat, now seems a marvel . . . Then I went to bed and am
still there. A good doctor diagnosed my trouble as, first, a severe dys-
entry and, then, diphtheria.

December 15, 1870
Even if we do not find many people to share our views, I still believe
that we can fairly—not without losses, of course—pull ourselves up out
of this stream and that we shall reach an island on which we shall not
need to stop our ears with wax any more. Then we shall be teachers to
each other, our books will be merely fishhooks for catching people into
our monastic and artistic community.

June 21, 1871
When I heard of the fires in Paris, I felt for several days annihilated
and was overwhelmed by fears and doubts; the entire scientific, scholarly, philosophical, and artistic existence seemed an absurdity, if a single
day could wipe out the most glorious works of art, even whole periods
of art; I clung with earnest conviction to the metaphysical value of art,
which cannot exist for the sake of poor human beings but which has
higher missions to fulfill.

December 27, 1871
When I saw the beautiful Russian leather, I thought you were really
spoiling me—where would such aristocratic tendencies land me! Such a
writing case was certainly something I needed, and the first letter I write
on it, my dear mother, is for you. Equally useful and delightful were
the good comb, the hairbrush, the clothesbrush (except it is somewhat
too soft), the nice socks and the large quantity of delicious gingerbread—
all of them beautifully and festively packed.

July 16, 1872
The goat legs are the true characteristic of the oldest idea; and without
any archaeological proof, I would maintain that Hesiod's ουτιδγυοι κγι
γμηχδυοενγοι were goat-legged, thus *capripedes*, As Horace says, Odes
2, 2, and other poets (Greek also) ογτυροι I explain, like τυνοι, as a
reduplication of the root τερ (as in the relation of ξιιουαοζ to οοσοζ);
τοροζ = "penetratingly bright"; σγτυροι = "those uttering penetrating
shrieks," as epithet for the goats, just as μηκγδεζ is the epithet for the
she-goat.

October 25, 1872
I see what you have *done for Wagner* by your act of friendship toward
me. When Gersdorff reads your book I am convinced he will stand on
his head two or three times for sheer joy!

October 18, 1873
Meanwhile another thing has waxed gigantic and really beyond our
control . . . The acute critic E. R. has no access to the whole *apparatus
criticus* (letters and statements from the female phantom R. N.). From
what we do know, even less experienced crytycs can draw a frightfully
definite conclusion, especially when they avail themselves of R.'s famous
speculative classroom void. . . . Incidentally, it is earnestly requested by
the dictator and writer of this letter that you burn it *at once*. . . . We are

living Samarow—thinking in terms of bombs and counterbombs, we sign only pseudonymous names and wear false beards.

May 23, 1876
It struck me that you said very little about pederasty . . . Perhaps as I read on I shall find some hints on this too; I have not got far yet—my eyes are too bad.

August 1, 1876
You can all stay together in the Giessels' house; for the rent we are paying, it's the cheapest lodging in Bayreuth. You should hear what the other prices are! . . . I have had enough of it all! . . . I do not even want to be at the first performance—but somewhere else, anywhere but here, where there is nothing but torment for me.

End of July, 1877
Wagner . . . is so averse to anything mathematical and strictly symmetrical (as is shown on a small scale in his use of triplets—I mean the excessive use of them) that he prefers to prolong four-beat phrases into five-beat ones, six-beat ones into seven-beat ones (in *Die Meistersinger*, Act 3, there is a waltz; check to see if it is not governed by seven-beat phrases). Sometimes—but perhaps this is a crime of *lèse-majesté*—it reminds me of Bernini's manner; he can no longer tolerate simple columns but makes them, as he thinks, come alive with volutes all the way up.

July 18, 1880
. . . a reflection: one ceases to love oneself *aright* when one *ceases* to give oneself exercise in loving others, wherefore the latter (the ceasing) is to be strongly advised against (from my own experience).

July 30, 1881 (postmark)
I have a precursor, and *what* a precursor! I hardly knew Spinoza: what brought me to him now was the guidance of instinct. Not only is his whole tendency like my own—to make knowledge the most *powerful passion*—but also in five main points of his doctrine I find myself: he denies free will, purposes, the moral world order, the nonegoistical, evil; of course the differences are enormous, but they are differences more of period, culture, field of knowledge.

End of August, 1882

Lastly, my dear Lou, the old, deep, heartfelt plea: *become the being you are*! First, one has the difficulty of emancipating oneself from one's chains; and ultimately one has to emancipate oneself from this emancipation too! Each of us has to suffer, though in greatly different ways, from the chain sickness, even after he has broken the chains.

September 16, 1882

Yesterday afternoon I was happy; the sky was blue, the air mild and clear, I was in the Rosenthal, lured there by the *Carmen* music. I sat there for three hours, drank my second glass of cognac this year, in memory of the first (ha! how horrible it tasted!), and wondered in all innocence and malice if I had any tendency to madness. In the end I said *no*. Then the *Carmen* music began, and I was submerged for half an hour in tears and heart beatings.

March 24, 1883 (Genoa)

Deep down, a motionless black melancholy. And fatigue. Mostly in bed—that is the best thing for my health, I had become very thin—people were amazed; now I have found a good *trattoria*, and will feed myself up again. But the worst thing is: I no longer see *why* I should live for another six months—everything is boring, painful, *dégoûtant*. I forgo and suffer too much, and have come to comprehend, beyond all comprehension, the deficiency, the mistakes, and the real disasters of my whole past intellectual life.

February 22, 1884 (Nice)

It is my theory that with this Z(arathustra) I have brought the German language to a state of perfection. After Luther and Goethe, a third step had to be taken—look and see, old chum of mine, if vigor, flexibility, and euphony have ever consorted so well in our language ... In any case I have remained a poet, in the most radical sense of the word—although I have tyrannized myself a great deal with the antithesis of poetry.

May 21, 1884 (Venice)

All my still existing relationships suffer from, and have been made absurd by, an irreparable fault at the root. Ultimately, though, my real *distress* lies elsewhere and not in my consciousness of this absurdity: a distress so great and deep that I am always asking if any man has ever suffered so. Who, indeed, feels as I do what it means to feel with every fiber of one's being that "the weights of all things must be decided anew." That from this situation, in the twinkling of an eye, all kinds of physical danger, prison and suchlike, could arise is the least important thing; or rather, it would comfort me if things were to go that far.

Mid-June 1884
But this solitude, ever since my earliest childhood! This secretiveness, even in the most intimate relationships! There can be no breaking it, even by kindness. . . . Meanwhile the situation has been changed by my radical break with my sister; for heaven's sake, do not think that you should mediate between us and reconcile us—there *can* be no reconciliation between a vindictive anti-Semitic goose and me.

Winter 1884–5 (Nice)
Wagner's expression "infinite melody" voices most sweetly the danger, the ruination of instinct and good faith, of good conscience. Ambiguity in rhythm, the effect of which is that one does not know, and *should* not know, whether something is this way or that way round, is doubtless a technique which can procure wonderful effects— *Tristan* is full of it— but as a symptom of an entire art, it is and remains the sign of dissolution. The part dominates the whole, phrase dominates melody, the moment dominates time (also the *tempo*), *pathos* dominates *ethos* (character, style, or whatever you want to call it); finally, even *esprit* dominates "sense." . . . Forgive me if I add: decadent taste is furthest of all from one thing, and that is the *grand* style: which the Palazzo Pitti has, for example, but *not* the Ninth Symphony. The grand style is the most intense form of the art of melody.

May 20, 1884 (Venice)
Almost all my human relationships have resulted from attacks of a feeling of isolation: Overbeck, as well as Rée and Malwida—I have been ridiculously happy if ever I found, or thought I had found, in someone a little patch or corner of common concern. My mind is burdened with a thousand shaming memories of such weak moments, in which I absolutely could not endure solitude any more . . . The feeling that there is about me something very remote and alien, that my words have other colors than the same words from other people, that with me there is much multicolored foreground, which is deceptive—precisely this feeling, of which testimony has lately been reaching me from various sides, is nevertheless the subtlest degree of "understanding" that I have till now found.

October 15, 1885 (Leipzig)
No praise can be too high when, among Germans, someone abjures, as Rée has always done, the real German devil, the genius or *daimon* of obscurity. The Germans think they are profound.

Spring 1886 (Nice)
Malwida, the dear soul, who with her rosy superficiality has always kept herself "on top" in a difficult life, once wrote me, to my bitterest delight, that she could already see from reading my *Zarathustra* the serene temple beckoning from afar, the temple which I would build on this foundation. Well, it's enough to make one die laughing; and by now I am content that people do not pay attention and do not see *what* kind of "temple" I am building.

January 9, 1887 (Nice)
I have just been reading . . . Simplicius's commentary on Epictetus; here one can see clearly before one the whole philosophical scheme in which Christianity became embedded, so that this "pagan" philosopher's book makes the most Christian impression imaginable (except that the whole world of Christian emotion and pathology is missing, "love," as Paul speaks of it, "fear of God," and so on). The falsifying of everything actual by morality stands there in fullest array: wretched psychology, the "philosopher" reduced to the stature of "country parson." And it is all Plato's fault! He is still Europe's greatest misfortune!

February 25, 1887 (Nice)
We are living, in fact, in the interesting expectation that *we shall perish*—thanks to a well-intentioned earthquake, which is making the dogs howl far and wide, and not only the dogs. What fun, when the old houses rattle overhead like coffee mills! when the ink bottle assumes a life of its own! when the streets fill with half-dressed figures and shattered nervous systems! Last night between two and three o'clock, *comme gaillard* as I am, I toured the various districts of the town to see where the fear is greatest . . . Except for an old, very pious lady, who is convinced that the good Lord is not entitled to do her any harm, I was the only cheerful person in the crowd of masks and "feeling hearts."

November 10, 1887 (Nice)
The second volume of the *Journal des Goncourts* has appeared—a most interesting new publication. It concerns the years 1862–65; in it, the famous *dîners chez Magny* are described in an extremely vivid way, the

dinners at which the most intelligent and skeptical troupe of Parisian minds at that time met together (Sainte-Beuve, Flaubert, Théophile Gautier, Taine, Renan, the Goncourt brothers, Schérer, Gavarni, sometimes Turgenev, and so on). Exasperated pessimism, cynicism, nihilism, alternating with a lot of joviality and good humor; I would have been quite at home there myself—I know these gentlemen by heart so well that I have actually had enough of them. One should be more radical; at root they all lack the principal thing—"*la force.*"

February 12, 1888 (Nice)
The days pass here in unashamed beauty; never was there a more perfect winter. And these colors of Nice—I would like to send them to you. All the colors permeated with a shining silver gray; spiritual, intelligent colors; no residue at all of the brutality of the dark tones. The advantage of this small piece of coast between Alassio and Nice is that it allows an Africanism, in color, vegetation, and the dryness of the air—this does not occur elsewhere in Europe.

March 20, 1888 (Nice)
This winter I have what I did not have before—a room which I like, a high one, with excellent light for my eyes, freshly decorated, with a large, heavy table, chaise longue, bookcase, and dark reddish-brown wallpaper, which I chose myself.... I walk for an hour every morning, in the afternoon for an average of three hours, and at a rapid pace— the same walk day after day—it is beautiful enough for that. After supper, I sit until nine o'clock in the dining room, in company mainly with Englishmen and English ladies, with a lamp, which has a shade, at my table. I get up at six-thirty in the morning and make my own tea and also have a few biscuits. At twelve noon I have breakfast; at six, the main meal of the day. No wine, no beer, no spirits, no coffee—the greatest regularity in my mode of living and in my diet.

April 10, 1888 (Turin)
Around 1876 my health grew worse ... There were extremely painful and obstinate headaches which exhausted all my strength. They increased over long years, to reach a climax at which pain was habitual, so that any given year contained for me two hundred days of pain. The malaise must have had an entirely local cause—there was no neuropathological basis for it at all. I have never had any symptoms of mental disturbance—not even fever, no fainting. My pulse was as slow as that of the first Napoleon (= 60). My specialty was to endure the extremity

of pain, *cru, vert*, with complete lucidity for two or three days in succession, with continuous vomiting of mucus.

April 20, 1888 (Turin)

The spacious tall Portici are the *pride* of the place: they extend over 10,020 meters, which means two good hours of walking. Big *trilingual* bookshops. I have never seen anything like them. . . . An excellent *trattoria*, where people treat the German professor most courteously; I pay for each meal, including the tip, one franc, twenty-five centimes. (Minestra or risotto, a good portion of meat, vegetable, and bread—all good to eat!) The water is glorious; coffee in the foremost cafés costs twenty centimes a pot; ice cream of the highest quality, thirty centimes.

August 26, 1988 (Sils Maria)

. . . this animation and enlivening of the smallest articulations, as it enters Wagner's *practice* in music and has spread from there to become almost a dominant performance system (even for actors and singers), with counterparts in *other* arts—it is a *typical symptom of deterioration*, a proof that life has withdrawn from the whole and is *luxuriating* in the infinitesimal.

October 18, 1888 (Turin)

. . . The Germans . . . This irresponsible race, which has all the misfortunes of culture on its conscience and at all *decisive* moments in history, was thinking of "something else" . . . There was never a moment in history—*but who knows a thing about it*? The disproportion here is altogether necessary; at a time when an undreamed-of loftiness and freedom of intellectual passion is laying hold of the *highest* problem of humanity and is calling for a decision as to human destiny, the general obtuseness *must* become all the more sharply distinct from it.

December 7, 1888 (Turin)

When your letter reached me yesterday—the first letter in my life to reach me—I had just finished the last revision of the manuscript of *Ecce Homo*. Since there are no more coincidences in my life, you are consequently not a coincidence. . . . It would take a poet of the first rank to translate *Ecce Homo* . . . On the other hand, it is anti-German to an annihilating extent; throughout, I side with French culture. (I treat all the German philosophers as "unconscious counterfeiters). . . . To secure myself against German brutalities, I shall send the first copies, before publication, to Prince Bismarck and the young emperor, with letters

declaring war—military men cannot reply to that with police measures.—I am a psychologist.—

December 9, 1888
Signs and wonders!
                    Greetings from the   Phoenix.

December 16, 1888
I never write a sentence now in which the whole of me is not present,
then the *psychologist's antithesis* will also be a way for people to understand me—*la gran via* . . .

. . . Evenings I sit in a splendid high room; a small, *very nice* orchestra
plays so quietly, just as I would wish—there are three adjoining rooms.
My paper is brought to me, *Journal des Débats*; I eat an excellent portion
of ice cream; costs, including the tip (which I pay, since it is the custom
here) forty centimes.

December 21, 1888
I have real geniuses among my admirers—today no other name is treated
with so much distinction and reverence as mine. You see that is the best
trick of all: without a name, without rank, without wealth, I am treated
here like a little prince, by everyone, down to my peddler woman, who
will not rest until she has found the sweetest of all her grapes for me.

December (no date) 1888
Now that my destiny is certain, I feel every word of yours with tenfold
sharpness; you have not the remotest conception of what it means to
be closely related to the man and to the destiny in whom the question
of millennia has been decided—I hold, quite literally, the future of
mankind in the palm of my hand.

December 29, 1888
With every glance I am treated like a prince—there is an extremely
distinguished air about the way people open the door for me or serve
me food. When I enter a large shop, all the faces change.

January 4, 1889
To my maestro Pietro,
Sing me a new song: the world is transfigured and all the heavens rejoice.
                              The Crucified.

January 5, 1889

I pay twenty-five francs, with service, make my own tea, and do my own shopping, suffer from torn boots, and thank heaven every moment for the *old* world, for which human beings have not been simple and quiet enough. Since I am condemned to entertain the next eternity with bad jokes, I have a writing business here which really leaves nothing to be desired—very nice and not in the least strenuous.

• • •

I've read these extracts from Nietzsche's letters with a view to loosening the logjam of abstractions which begins, sooner or later, to make itself felt during such symposia as this. Besides, I thought it would be proper for us to hear Nietzsche, albeit muted, snipped asunder, and in translation.

The extracts mark vestigially the stages of his life. The markings are vestigial because the extracts are short, but also because Nietzsche is not as revealing or pungent in his letters as one might wish he might have been. Mostly he contains himself strictly within the epistolary decorum of his time. Since translating some of his letters almost twenty years ago, I've often wondered about the discrepancy, real or apparent, between the writer of the letters and the philosopher of the books. The writer who regarded himself as an arch-psychologist fathoming the murkiest motives of the European soul, simply declined to offer to his correspondents any portion of himself that might allow them to fathom him. In his letters one misses the audacities, the prismatic scintillations, the ironies and the electrifying insolence of his books.

Whether he was, as a writer, self-intoxicated and word-intoxicated or not, is probably beside the point. But don't we tend, ourselves intoxicated by his prose, so spellbound that we experience through his prose a vicarious intellectual liberation, don't we tend to forget how few people he actually knew, or how many he never cared to know, at first hand? The anthropological basis of his towering insights was, I'm suggesting, insufficiently diverse—at least as regards individuals and groups not of his nation, his social class and intellectual rank.

What then is it about us that rivets us to his critique of morals, to his conceptions of the *übermensch* and the "will to power"? Are we so strapped into our cockpits of abstraction, such captives of our own constructions, that we nosedive into a central fact—without even sensing the explosion all around us? Nietzsche's fabulous conceptions of human fate, these truths or chimeras of a speculative genius enshrined in such bewitching prose, do not gibe at all with other mysteries that are always close at hand and are perhaps even less time-bound, certainly more extralinguistic, than his elegant arguments. I mean the concreteness and the obscurity of ordinary laboring individuals.

Perhaps we are so riveted because we recognize Nietzsche as the Columbus of the America of Abstractions in which we live. Even his insistence on revering the earth is an abstraction, even his refusal of compassion is. Perhaps, too, we are so riveted to his abstractions—which would make an even moderately enlightened social anthropologist of our time throw up his hands, or at least wring them—because we are under pressure from peculiar academic anxieties. Different from the unreflecting masses, different from the earth which our overlords around us mutilate with our connivance, but also ordinary in our peculiar ways, we are powerless to make our differences effectual even locally, let alone in a world whose will to power has made giant strides, since Nietzsche, toward a self-destruction beyond even his imagining; a world whose lords are ignorant, while they pretend to be loaded with information, and who are pitiless, while they pretend to mean well.

There it is again: the generalizing. Nevertheless, to loosen a little more the logjam, here is a poem which portrays a man. He's the kind of man whose like, I suppose, Nietzsche never reckoned with. And the poem is an undoctored one, to suit the man. It was an old scribble without focus until last night when I took it up again. For I had a hunch it might have a glancing relevance, the kind of glancing that Nietzsche commends. Or at least I might now have made it so, without injustice, in that room over there, scribbling to the last minute.

A Portrait of J. L. M.

We called him spirit of the place,
But he's more like a good old tree root.
Went off, a year gone, back to Rockport.
It seems, when he'd gone, us not even
Knowing it, everything fell apart.

Wish I remembered
What he told me. This bit of town I landed in,

These railroad tracks he'd known, secret
Signs chalked on the freight wagon doors,
Hobos bivouacking, and how he'd drift across,
Talk with them. That was far back
In the Thirties, near enough to the yard on Seventh
He got our big old bamboo from, planted it.

            Wanderings, the split rail
Fences he built, him wiry then as now, bird faced,
Out west of Sanantone; any job he could find
He put both hands to. He belonged with
Boilers of big ships, blue clouds
Of working people on the move, tumbleweed;
You do the most you can.

            Far out hereabouts
He'd gone courting, before big money
Rolled the roads in. Remember now,
Hummed the tune once, he did. They walked out
Through live oaks together, rocks, and cedar,
Listening to the trickle of the creek in Spring.
He sat his Mildred down, kissed her,
Same old tune in their heads.

            I ate her cakes
She'd later bring at Christmas down the hill,
Stopping to chat a while, propped against
The doorpost, she'd laugh like anything
But sometimes she took ill.

            Drains, spigots, carburetors,
The pump, I saw his knuckles whiten
When he fixed them, and later his hand
Shook, breath caught, and as he worked
His mouth helped, with twists and lippings.

            Rolled his own cigarettes; told me—
Here's this old song book, found it at the county dump,
You want it? 1865—Irish songs. Irish
As his Indian scout grandfather had been. He'd
Told him of hilltops hereabouts

            Where the Indians hunkered,
Yawning. And how a coach might rumble by,
Gold or guns in it, stuff they could use. And how
Into this cave his grandfather went once, deep,

Now they've blocked it, but it goes underground
All the way from the lake to Tarrytown.
A volcano, too, he said

                I might not believe it,
Not so far off, east, he found obsidian there,
Beyond where the highrise banks and turnpikes
And the military airport are. Trees,
He loved trees and drove miles to see them
At their best, the right time of the year.
Buckeye and catalpa in their first flower,
Chinaberry, dogwood.

             All birds had ordinary names,
Like redbird, but once in a while he'd speak
Old words, not from books but from Tennessee,
Like once he said "quietus." Always
Flesh in his words, and bone, and in his doings,
Not absent even from the way he'd knock
A bourbon back, straight, that was the way
He liked it, then roll another cigarette.

            For Mildred when her teeth
Fell out he whittled deer horn so she'd have
A biting edge up front. When he came by, dressed
Smart for a visit, he'd be wearing false
Rat teeth up front and give a wicked grin.
There was this park he kept,

            He knew all the weeds in it,
All, and told how some weed sent
Cows mad and was taken too much liberty with
By them young folks as went out there
For a high time.

            Well, then he'd push off
In his battered pickup, headed for a honkytonk
Some place down the line. Why don't folks look at
That kind of man? Some say insight
Comes when you tell the individual
Get lost. What's all their deep droning talk
To him? He's too smart to think up
Revolutions, what's it, that perspective stuff?
Maybe he's nobody

            But he made things work,
Never slaving, nor ginrollizing. Made things

Shift and level with every breath he drew.
Had no grievance, spoke no ill of anyone
Or anything save spindly offshoots
Of tree roots that split drainpipes in the country,
Having ballooned in them, like brains
Got swole, so he'd say, with all the excrement.

The "gists" from Nietzsche's letters are reprinted from *Selected Letters of Friedrich Nietzsche*, ed. and trans. C. M. Middleton (Chicago: University of Chicago Press, 1969), with the permission of the publisher. "A Portrait of J. L. M." originally appeared in *Two Horse Wagon Going By* (New York: Carcanet Press, 1986) and is reprinted with the permission of the publisher.

Pessimism and the Tragic View of Life: Reconsiderations of Nietzsche's *Birth of Tragedy*

IVAN SOLL

Nietzsche's Rejection of Schopenhauer

Reconsideration of Nietzsche's first book, *The Birth of Tragedy*, begins with his own repeated reassessments of it and his persistent reworking of its central ideas and concerns.

When in 1886, fourteen years after the original publication of *The Birth of Tragedy*, Nietzsche brought out a new edition, he saw fit to furnish it with a preface called "Attempt at a Self-Criticism." This self-criticism, being the criticism of a much earlier self, serves, like most retrospective self-criticism, to disassociate its author from what he perceives to have been his previous errors and follies. Among Nietzsche's principal repudiations, here and in other critical retrospections, is his sweepingly stated rejection of any previously held allegiance to Schopenhauer's philosophy and of any previously felt affinity for Schopenhauer's spirit. Certainly by the 1880s Nietzsche tended generally to emphasize his divergence from Schopenhauer, indeed to define himself in some important sense as Schopenhauer's antipode. He also tended to represent his early infatuation with Schopenhauer and the influence of Schopenhauerian ideas on his own work as having been transitory and superficial. Two years later in 1888, in *Ecce Homo*, there is once again a section devoted to a retrospective evaluation of *The Birth of Tragedy*. Here he describes this first book of his, the one generally conceded to be the most profoundly influenced by Schopenhauer, as one which "smells offensively Hegelian, and in which *the cadaverous perfume of Schopenhauer sticks only to a few formulas.*"[1]

This assertion by Nietzsche that Schopenhauer's influence upon his work was minimal where it was presumably greatest is patently a bit of rhetoric used to remove himself as completely as possible from all association with Schopenhauer. It would be safe and conventional to remark at this point that Nietzsche's own assessment of Schopenhauer's influence upon him "must be taken with a grain of salt." It would be less cautious, but closer to the truth to counsel simply rejecting Nietzsche's assessment, which in fact grossly, even grotesquely, understates and represses the influence of Schopenhauer on *The Birth of Tragedy*. A careful comparative study of Schopenhauer's *World as Will and Representation* and Nietzsche's *The Birth of Tragedy* would reveal the extent and nature of an influence, which is far more substantial than Nietzsche allows. Moreover, such a study would illuminate the more general issue of what was the actual influence of Schopenhauer on Nietzsche's entire philosophic development and production, as opposed to what Nietzsche represented it to be.

If Nietzsche indeed misrepresented Schopenhauer's influence in the case of *The Birth of Tragedy*, could he not also have misrepresented the influence of Schopenhauer upon his later work? And if Nietzsche's underassessment of Schopenhauer's influence upon him is an aspect of a more general campaign to disassociate himself from Schopenhauer, might we not also expect him to have exaggerated the divergence of their views and the difference in their characters? It is my thesis that Nietzsche does just that. In the attempt to reconstitute Schopenhauer one-dimensionally as his antipode in all matters, Nietzsche had to resort to oversimplification occasionally bordering on the ridiculous. A few lines before reducing Schopenhauer's influence on *The Birth of Tragedy* to a "cadaverous perfume" which "sticks only to a few formulas," he rejects Schopenhauer's view of tragedy by saying, "Schopenhauer went wrong at this point, as he went wrong everywhere." Let us note *en passant* the implausibility of there being anyone who goes wrong everywhere, and ask the question, why was Nietzsche interested in defining himself as Schopenhauer's opposite in every way?

Nietzsche's tendency to disown Schopenhauer completely, rather than to delineate with more sensitivity and detail the extent and limits of their affinity and agreement, was in part due to Wagner's enthusiasm for Schopenhauer. Because Nietzsche was in the painful and difficult throes of working his way free of Wagner, he brought to his critical evaluation and reevaluation of Schopenhauer the same stance of hyperbolic and somewhat monolithic repudiation that he had needed to escape Wagner's oppressive domination. This mode of discourse and intellectual procedure, characterized by exaggeration and oversimplication, readily recognizable and comprehensible in the context of establishing autonomy vis-à-vis an overwhelming father figure like Wagner, becomes puzzling and not so easily recognized in Nietzsche's relation to Schopenhauer in which there seems, at first, less at stake psychologically and existentially. It is my hypothesis that Nietzsche treated Schopenhauer in a manner he had developed to deal with the threat Wagner had posed to his personal autonomy. Although this hypothesis, even if true, in no way justifies Nietzsche's behavior, it does help to explain why he seems so insensitive and often so off the mark in his comments on Schopenhauer.

The "Attempt at a Self-Criticism" and the section on *The Birth of Tragedy* in *Ecce Homo* serve not only to repudiate some of the ideas, styles of presentation, and personal allegiances of the earlier book, but also to locate and emphasize what Nietzsche in the late 1880s had come to see as the most important and valuable aspects of the book. Clearly his later view of what is particularly valuable in the book need not and does not match his conception of these matters at the time he wrote it. Nietzsche wanted to focus upon what in his first book had proven to be of central and lasting importance in the course of his philosophical development.

What he did take to be central is indicated by the new title he furnished for the edition of 1886. The original title, *The Birth of Tragedy out of the Spirit of Music*, is supplanted by *The Birth of Tragedy: or the Greek World (Griechentum) and Pessimism*.[2] There are at least two reasons for the change. First, by removing any mention of music from the title he was in effect removing Wagner from the center of consideration. Nietzsche wanted to make clear that the book was only peripherally concerned with Wagner, particularly because he felt that Wagner had often been perceived as the focus of the book. "Several times I saw this book cited as '*The Rebirth of Tragedy out of the Spirit Music*': what people had ears for was only a new formula for the art, the intentions, the task of *Wagner*—and what was really valuable in this essay was ignored."[3]

Secondly, by the 1880s he clearly conceived the most philosophically significant issue in the book to be the problematic nature of human existence, what he calls in the new preface "the big question mark concerning the value of existence." What raises the question mark about the value of human existence, both in *The Birth of Tragedy* and throughout the later work, is the apparent universality and ineluctability of frustration, dissatisfaction, and suffering in life. With the focus upon the problem of suffering or pain as the central philosophical issue of *The Birth of Tragedy*, pessimism, as an expression of the despair commonly resulting from the recognition of the inevitability of suffering, becomes one of the central topics of the discussion and is moved into the title. The new formulation somewhat tentatively offers a choice of titles: *The Birth of Tragedy or: the Greek World and Pessimism.* The first option, *The Birth of Tragedy*, indicates the historical and philological aspect of the work; the second, *The Greek World and Pessimism*, expresses better what the book is about from a philosophical perspective. In *Ecco Homo* Nietzsche actually proposes this second half alone as a "less ambiguous title."

I would like to examine more closely those ideas and problems which Nietzsche himself took to be at the heart of his first book and which I believe are the heart of his entire philosophical enterprise. In doing this I shall attempt to clarify to some extent the relation between Nietzsche and Schopenhauer, showing that Nietzsche's repeated rejection of Schopenhauer's pessimism masks its substantial similarity to his own. I hope to demonstrate that Nietzsche to a great extent accepted and utilized Schopenhaurian arguments in constructing just those positions by means of which he defined himself as diametrically opposed to Schopenhauer.

Schopenhauer's Pessimism

These Schopenhaurian arguments occur in their fullest form in the early sections of volume 1, book 4, of *World as Will and Representation*.[4] Here Schopenhauer attempts to demonstrate that in life suffering is fundamental, universal, and unavoidable, and real satisfaction unobtainable. These arguments constitute the core of Schopenhauer's pessimism. Although Nietzsche neither presents nor even explicitly refers to them, their presence in his mind clearly manifests itself in his writings. There is much in *The Birth of Tragedy* and in the later writings that simply relies upon the positions argued by Schopenhauer as already established points of departure for further development and application, and typically neither their Schopenhaurian origin nor Schopenhauer's supporting argumentation are mentioned by Nietzsche. There is also

much in Nietzsche which is best understood as a rejection of Schopenhaurian arguments or at least as a response to the challenge of Schopenhaurian positions, again presented without delineating the arguments
rejected or mentioning their provenance.

Book 4 of the *World as Will and Representation* begins with a discussion of death in which, interestingly enough, it is dismissed as a
pseudo-problem.[4] Mortality as an ineluctable condition of human existence, which has been a fundamental source of existential dismay for
many, does not at all contribute to the construction of Schopenhauer's
pessimistic worldview. In dismissing the problem of death as specious,
Schopenhauer relies upon his reworked and streamlined version of
Kant's distinction between phenomena and noumena, between appearance and reality. The death which concerns us, he argues, is our death
as individuals. But our existence as individuals is itself only an illusion
of the world of appearance, since it is only in the illusory world of
spatiotemporal appearance that individuation can occur. Thus death,
like the individuality whose end it marks, is only an illusion of the
phenomenal world and has no ultimate reality.

Schopenhauer's other line of argument rests upon the Kantian doctrine of the merely phenomenal nature of time. The fear of death is a
fear concerning the future; and the future, as an aspect of the phenomenal structure of time, has no ultimate reality. Only an eternal, that is,
timeless, present does. Thus, the fear of death, as the fear of a particular
eventuality in a figure which is unreal, is argued to be unfounded. In
The Birth of Tragedy, as in *The World as Will and Representation*, the
problem of human existence has nothing to do with its limitation through
death. In both cases, it is the texture of life itself, the purported prevalence of suffering and lack of real satisfaction within it, which renders
it problematic.

Against the background of this problem death makes its appearance
in both philosophies, not as itself a problem but rather as the promise
of a possible, though ultimately unacceptable, solution to the problem
of existence. Nietzsche presents this positive aspect of death in the story
of the wise Silenus, whose message is: "What is best of all is utterly
beyond your reach, not to be born, not to *be*, to be *nothing*. But the
second best for you is to die soon."[5] Silenus's message is presented by
Nietzsche as "folk wisdom"—one might also call it "folk revelation"—
in any event, aṣ true. The Greeks were, according to Nietzsche, aware
of this truth in an immediate and intuitive way. "The Greek knew and
felt the terror and horror of existence."[6] Unlike the attempted philosophical demonstration of this same vision of existence in *The World as*

Will and Representation, there is, on Nietzsche's account, no argument or even any discernible structure of inference involved in the Greeks's awareness of the horror of existence.

What is there then about the Greek vision of the terror and horror of existence, as presented by Nietzsche, that links it specifically to Schopenhauer? After all, other philosophers had entertained and espoused negative views of human existence which had been based upon overall intuitive assessments rather than upon analysis or argument. Even the notoriously rationalistic Hegel's well-known characterization of history as a "slaughterbench upon which the happiness of peoples, the wisdom of states, and the virtue of individuals have been sacrificed"[7] was never supported by argumentation, nor does there seem to have been any unstated argument or systematic analysis behind it.[8] What reason is there to think that Nietzsche's endorsement of Silenus's bleak assessment is in any way derived from Schopenhauer's more argumentative and analytic construction of a negative view of existence?

To begin with, the grim vision Nietzsche attributed to the Greeks is described in a Schopenhaurian idiom as being not merely a correct assessment of the empirical world but an insight into the essential nature of a deeper, underlying reality. Nietzsche's immediate comment upon Silenus's message is: "How is the world of the Olympian gods related to this wisdom? Even as the rapturous vision of the tortured martyr to his suffering. *Now it is as if the Olympian magic mountain had opened up before us and revealed its roots to us.*"[9] Silenus's wisdom, that existence is basically suffering, is thus presented by Nietzsche as a metaphysical truth about the world as it is "in-itself" (to use Kant's formulation), that is, about the world as it really is as opposed to the way in which it superficially appears, inevitably distorted in being perceived.[10]

Nietzsche refers to "the truly existent primal unity, eternally suffering and contradictory."[11] The emphasis upon the world of things as they really are in themselves as being a "primal unity" is almost a sure sign that Nietzsche had accepted and was working with Schopenhauer's revision of Kant's theory. Kant had argued that human beings, in perceiving the world, produce the structures of space, time, causality, and substance. From this, he inferred that these structures are consequently not true of reality as it is "in-itself," but imposed upon reality by the perceiver in the act of perception. Schopenhauer had further developed the Kantian position by demonstrating that individuation can take place, and consequently there can exist a plurality of individuals only within the structures of space and time, which are supplied to the phenomenal world by its perceivers.[12] Correspondingly, he argued that reality as it is in-itself, apart from the mode in which it is perceived, being free of the structures of space and time, which appear only in the process of perception, must lack all individuation and thus any plurality of individuals. Ultimate reality, he reasoned, must be a "primal unity" without individual (or individuatable) parts.

This ultimate reality as it is apart from the ineluctable contributions and thus distortions of the perceiving consciousness, the "thing-in-itself," Schopenhauer argued to be the will. And he further argued that human existence offers no real satisfaction for the very reason that in its fundamental metaphysical nature it is will. Before examining his arguments that human existence, being basically will, cannot obtain true satisfaction, let us note that in *The Birth of Tragedy* Nietzsche, following Schopenhauer, holds the view that life is essentially characterized by suffering because this suffering is rooted in our true being. Both differ from claims about the prevalence of suffering like Hegel's, which is rather an intuitive and empirical assessment of human life.

Schopenhauer's first argument for the thesis that satisfaction is impossible in life is directly derived from his voluntaristic metaphysics, from the premise that what we really are is will: "The will dispenses entirely with an ultimate aim and object. It always strives because striving is its sole nature, to which no attained goal can put an end. Such striving is therefore incapable of final satisfaction."[13] This argument considered in isolation does not initially seem to present a very pessimistic picture of the human condition, in that it seems compatible with an existence in which there are numerous satisfactions and pleasures. It only rules out reaching a goal that puts an end to all further striving. One might naturally conceive of the ultimate goal of all of one's striving as the achievement of that which will keep one happy and satisfied for the rest of one's life. Only if one dimly conceives of this desired state of lasting happiness and satisfaction as being completely free of further striving, however, does the conclusion of Schopenhauer's argument present an existential difficulty. But is this state of satisfied statis really what all or most of us ultimately and inevitably strive toward? That we do is Schopenhauer's implicit and unargued thesis, one that appears to require a defense, and perhaps to be indefensible, as soon as it is made explicit and considered critically. There are indications that Nietzsche consciously considered it, found it to have some force, and tried to reply to it. For example, among the reasons that supposedly make the idea of eternal recurrence so difficult to embrace, is that, according to it, there is no final end state and resting place either for the individual or for the world—the same difficulty implicitly posed by Schopenhauer's argument.[14]

Even if, as Schopenhauer claims, we human beings had as our ultimate and unachievable goal a lasting state of satisfaction in which there were no further longings and strivings, how bleak would our condition be? Although our ultimate goal would be unobtainable, could we not reconcile ourselves to this limitation by at least achieving a series of passing but nevertheless substantial satisfactions? To defend a pessimistic construal of human life, Schopenhauer had to argue that one does not really attain any substantial satisfaction even in what would normally be considered a successful life of striving for and achieving a series of goals. He does exactly that in the following crucial passage, where he asserts with respect to any "animal or man": "Willing and striving are its whole essence, and can be fully compared to an unquenchable thirst. The basis of all willing is need, lack, and hence pain. If, on the other hand, it lacks objects of willing because it is at once deprived of them by too easy a satisfaction, a fearful emptiness and boredom comes over it, in other words, its being and existence become an intolerable burden for it. Hence its life swings like a pendulum to and fro between pain and boredom, and these two are in fact its ultimate constituents. This has been expressed very quaintly by saying that, after man had placed all the pains and torments in hell, there was nothing left for heaven but the boredom."[15]

The argument seems to be that, while one is striving for something, one does not yet, by definition, have what one wants, and one experiences this lack of what one wants as a kind of suffering or pain. The aim of this argument to convince us that even what would normally be considered a successful life of striving for and achieving a series of goals is actually a dismal alternation between the pain of lacking what is being sought and the boredom that sets in almost immediately upon achieving it.

If one took up the task of dismantling Schopenhauer's pessimistic vision of human existence, one might attack his arguments in a number of ways: First, one might reject the idea that what we ultimately want is a satisfaction which would put an end to all further striving. And, in rejecting this, one might naturally also want to attack the auxiliary idea that Schopenhauer implicitly relies upon in arriving at his negative conclusions, namely, that a satisfaction that is not permanent is not real. These ideas are crucial for Schopenhauer's construction of a pessimistic worldview, and he uses them as implicit components of his argument without ever arguing for them. As soon as they are subjected to critical scrutiny, however, they reveal themselves to be highly questionable.

Secondly, one could object to Schopenhauer's characterization of all states of striving as being essentially states of suffering the lack of that toward which one strives. It could be pointed out that we do indeed by definition "suffer" all lacks, but only in the minimal sense of undergoing them, not necessarily in the stronger sense of feeling pain in the process, the sense required for Schopenhauer's pessimistic view of the human condition. One could begin the rebuttal by appealing to the pleasure commonly experienced in making progress toward an as yet unrealized goal.

Finally one could attack Schopenhauer's contention that boredom inevitably sets in almost immediately after achieving any goal. That Schopenhauer says this immediate onset of boredom occurs upon "too easy" a satisfaction unfortunately just confuses the issues and begs the question. Only those satisfactions that produce emptiness and boredom would be counted as "too easy." And nothing is thereby said about the all those satisfactions that are achieved only with considerable effort and thus not, if seems, too easily. Schopenhauer obviously wanted to make a more radical and relevant claim than the trivial one that emerges from his unfortunate formulation. He probably meant to assert that all satisfactions, easy or not, inevitably and promptly transform themselves into boredom. This is the position he would have had to propound in order to support his general, pessimistic conclusions. The thesis that all satisfactions very quickly dissolve into boredom rests upon the metaphysical position that what constitutes our most essential and profound being is the will and that the will, being by its very nature a ceaseless striving, is incapable of true satisfaction, which requires the stilling of such striving. Schopenhauer's pessimistic view concerning the extreme transitoriness of all satisfaction ultimately rests upon his voluntaristic metaphysics, so any criticism of his general metaphysical position would also undermine his pessimistic conclusions.

Aspects of "Pessimism"

As vulnerable to rebuttal as Schopenhauer's arguments seem to be, there is little or no reason to think that Nietzsche, at least at the time he wrote *The Birth of Tragedy*, was aware of the weaknesses of these arguments; nor is there any evidence to believe that he was at any time in disagreement with their conclusion, that in human life suffering and pain predominate. Let us remember that in *The Birth of Tragedy* he cites with approbation what he takes to be a similarly negative view of human existence among the Greeks and reformulates this purportedly Greek insight in a peculiarly Schopenhaurian fashion, and that he continues throughout his writings to admire the Greek tragedians for having had the courage to maintain a clear awareness of the horror of existence. Despite Nietzsche's continually growing tendency in his later works to disavow his affinities with Schopenhauer and to treat what he designates as "pessimism" more and more negatively, I want nevertheless to maintain that Nietzsche never rejected Schopenhauer's pessimistic conclusion, that life is basically suffering.[15] In rejecting "pessimism" Nietzsche was actually rejecting certain types of human beings, psychological attitudes, value judgements, and recommendations for life, which have often been associated with the pessimistic doctrine that life is predominantly suffering, but which are neither intrinsic parts of this doctrine nor its necessary concomitants.

Schopenhaurian pessimism and the pessimism of classical Greek culture, though essentially identical in descriptive content, had resulted in diametrically opposed evaluations of life and correspondingly divergent recommendations concerning the appropriate attitude toward life and the appropriate manner of living it. Schopenhauer, on the basis of his pessimistic conclusions, had denied the value of life and advocated the most radical withdrawal from it short of suicide. The Greeks, despite their acceptance of the same view of life, had affirmed the value of life and advocated living as intensely as possible.

What emerges from these comparisons and contrasts is the methodological importance of distinguishing at least three aspects of the phenomena Nietzsche has in mind when he comments upon what he calls "pessimism." First, there is a negative view that in human existence pain and suffering predominate over pleasure and satisfaction. This is the *descriptive aspect* of pessimism in that it consists of a negative description of the nature of life. In the historically important examples of pessimism considered by Nietzsche, the negative description is largely formulated in hedonistic terms, such as pain, suffering, and the absence of pleasure. Although other varieties of descriptive pessimism are conceivable, such as that in which existence would be viewed as lacking any meaning, the pessimistic description of existence in hedonistic terms has

been the historically prevalent version and the one that Nietzsche confronts in the doctrines of Schopenhauer, the ancient Greeks, and the
Buddha.

Secondly, there is in some cases a negative assessment of the overall
value of life based upon the negative description. It might, for example,
be inferred that life, because it is basically suffering, has no positive
value. This *evaluative aspect* of pessimism depends upon the descriptive
aspect, in that the negative evaluation of life draws its support from a
negative description of what life is like.

Third, there are recommendations concerning the proper attitudes
and actions to take, based upon either the pessimistic description or
evaluation of life, or both. Schopenhauer recommends that we reject
and withdraw as much as possible from life, while the Greek tragedians,
fully recognizing that life is essentially suffering, still recommend embracing it. This is the *recommendatory aspect* of the phenomena
Nietzsche includes in his discussion of "pessimism."

It is in part Nietzsche's failure to draw and maintain such distinctions
that obscures his discussion of pessimism and allows him to obscure from
himself and others his continued agreement with a central aspect of
Schopenhauer's philosophy.

A Pessimism of Weakness versus a Pessimism of Strength

In *The Birth of Tragedy* itself, the central contrast between Schopenhauer and the Greek tragedians is not emphasized or even explicitly
drawn. The Greeks are praised for having had the courage both to look
clearly at the terror and horror of existence and, in spite that, to embrace
it. That Schopenhauer, having similarly accepted the horror of existence,
did not nevertheless embrace it, is not mentioned. Nietzsche could not
have been unaware of this major divergence when he wrote *The Birth
of Tragedy*, but it did not then suit his mood, rhetoric, or strategies for
lasting friendship with Richard Wagner to dwell upon this crucial difference. Later he came to feel that this divergence was philosophically
crucial and necessary to mention explicitly, indeed, to emphasize. He
probably also came to feel with some embarrassment that in *The Birth
of Tragedy* his admiring and uncritical treatment of Wagner, which the
older, charismatic, and domineering friend had mesmerized and bullied
him into, had been extended as a consequence to the musical master's
favorite philosopher, and that it was necessary to redress the imbalance

of his early and somewhat blind enthusiasms and allegiances with withering and repeated criticisms.

Associations of Schopenhauer with Wagner aside, Nietzsche came to find it also important for philosophical reasons to distinguish a pessimism that is, like Schopenhauer's, combined with a recommendation to renounce life, from a pessimism that is combined with a recommendation to affirm and embrace life—and to reject the former. As he came to identify the very center of his own philosophical position with the affirmation of life, despite a recognition of the prevalence and ineluctability of suffering in it, he tended more and more to identify Schopenhauer, who had advocated the denial of life, as his antipode in all things and thus to forget and obscure their basic agreement about the preponderance of suffering in human existence. Having given his highest endorsement and allegiance to those who affirm life while accepting the pessimism of a view of life in which suffering prevails, Nietzsche turned to the tandem tasks of criticizing any pessimism that rejects life and of separating this objectionable pessimism from the kind he endorsed.

Nietzsche draws this distinction in his preface to the second edition of *The Birth of Tragedy* in terms of a pessimism of weakness versus a pessimism of strength. He poses the rhetorical question, "Is pessimism *necessarily* a sign of decline, decay, degeneration, weary and weak instincts—as it once was in India and now is, to all appearances, among us, "modern" men and Europeans? Is there a pessimism of *strength*? An intellectual predilection for the hard, gruesome, evil, problematic aspect of existence, prompted by well-being, by overflowing health, by the *fullness* of existence?"[16] Nietzsche is clearly suggesting that there is such a pessimism of strength, and that Greek tragedy exemplifies it.

Let us examine more closely, however, the nature of Nietzsche's distinction between a pessimism of strength and a pessimism of weakness. It clearly does not consist of a difference in the descriptive content of the two kinds of pessimism distinguished. It is a distinction that manifests itself rather in the evaluative and recommendatory aspects of the two kinds of pessimism Nietzsche wants to separate, but the distinction is nevertheless not defined or constituted by these differences. Although a negative overall evaluation of life and a recommendation to withdraw from it are for Nietzsche the characteristic consequences and indications of a pessimism of weakness; what determines and defines the two types of pessimism is a difference in the character of the persons who are drawn to espouse the pessimistic doctrine that life is characterized by suffering. A pessimism of strength cannot be distinguished from a pessimism of weakness by its description of life. And even though it diverges from a pessimism of weakness in its positive evaluation of life and its recommendation to embrace life, it is not defined in terms of these distinguishing features. As a pessimism *of the strong* and a pessimism *of the weak*, they are categories that essentially concern the character of their advocates rather than the content of their doctrines. In his analysis of pessimism, Nietzsche came to focus more upon the character of the human beings who typically embrace the doctrine than upon anything else concerning it.

Philosophy as Symptom: Nietzsche's Method

It is important to be clear about the nature of this distinctively and characteristically Nietzschean inquiry. It is not directly concerned with the truth of the doctrine under consideration nor even with the amount and nature of the evidence for its truth. It is rather an analysis of what it is about the doctrine, apart from the amount of evidence for or against its truth, that makes it *attractive* or *unattractive* to different types of people. Being an inquiry about what in a doctrine under consideration, apart from the evidence in its favor, makes different types of people *tend or want to believe* the doctrine, it is not exclusively or directly an inquiry about what different types of people do in fact believe; for what they in fact believe is, at least to some extent, affected by the evidence and the cogency of the arguments for the positions under considerations. Just as our actual beliefs, because of the intrusion of prejudice and predilection, are not a simple function of the evidence pertaining to them or of their plausibility, the unimpeded and unequivocal expression of our prejudices in our beliefs is correspondingly hindered and clouded by the interference of considerations of evidence and plausibility. What we *want to believe* or *have a tendency to embrace* is, fortunately and unfortunately, not what we inevitably end up believing or embracing. Nietzsche in his consideration of pessimism is interested, as he is elsewhere, primarily in what we want to believe rather than in what we actually believe. Of course the two considerations tend to merge. In as much as what we want to believe influences what we actually do believe, our actual beliefs are justifiably used as indications, though partial and imperfect ones, of our predilections.

Nietzsche concentrates upon what makes pessimism attractive or unattractive to various human types, because it is this that seems to reveal most about the kinds of people they are. He is interested in utilizing pessimism and other philosophical doctrines to analyze the character or condition of the individuals or groups who react in one way or another to them. Whether a doctrine like pessimism is attractive or repugnant to someone seems to reveal more about the person than whether he actually accepts or rejects it. Someone's actual acceptance or rejection of a doctrine might be as much a reflection of the evidence for it as of anything else.

Approaching theories, doctrines, and ideas primarily as signs or symptoms of the human or social conditions from which they emerge, while marginal to our philosophical tradition, has affinities to standard ways in which philosophical ideas have been treated by historians, sociologists, political scientists, psychologists, and psychoanalysts. Nietzsche's consideration of pessimism as a means of diagnosing the important human realities revealed in various reactions to the doctrine, though it deviates from the philosophic tradition narrowly defined, and thus is easily misunderstood within this context, is more easily recognized when illuminated by comparisons to similar analyses of ideologies, theories, and doctrines in other humanistic disciplines.[17]

Proof and Prejudice

This shift in philosophical focus away from the standard concern for the truth and plausibility of a theory to a concentration upon its attractiveness and repulsiveness is bound up with Nietzsche's conviction that considerations of truth, evidence, and the cogency of arguments have counted for less in the acceptance and rejection of philosophical theories than has been generally supposed.[19] With the belief that other considerations have to a very large extent determined the genesis and reception of philosophical ideas, one naturally tends to turn one's attention away from the traditional evaluation of the truth and evidence. The investigation of other factors, those that, by rendering philosophical ideas attractive or repugnant, largely determine the human reaction to various philosophical ideas, gains in importance as a method of understanding the history of philosophy and of analyzing the character of individuals and cultures.

Apparent truth and evidence, to the extent that they are efficacious, compel us to accept or reject particular doctrines independent of our desires; they are reasons and causes for believing even what we do not want to believe. Other motivations for accepting or rejecting doctrines are normally more closely allied with our desires; they usually become efficacious in influencing our beliefs only by influencing what it is we want to believe. Thus, Nietzsche's refocussing of the inquiry upon what, apart from the supporting evidence, brings us to believe something, is at the same time a refocussing upon what brings us to *want* to believe it.

The centering of the inquiry upon what makes a belief desirable or attractive, rather than upon what makes it plausible or true, is clearly illustrated in Nietzsche's treatment of pessimism. There is a remarkable and distinctively Nietzschean failure to examine critically the claims and arguments for the truth of the pessimistic description of the world. Since Nietzsche presents the Greeks as having directly intuited, rather than argued for, the fundamental horror of the world, there are no arguments to criticize. But one can also take issue with claims that are made without argumentation, or at least raise the issue of their truth. Nietzsche does not do this for two reasons: first, he finds the pessimistic description of the world so overwhelmingly plausible and so obviously true as not to require any critical examination of the evidence for it; second, he was more intent upon analyzing the Greeks' embracing of this *Weltanschauung* as a symptom of what sort of human beings they were then he was in evaluating the plausibility of the view itself.

That Nietzsche neither presents nor assesses the Schopenhauerian arguments for pessimism is also, in part, a consequence of his general method. Unquestionably, he was aware of these arguments and agreed with their conclusion that life is predominantly suffering. Arguably, his interpretation of the tragic worldview of the Greeks as resting upon this same conclusion was influenced and reenforced by his reading of these Schopenhauerian texts. That Schopenhauer's arguments are not adduced to support the Greeks's pessimistic conclusion is not surprising given Nietzsche's belief in the obvious and intuitive plausibility of these conclusions and his general tendency not to analyze evidence or arguments explicitly.[20]

Pessimism and Eternal Recurrence

It is illuminating to compare Nietzsche's treatment of pessimism with his treatment of "the eternal recurrence," the doctrine that everything that occurs has already occurred an infinite number of times in the past and will occur again an infinite number of times in the future, that our individual lives and the history of the world as a whole repeat themselves *ad infinitum.* The singular significance that Nietzsche attributed to this idea had, as in the case of pessimism, nothing to do with the question of its truth (of which he was also convinced) nor with the cosmological grandeur of its scope. What makes this idea, for Nietzsche, "the thought of thoughts" and "the mightiest of thoughts" is rather that it is so extremely attractive to those who, having positively embraced or "affirmed" their lives, rejoice at the prospect of infinitely repeating them, and so extremely abhorrent to those who, having not been able to affirm their lives, find this prospect a hellish condemnation. Confrontation with the idea of eternal recurrence thus serves as a crucial test of human strength and one's attitude toward life.

Both Nietzsche's treatment of pessimism and of eternal recurrence focus upon the features of the doctrines that make some people want to accept them and some want to reject them, apart from the intrinsic merit of the argumentation and evidence for or against them. In both cases there is a notable absence of any critical evaluation, or even presentation, of arguments for the view under consideration. Just as Nietzsche fails to present and evaluate the Schopenhauerian arguments supporting pessimism, he fails to present in his published work the arguments he himself had developed in support of eternal recurrence. The absence in the published work of these arguments, which are to be found in Nietzsche's unpublished *Nachlass*, is not to be understood, as some mistakenly have, as an indication that he was not satisfied with them. There is no direct evidence that he ever doubted these arguments; his description of the eternal recurrence as "the most scientific of all hypotheses" indicates rather that he thought (though mistakenly) them to be very strong.[21] Similarly, the absence of a discussion of the Schopenhauerian arguments for pessimism does not indicate his disagreement or dissatisfaction with them. Given his approach to these philosophical ideas as symptoms of the kinds of people who are drawn to or away from them, all arguments supporting them, even his own, became peripheral to his enterprise.

Considering Nietzsche's treatments of pessimism and of eternal recurrence together, one is struck by their essential similarity and the working of a characteristic, Nietzschean philosophic method. Contrasting them is also illuminating. Although his approach to both is basically identical, the results of the two analyses diverge significantly. Since eternal recurrence is supposedly attractive to the strong human beings, who have affirmed their lives, and abhorrent to the weak, who have not been able to do so, one's attitude toward the doctrine serves to determine who is strong and life-affirming and who is weak and life-negating. This

determination of who is strong and who is weak by the doctrines that
affirm life or negate it is at the heart of Nietzsche's philosophical
enterprise.

Pessimism and Paradox

Pessimism turns out to be, unlike the eternal recurrence, a doctrine
attractive to both the strong and the weak, the affirmers and the negaters
of life. Nietzsche's distinction between a pessimism of strength and a
pessimism of weakness calls attention to a complexity in the analysis of
pessimism as a symptom of individual and cultural strength or weakness,
which one does not confront in the same kind of analysis of the doctrine
of eternal recurrence. Since both the strong and the weak can be attracted to pessimism, the doctrine cannot serve, as the idea of eternal
recurrence did, as a crucial test of one's strength and attitude toward
life.

Moreover, how can the same doctrine, the pessimistic assessment of
life as basically suffering, attract diametrically opposed human types?
This situation would be unproblematic if there were nothing in the
doctrine that appealed to the strong or the weak as such. There are
many things that appeal unproblematically to members of two opposed
categories of people, where the appeal has nothing to do with what
distinguishes the groups. That both strong and weak people like to eat
fruit, that both intelligent and stupid people like to travel, that both the
energetic and the lazy like to listen to music, poses no conceptual problem. But the attraction of pessimism for both the weak and the strong
becomes somewhat paradoxical, in as much as Nietzsche suggests that
its appeal for the strong has something to do with their being strong,
and its appeal to the weak has something to do with their being weak.
How can a pessimistic description of life appeal both to the strength of
the strong and to the weakness of the weak?

It is also unclear initially why anyone, strong or weak, would find a
pessimistic description of life attractive. It seems plausible that a more
optimistic view might have greater appeal for everyone, and that those
who accept pessimism do so only reluctantly, compelled, contrary to
their predilections, by the force of argument. Nietzsche was well aware
of, and pleased with, the counterintuitive and even paradoxical aspect
of the claim that this apparently unappealing view is actually attractive
to some, and, indeed, somehow both to the strong because of their
strength, and to the weak because of their weakness. After all, the less

obviously true the analysis, the more profound and enlightening it is if correct.

Nietzsche's explanation of why the "weak" or "decadent" find pessimism an attractive doctrine hinges upon the notion that these people, having little energy and vigor, tend to shun exertion and struggle. Any view that can offer a justification for not making the exertion or engaging in the struggles required by life is attractive to this sort of person. In arguing that no amount of exertion can possibly ameliorate one's fundamental misery, a pessimism like Schopenhauer's furnishes just such a justification for inaction. Let us remember that Schopenhauer's arguments for pessimism had emphasized both the futility and painfulness of all striving.

Pessimism versus Futilitarianism

What makes a pessimism like Schopenhauer's attractive to the weak on Nietzsche's analysis is actually not that its view of life is negative, but that it presents all action as futile, that it rejects the efficacy of action. If this analysis is correct, any view of life in which striving and exertion make no difference should have the same appeal. This would even be true of a diametrically opposed, optimistic view of the world, in which everything inevitably works out for the best, no matter what anyone does or does not do. The same would also hold for any value-neutral fatalism, which claimed that *che sarà, sarà*, that the fated course of personal and political history will take place, for better or worse, no matter what anyone tries to do to influence it. In as much as these nonpessimistic views also seem to undermine the efficacy and thus the sense of all action, they would hold the same attraction for those whose low vitality makes them desire to avoid all exertion. Nietzsche's attempt to analyze the appeal of pessimism for the weak inadvertently reveals that it is not the pessimism itself that exerts this attraction. Although he has argued that the futilitarian character of a view like Schopenhauer's can appeal to those too weary and weak to want to "take arms against a sea of troubles," he has not thereby shown that it is its pessimistic character that holds the appeal.

Pessimism, Hedonism, and the Will to Power

If the weak are supposed to be attracted to pessimism by what they perceive as its release from action and striving, why are the strong supposed to be attracted to pessimism? The strong, according to Nietzsche, delight in exertion and struggle, because only in this way can they experience their own strength. How can they be drawn to a philosophical view that seems, to some, to imply a quietism, which they abhor? They must be drawn to a pessimism that does not imply withdrawal from the struggle of life. Indeed, after posing the possibility of a "pessimism of *strength*" as an "intellectual predilection for the hard, gruesome, evil problematic aspect of existence, prompted by well-being, by overflowing health, by the fullness of existence," Nietzsche goes on to describe it as, "the sharp-eyed courage that tempts and attempts, that *craves* the frightful as the enemy, the worthy enemy against whom one can test one's strength."[22]

But how can a pessimistic view of the world serve as a challenge, an invitation to test one's strength? If it denies all possibility of ever struggling successfully, as does Schopenhauer's view, it makes all struggle futile. If a pessimistic worldview is to be an invitation to struggle, it must hold out some possibility of success. But it would seem that a worldview ceases to be pessimistic in as much as it allows for success. How then can a view remain pessimistic and allow for success or satisfaction?

There are at least two ways to escape from this dilemma. First, one might envision the strong drawn to a view of human existence according to which life is essentially characterized by suffering, but in which one can struggle against this suffering with the possibility of modest and limited success. Such a view would remain pessimistic in maintaining that life at its best is still filled with pain, but, by allowing for the possibility of somewhat diminishing the pain, it would not undermine the meaningfulness of action. On this view, life is a poor thing at best, but there are significant differences in how bad it can be. This is not, however, what Nietzsche has in mind when he envisions the possibility of strong, energetic, life-affirming people being attracted to pessimism.

His solution does not depend upon allowing for a limited amount of variation in an escapably dismal existence, but upon radically changing the criteria of what makes an existence dismal or not. The pessimistic description of human existence as basically characterized by pain and suffering, the position of Schopenhauer and the Buddha, as I have already noted, is conceived and formulated in hedonistic terms. It is the claim that life, when considered from the hedonistic perspective of whether pleasure or pain is prevalent in it, is an irremediable failure. Whether or not one proceeds to infer from this state of affairs that life is of no value clearly depends on whether or not one evaluates life according to hedonistic criteria. Similarly, any recommendations to withdraw from life and striving, like those of Schopenhauer and the Buddha, based upon the prevalence of suffering in human existence, must also rest upon hedonistic criteria of value. The pessimism of Schopenhauer, the Buddha, and Christianity, the pessimism of the weak in general, consists of a hedonistically negative description of life.

In contrast, the pessimism of the strong, which embraces the same hedonistically negative description of life, neither infers the worthlessness of life from its inescapable painfulness nor recommends rejecting it. In this case, hedonistic criteria of evaluation have obviously not been applied to the pessimistic description of life. The strong are able to affirm life while subscribing to a description of it as characterized by suffering and struggle, because suffering is not for them the ultimate evil. And if suffering is not the ultimate evil for them, they obviously do not evaluate existence with hedonistic standards.

While the rejection of hedonistic standards by the strong explains how they can consistently accept pessimism and still affirm life, it leaves unanswered the question of why the pessimistic description of life is *attractive* to these affirmers of life, not simply consistent with their positive attitudes.[23] The answer lies in their replacement of hedonistic values with values based upon power. One of the central developments in Nietzsche's philosophy was to replace what he took to be the prevailing hedonistic or utilitarian account of the ultimate motivations of human behavior and of the ultimate sources of human values with an alternative account of both in terms of a "will to power."[24]

For Nietzsche the doctrine of "the will to power," like those of pessimism and the eternal recurrence, in addition to being true, was interesting and important in its attractiveness and repellence for different types of human beings. It is, like the eternal recurrence, more appealing to the strong. In distinguishing between a pessimism of the weak and a pessimism of the strong, he presents the weak as intellectually adhering to hedonism and the strong as having transcended it for some more or less consciously reflected and articulated version of a *Weltanschauung* in which power is the ultimate value. Whether one is attracted by values based upon pleasure or power is, like one's attitude toward the idea of eternal recurrence, an important diagnostic test of the type of person one is.

It is because the strong tend to be oriented toward power rather than pleasure that they find pessimism appealing. A view of existence as fraught with difficulty, pain, suffering, struggle, exertion, and striving is not only tolerable but attractive to someone who places the highest value upon power and *the experience of power*, because it is only in overcoming difficulty, pain, and suffering, in successfully struggling and striving, that one experiences one's power. The powerful "crave" a world which allows them to experience their power, and the world as described by pessimism promises just that.

Nietzsche came to believe that all men, weak and strong, whether they are conscious of it or not, are really motivated by considerations of power rather than pleasure. There is, of course, no contradiction between his general advocacy of the will to power and his analysis of the weak as embracing hedonism. What really motivates human beings and is the source of their values need not be what they take to be their motivations and sources of their values.

According to a theory that posits the experience of power as the ultimate satisfaction and goal of human behavior, the weak can be understood as wanting to avoid struggle, not just from laziness or lack of vitality, but more fundamentally because in unsuccessfully struggling they experience their impotence. Their tendency to embrace hedonism can be understood, in part, as a way to avoid accepting a standard of value, namely power, according to which they would be of little worth.

Life as Painful, Life as Worthless

Let us now consider the distinction between the pessimism of the weak and of the strong with respect to the descriptive, evaluative, and recommendatory aspects of pessimism, which I previously distinguished. The pessimism of the strong and of the weak are identical in the descriptive aspect and diverge sharply in both the evaluative and recommendatory aspects. The pessimism of the weak describes life as dominated by suffering and infers from this that life has no value, and that one should avoid it as much as possible. The pessimism of the strong describes life in the same way, but still holds it to be valuable and recommends living fully. In as much as Nietzsche takes both to be versions of pessimism, he implicitly locates the essence of pessimism in what the two have in common, i.e., in their descriptive rather than evaluative or recommendatory aspects. In positing that there are two forms of pessimism, Nietzsche clearly identifies the essence of pessimism with a view of existence as characterized by suffering, and not with any overall evaluation of life or recommendations concerning how one should live. *Pessimism, understood in this way, is a view shared by*

Schopenhauer and the Greek tragedians—and by Nietzsche throughout his philosophical development.

This unchanging affinity was obscured by Nietzsche's growing anti-Schopenhauerian rhetoric and by an important inconsistency in the way that Nietzsche used the term "pessimism." This shift in meaning can be traced across Nietzsche's two most important written reconsiderations of *The Birth of Tragedy*, the preface to the second edition of 1886, the "Attempt at a Self-criticism," which we have been considering, and the section on *The Birth of Tragedy* in *Ecce Homo*, written about two years later, a book in which he devotes himself to a reconsideration of all his previous work.

In *Ecce Homo*, Nietzsche no longer describes the tragic view of the Greeks as a pessimism that is admirable, a "pessimism of strength," or a "Dionysian pessimism," in contrast to an objectionable "pessimism of weakness" or "romantic pessimism." He asserts instead that the Greeks were not really pessimists at all: "'The Greek World and Pessimism'" would have been a less ambiguous title—suggesting the first instruction about how the Greeks got over their pessimism, how they *overcame* it. Precisely their tragedies prove that the Greeks were *not* pessimists: Schopenhauer went wrong at this point, as he went wrong everywhere."[25]

This startling shift in Nietzsche's description of the Greek's tragic view of life is the result of a change in the use of the term "pessimism," rather than of a substantive reassessment of the Greeks. In drawing a distinction between an admirable pessimism of the strong and a despicable pessimism of the weak, Nietzsche had implicitly identified pessimism with what was common to the two types, namely, the description of life as being predominantly suffering, what I have called the descriptive aspect of pessimism. When he denies, in *Ecce Homo*, that the Greeks were pessimists, what he means by "pessimism" has changed and is now identified with an overall negative evaluation and rejection of life, what I have distinguished as the evaluative and recommendatory aspects of pessimism. That he redescribes the Greeks as not being pessimists does not mean he has revised his view of their acute awareness of the prevalence of suffering, but rather that he has reidentified pessimism with the negative evaluation and rejection of life, which Schopenhauer and others had attached to their description of life as suffering, but which the Greeks, according to Nietzsche, had not. The Greeks had "gotten over" and "overcome" their pessimism by refusing to reject life, despite their view that it was filled inevitably with pain. It is only because Nietzsche implicitly no longer identifies pessimism with such a hedonistically negative description of life, that he is able, in *Ecce Homo*, to deny that the Greeks, who espoused such a view, were pessimists. The change in Nietzsche's characterization of the Greeks, then, results not from a substantial reassessment of them, but from a deliberate or inadvertent shift in terminology.

Nietzsche also uses "pessimism" to refer primarily to a negative evaluation and rejection of life, rather than to a description of it as suffering, elsewhere in his writings. In *The Gay Science*, for example, he takes up the case of Socrates, who requested just before dying that one of his followers sacrifice a rooster to Asclepius, the god of medicine, indicating that he considered life a disease and death it cure. When Nietzsche here ponders the dismaying possibility that Socrates had been a pessimist, he is actually considering whether Socrates' overall evaluation of life had been negative, not whether he thought it painful. He asks whether "Socrates *suffered life*," not whether he suffered *in* it. He wonders whether Socrates "had merely kept a cheerful mien while concealing all his life long his *ultimate judgment*."[26] Again, a few sections later, he implicitly defines pessimism as a total rejection of life, when, in discussing the affinities between modern pessimism, Buddhism, Christianity, and all views which contrast our worldly existence with a superior otherworldly one, he describes pessimism as "the contempt for that existence which is knowable by us."[27]

In section 370 of *The Gay Science*, he speaks approvingly, however, of a "Dionysian pessimist," contrasting Schopenhauer's "romantic pessimism" with a "*Dionysian* pessimism," which he sees both a "pessimism of the future" and as a "classical type," that is, as the type he attributes to the tragic view of the Greeks, and as a view that might return to replace the despicable Schopenhauerian pessimism of the nineteenth century. In this section, with its distinction between an admirable and a despicable pessimism, he has obviously, but perhaps not deliberately, shifted back to using pessimism as a term for a certain description of the world.

The Gay Science was originally published in 1882, but sections 343 to 384 were among the additions to the second edition of 1887. Thus, the distinction between a pessimism of strength and of weakness in the second preface to *The Birth of Tragedy* of 1886 is echoed in the distinction between a romantic, modern pessimism and a Dionysian pessimism in that part of *The Gay Science* written for the second edition of 1887. In both of these roughly contemporaneous texts pessimism is identified with its descriptive aspect. Yet, in the section in *The Gay Science* on Socrates, written for the first edition, and in the section on otherworldly views, written for the second edition, pessimism is identified with its evaluative and recommendatory aspects and treated pejoratively. These texts, taken together, indicate that in this period Nietzsche shifted back and forth between two significantly different concepts of pessimism, probably unaware of the distinction between the two and of the fact that he was vacillating between them.

Nietzsche's Final Rhetorical Rejection of Pessimism

Section 370 of *The Gay Science* was, however, revised by Nietzsche and included under the title "We Antipodes" in his last book, *Nietzsche contra Wagner*, written immediately after *Ecce Homo* in 1888. Some of the revisions, interestingly enough, show the same shift in the use of the concept of pessimism that occurs between the second preface to *The Birth of Tragedy* and the reconsideration of this book in *Ecce Homo*. In both the original and revised versions of the text, Nietzsche confesses that he had for a time "approached the modern world with a few errors and overestimations" and "understood the philosophical pessimism of the nineteenth century as if it were a symptom of a superior force of thought, of more audacious courage, and of a more triumphant fullness of life than had characterized" the previous age. And he admits that he had misunderstood it as "tragic insight," that is, he had mistakenly identified the worldview of Schopenhauer with that of Greek tragedy. In *The Gay Science*, he goes on to rectify this confusion by distinguishing romantic pessimism from Dionysian pessimism. In *Nietzsche contra Wagner*, however, he drops all references to Dionysian pessimism.

The change in his language and approach between the two versions is well illustrated in his criticism of Epicurus. In *The Gay Science*, he writes, "Thus I gradually learned to understand, Epicurus, the opposite of a Dionysian pessimist." What defines Epicurus here, for Nietzsche, is his optimism, which Nietzsche understands here and elsewhere as the denial that life is ineluctably characterized by suffering. He generally spurns it as a view embraced by those too weak to accept the world as it really is. Nietzsche's unwavering rejection of "optimism," which he understood as the denial of the descriptive aspect of pessimism, further supports by claim that Nietzsche, despite misleading shifts in terminology, never wholly rejected the descriptive aspect of pessimism.[28]

In the revised version included in *Nietzsche Contra Wagner*, Nietzsche comes to understand Epicurus as the opposite, not of "the Dionysian pessimist," but of "the Dionysian Greek," and he faults him not for his "optimistic horizons," but for his "hedonism." The two revisions are integrally connected. Criticizing Epicurus as an optimist naturally suggests an approval of at least some form of pessimism, in this case called "Dionysian pessimism." With the decision not to characterize his ideal type of man as "pessimistic," Nietzsche no longer wants to characterize his opposite as "optimistic."

The refocussing of the criticism upon Epicurus's hedonism is, once again, to a large extent a change in rhetoric rather than substance. The pessimistic description of the world as one in which suffering predominates is formulated in hedonistic terms. Optimism, as the denial of pessimism, is correspondingly understood as the doctrine that it is, on the contrary, possible to lead a life in which pleasure prevails over pain. It is this optimistic hedonism that Nietzsche most often has in mind when he speaks of "hedonism," and he seems to have it in mind here.

Strictly speaking, hedonism is the view that life is to be judged by whether pleasure or pain prevails in it, not an assertion of which in fact prevails. Understood in this way, hedonism has both pessimistic and optimistic variants, and indeed traditional pessimistic descriptions of the world, like Schopenhauer's, are hedonistic, though negatively so. But Nietzsche tends to use "hedonism" to refer to views according to which life is both to be evaluated in terms of pleasure and pain and, at least in some cases, to be judged positively in these terms. Thus, in both versions of the text Nietzsche is referring to the same philosophical position, the optimistic hedonism of Epicurus, but mentioning in each a different aspect of it.

The parallel changes in rhetoric from the preface to the second edition of *The Birth of Tragedy* of *Ecco Homo*, and from section 370 of *The Gay Science* to its revision in *Nietzsche contra Wagner*, indicate a systematic and deliberate reformulation of language at the very end of Nietzsche's philosophical development. In part, it was based upon the realization that the distinction between those who are attracted to optimism and those who are attracted to pesimism, like the distinction between those who are attracted by pessimism and those who are not, cannot be used as an indication of those who affirm life and those who reject it. Both the strong and the weak are attracted to pessimism, but for different reasons. Optimism, though the apparent opposite of pessimism, attracts the same weak types as does the prevalent form of pessimism. One's preferences regarding these positions cannot therefore serve to draw a clear distinction between the vital and the decadent, the strong and the weak, the life-affirming and the life-denying, which Nietzsche came to see as the only distinction worth pursuing.

When he speaks in the section on *The Birth of Tragedy* in *Ecce Homo* of "the wretched and shallow chatter about optimism versus pessimism," he is not rejecting the categories completely. After all, this comes just after he suggests that the title of the book should have focussed upon the concept of pessimism. He is feverishly overstating the idea that the opposition of pessimism and optimism does not mirror or reveal what he sees as "the real opposition: the degenerating instinct that turns against life with subterranean vengefulness . . . versus a formula for the highest affirmation . . . "

Nietzsche's apparently deliberate omission of the pessimistic aspect of his Dionysian ideal in his last descriptions of it also serves his campaign to distance himself a much as possible from Schopenhauer (and thereby from Wagner). The dropping of all reference to pessimism in his description of his Dionysian ideal in the revision of section 370 of *The Gay Science*, let us remember, occurs under the title, "We Antipodes," in a book called "*Nietzsche contra Wagner.*"

Nietzsche's continual reworking of his definition of a human ideal, an enterprise which stretches from his first to his last book, was influenced, and, unfortunately, to some extent warped, by his equally protracted attempt to redefine himself too simplistically as the antipode of those who had threatened his personal and philosophical autonomy. His final formulations of this Dionysan ideal are designed to obscure those features shared by pessimism and the tragic view of life, by Schopenhauer and the Greeks, and by Schopenhauer and Nietzsche himself.

Notes

1. *EH*, "The Birth of Tragedy," sec. 1, my italics.

2. I diverge from the Kaufmann translation of "Griechentum" as "Hellenism." "Hellenism" has several meanings that are not appropriate translations of "Griechentum." The German word refers to the entirety of Greek culture, not the Hellenistic period in particular, and not to the devotion to Greek culture by later periods. Besides, there is the German term "Hellenismus," which corresponds to the English "Hellenism."

3. *EH* 1

4. *The World as Will and Representation*, trans. E. F. Payne (New York: Dover Press, 1969), vol. I, bk. 4, sec. 54.

5. *BT* 3.

6. Ibid.

7. *Vernunft in der Geschichte*, ed. J. Hoffmeister (Hamburg: Meiner Verlag, 1955), p. 48.

8. While the purported preponderance of suffering in the world constitutes a basis and starting point for philosophical argument in Hegel's work, it is not the result of such argumentation. See my "*Hegels* Rechtfertigung der Geschichte," *Hegel Jahrbuch für 1968–69* (Meisenheim am Glan: Verlag Anton Hain, 1970).

9. *BT* 3, my italics.

10. In the preface to the second edition, Nietzsche speaks of "the image of everything *underlying existence [auf dem Grunde des Daseins]* that is frightful, evil, a riddle, destructive, fatal (sec. 4, my italics)." Again, the suggestion is that the horrors of existence belong to its deeper levels, not to its surface.

11. *BT* 4.

12. *World as Will and Representation*, vol. 1, bk. 2, sec. 23.

13. Ibid., vol. I, bk. 4, sec. 56.

14. "Let us think this through in its most terrible form: existence as it is, without any meaning or aim, yet recurring inevitably *without any finale of nothingness*: 'the eternal recurrence.'" (*WP* 55, my italics)

15. Ibid., vol. 1, bk. 4, sec. 57.

16. Although Nietzsche seems to have remained in agreement with Schopenhauer's description of existence as essentially painful, he did later develop a critique of Schopenhauer's view that there was no substantial satisfaction in life. He was able to accept both the prevalence of suffering and the possibility of real satisfaction in life by detaching the notion of satisfaction from the notion of escaping from suffering. This separation of the concept of satisfaction from that of pleasure (or the absence of pain) was one of the results, and motives, of his rejecting hedonism for the theory of the will to power. I discuss some of these connections in my essay, "The Hopelessness of Hedonism and the Will to Power," *International Studies in Philosophy* 18.

17. Sec. 1.

18. I have analyzed this same aspect of Nietzsche's philosophic method with respect to his theory of the eternal recurrence in "Reflections on Recurrence," in *Nietzsche*, Modern Studies in Philosophy, ed. Robert Solomon, (Garden City, Doubleday: 1973).

19. See, for instance, *BGE*, "On the Prejudices of the Philosophers," sec. 6: "I do not believe that a 'drive to knowledge' is the father of philosophy; but rather that another drive has, here as elsewhere, employed understanding (and misunderstanding) as a mere instrument."

20. In the "Attempt at a Self-Criticism" Nietzsche rejects *The Birth of Tragedy*, among another reasons, for being "disdainful of proof, mistrustful even of the *propriety* of proof (sec. 3)." This criticism, while true of *The Birth of Tragedy*, does not clearly distinguish it from his other works. They are all, to one extent or another, notable for their lack of detailed and sustained argumentation.

21. This issue is taken up more fully in my "Reflections on Recurrence."

22. *BT*, "Attempt at a Self-Criticism," sec. 1.

23. For Nietzsche, the Greeks not only accepted but embraced pessimism. In the preface to the second edition of *BT*, he speaks of their *"craving for the ugly*; the good, severe will of the Greeks to pessimism, to the tragic myth."

24. I discuss Nietzsche's espousal of the theory of the will to power, because it allowed him to accept a pessimistic description of life and still affirm it, in my "The Hopelessness of Hedonism."

25. *EH*, "The Birth of Tragedy," sec. 1.

26. *GS* 340, my italics.

27. *GS* 346.

28. In the first edition of *The Birth of Tragedy*, optimism is associated with Socrates, with a "theoretical optimism" that is confident in man's ability to know whatever he wants to know, and with the belief that this knowledge brings virtue and happiness (secs. 14 and 15). It is also associated with the death of tragedy and the decadence of Greek culture.

In the preface to the second edition it is criticized further as a doctrine of the weak and associated with Greek culture in decline. "Could it be possible that ... the triumph of *optimism*, the gradual prevalence of *rationality*, practical and theoretical *utilitarianism*... might all have been symptoms of a decline in strength, of impending old age, and of physiological weariness? (sec. 3)"

In *Ecce Homo*, even after having rejected "the wretched and idle chatter about optimism versus pessimism" in his discussion of *The Birth of Tragedy*, he still writes: "I shall have a major occasion to demonstrate how the historical consequences of *optimism*, this abortion of the *homines optimi*, have been uncanny beyond measure. Zarathustra... was the first to grasp that the optimistic is just as decadent as the pessimist, and perhaps more harmful." ("Why I am a Destiny," sec. 4)

Reading *Zarathustra*

KATHLEEN HIGGINS

Thus Spoke Zarathustra was recommended to me when I was a high school senior, and I asked a fellow teenager who was reading it what the book was like. "Nietzsche's kind of like a perverted Kahlil Gibran," she told me. And when I perused the book for myself, I saw what she meant. Zarathustra was a prophet, and his sermons, although filled with blasphemous precepts, were pretentiously biblical in tone. I was annoyed even before I finished the prologue. The surreal plot seemed more theater of the absurd than philosophy, and I was appalled when Zarathustra tossed off his famous "God is dead" as a mere subordinate clause. ("Could it be possible? This old saint in the forest has not yet heard anything of this, that *God is dead*!"[1]) Interesting as some of Zarathustra's comments were, he was too smug for me. I lasted only somewhere into part I. Setting the book aside, I did not reopen it for nearly a year.

I doubt that my first encounter with *Zarathustra* is atypical, at least among contemporary Americans. We, as a culture, are not taken with pompous prophets or ponderous maxims. We find them offensive, forgivable only if they possess tremendous charisma—and charisma is something that Zarathustra lacks. His single effort to sway the masses is so unsuccessful that his audience literally mistakes him for a circus performer. Zarathustra is not our type of hero.

To aggravate our difficulty, Nietzsche has not made *Zarathustra* a very easy book to read. It is unwieldy. The story line is discontinuous. A wide range of narrative approaches are employed. Nietzsche even seems to take pride in the book's inaccessibility; in *Ecce Homo*, for instance, he remarks:

> When Dr. Heinrich von Stein once complained very honestly that he didn't understand a word of my *Zarathustra*, I told him that this was perfectly

in order; having understood six sentences from it—that is to have really experienced them—would raise one to a higher level of existence than 'modern' men could attain. . . .

   My triumph is precisely the opposite of Schopenhauer's: I say, "*non legor, non legar.*"[2] ["I am not read, I *will* not be read."]

Nietzsche's megalomaniacal pretensions are hardly a source of comfort to someone who wants to make sense out of the book. And long before Nietzsche abandoned all semblance of modesty, he subtitled *Zarathustra* "A Book for All and None." He obviously wanted the book to be a puzzle; but it is not superficially obvious that the book is a puzzle we can solve.

My basic suggestion in what follows is that by isolating some of the elements that are basic to the book—formal components, central themes, and organizing strategies—we can recognize a coherent design. In the first section, I will concentrate on three sustained projects that guide the narrative—those of parodying Scripture, parodying Plato, and presenting Zarathustra as a tragic hero. While these projects operate independently, they converge in supporting Nietzsche's endeavor to undercut the Platonic-Christian tradition and to provide an alternative worldview, which he associates with tragedy. The book's central themes, which I will consider in the second section, cooperate with this endeavor by clarifying Nietzsche's tragic vision of the world. I will focus particularly on Nietzsche's doctrinal notions of "the overman" and "eternal recurrence" in this capacity. In the third section I will consider a complicating feature of the book's construction, Nietzsche's systematic project of qualifying the force of Zarathustra's doctrines and even suggesting that they can have pernicious effects. I conclude that one of the central points implied by the book's literary structure is that the value of Zarathustra's doctrines is limited, that they can mislead when interpreted too rigidly.

Who Is Zarathustra?

Zarathustra as Prophet

Before we focus on these formal and thematic elements, however, let's return for a moment to Zarathustra's stance as a prophet. If Nietzsche is trying to supplant the Platonic-Christian worldview with a worldview of his own, are we not right in taking Zarathustra to be a traditional prophet with a new gospel? In a sense, Zarathustra does have a prophet's traditional role: he is a bearer of news who hopes to change people's minds. As we will see shortly, Zarathustra's role as a prophet suits him to serve as a parodic counterpart to Christ and to Plato's Socrates.

To the extent that the traditional prophet unerringly speaks the truth, however, Zarathustra's role is decidedly untraditional. The very fact that Nietzsche presents Zarathustra in the foolish situation of being mistaken for a clown early in the prologue reveals that Zarathustra is no unerring wiseman. Nietzsche is not courting a response of awed admiration for Zarathustra.

What he is courting is our response to another individual, someone who is like ourselves but who has his own idiosyncracies. Zarathustra, although the harbinger of a new worldview, is presented as an ordinary human being. He has limitations, and often enough we see his limitations turning his adventures into foibles. The significance of this will be evident after we have considered the details of Nietzsche's portrayal of Zarathustra's as a tragic hero.

Zarathustra's Context

At this juncture, however, we should clarify Zarathustra's role as a paradigm of individual existence by making a few observations about the context in which he is presented, one in which existence is unavoidably problematic. Platonism and Christianity granted human beings a sense of security as individuals. Christianity did this by promising a beatific afterlife as a reward for the proper conduct of *this* life. Platonism gave the individual the hope that individual limitations could be transcended by rational insight which, when fully developed, could transport the soul to an experience of the ultimate, atemporal reality. Christianity and Platonism offered the individual a sense that the activities of this life were meaningful by referring them to unchanging realities outside life.

The Platonic-Christian interpretation of individual existence is, in a sense, already dead, according to Nietzsche. The members of the modern world do not really experience their lives as meaningful as a consequence of these traditions' extraworldly visions. But modern human beings who have come to believe that this world is the only world, this life the only life the individual will ever experience, are likely to be disturbed by this insight. Our Platonic and Christian background has given us the sense that our activities have meaning, yet the ground of that meaning no longer seems available.

Zarathustra is presented as someone who finds his activities meaningful on different terms than those of the Platonic-Christian tradition.

The three projects that I mentioned as basic to the structure of the book all support this effort. The parodies of Christ and Socrates both function to undercut the traditions' understanding of meaning in human life.

Parodies of Christ and Socrates

Of the two, the parody of Christ does this most obviously. This parody is evident from the very first lines of the prologue: "When Zarathustra was thirty years old he left his home and the lake of his home and went into the mountain. Here he enjoyed his spirit and his solitude and did not tire of it."[3] We are ambivalently reminded of the thirty-year-old Christ, who also withdrew from human society by going into the desert, but who returned almost immediately to begin the mission that led to his death at age thirty-three. And throughout the book we experience the essential ambivalence provoked by parody, which simultaneously emphasizes and satirizes its model, with the satirical element ultimately dominating.

In accordance with the ambivalent character of the parodic project, Zarathustra directs attention to Christ's mission by sharing many aspects of it. Like Christ, he grapples with the problem of the ultimate meaning of human existence, reaches a certain resolution while in solitude, and returns to society to teach others what he has discovered. But Zarathustra's gospel diverges from Christ's in its insistence that if human life is to have meaning, this meaning must be found in earthly existence. This basic divergence informs the parodic allusions to Christ that occur throughout the book to the final scene. The last episode involves a surrogate Last Supper, a dinner party at which Zarathustra entertains the disciples in whom he has placed his greatest hopes, all of whom subsequently fail him. Zarathustra leaves the site of the party in the morning, not to go die, as Christ does when he leaves his disciples, but to renew the work of his life by beginning his mission again.

The final image, besides emphasizing Zarathustra's differences from Christ, also introduces the second parodic scheme that I mentioned. Zarathustra's morning departure from the site of a dinner with his disappointing disciples calls to mind Plato's *Symposium* and its hero, Socrates. Zarathustra is markedly a parodic counterpart to Socrates in the book's final image; but a structure of parodic allusion to Plato's dialogues is developed from the beginning. The Platonic Myth of the Cave is invoked by Zarathustra's opening emergence from his own cave to sing a hymn to the sun, a hymn in which he dedicates himself to the mission of returning to his community to share his insights.

This allusion to the Myth of the Cave urges us to compare Zarathustra to the philosopher that Socrates describes and presumably instantiates; but at the same time the opening image of Zarathustra inverts the detail of Socrates' parable. Zarathustra's flight from his former home did not involve a movement from a cave into the sun, comparable to that of Socrates' philosopher, but from a valley illuminated by the sun to the haven of his own cave. Furthermore, the cave and proximity to the sun's light do not stand in opposition as they do in the diagram drawn by Plato's Socrates. Zarathustra's cave, while it harbors darkness, is a mountain cave, representing a closer point of access to the sun than is afforded to the community in the valley.

I do not plan to probe the wide range of suggestions that Nietzsche is making with this parody of Plato. Nevertheless, I see *The Birth of Tragedy*, Nietzsche's first work, as a useful interpretive tool for understanding both this parodic project and the role of Zarathustra as a tragic hero. For this reason, I will linger on the opening image momentarily in order to indicate its allusion to *The Birth of Tragedy*.

The Birth of Tragedy *as Background: Apollo and Dionysus*

Nietzsche depicts Zarathustra in the opening scene as equally comfortable inside his cave and in the sunlight outside it. The cave and the sunlight suggest *The Birth of Tragedy*'s concepts of the Dionysian and the Apollonian, concepts which Nietzsche employs in analyzing the structure of Greek tragedy. Tragedy, according to Nietzsche, afforded a vision of life as meaningful despite the inevitability of human suffering; and this achievement depended on tragedy's use of both Apollonian and Dionysian perspectives on the individual's relationship to the world. Zarathustra's comfort with both the sun and the cave, therefore, seems to recall tragedy's conjunction of perspectives.

But what are the Apollonian and Dionysian perspectives? The Apollonian perspective is sunlike, portraying the world as an orderly whole that can be clearly understood by the human mind. Because the world is orderly, the individual can use his rational faculties to orient himself within it. On Nietzsche's view, the Dionysian perspective offers a more faithful but darker portrait of individual existence. It shows life as a tumultuous flux that has no ultimate respect for anything individual or orderly, although this flux is the substratum of every individual life.

The Dionysian perspective reveals the more fundamental truth about human reality, but each of the two perspectives reflects something important about the nature of individual existence. The Dionysian perspective reveals the precariousness of the individual's actual status in the world; but the Apollonian perspective offers a vision of the individual's ability to grasp the world, a vision that is essential if the individual is to be able to function. The only healthy perspective one can take on one's role as an individual in the world is to recognize the fragility of one's position but to continue to dream the Apollonian dream that reality is orderly, graspable, and beautiful. One must, in other words, integrate the Apollonian and the Dionysian perspectives in order to live a healthy life. Reconciling these perspectives is problematic, however, and to integrate them in a healthy perspective on individuality is a significant achievement.

Greek tragedy's attainment was to integrate the Apollonian and Dionysian visions of human reality. It portrayed the Dionysian flux as the fundamental reality; but this reality was portrayed as so indomitably powerful and joyous that transient human individuals could find satisfaction just in being part of it. The individual's participation in the flux necessarily involved the Apollonian illusion that the world is orderly and controllable. But this illusion itself is an expression of human vitality amidst the chaotic flux.

This analysis may seem far removed from Nietzsche's later parody of Plato, but the Socrates of Plato's dialogues plays an important role in Nietzsche's first work. Socrates figures there as the founder of the worldview that destroyed Greek tragedy. Greek tragedy confronted the threat that life's dynamic chaos posed to a conviction that human life is meaningful. It did so by embracing the irrational ground of life. Socrates confronted this threat by denying the reality of the flux and insisting that persistent rational inquiry can make all of existence intelligible. With this doctrine he fortified the delusion that individual well-being could be secured against the apparent chaos of the world, which might threaten it. But this is a nontragic notion that Nietzsche emphatically denies in *The Birth of Tragedy*. Socrates is the target of Nietzsche's second parodic attack in *Zarathustra* because Socrates represents a notion of human individuality that Nietzsche wants to repudiate.

Zarathustra as Tragic Hero

The more positive analysis of *The Birth of Tragedy* is reflected in the third project that I mentioned: the portrayal of Zarathustra as a tragic hero. Nietzsche's intention of portraying Zarathustra in this role is signaled by his inclusion of the first section of *Thus Spoke Zarathustra* in

The Gay Science under the title *"Incipit tragoedia"*—"The tragedy begins."[4]

The beginning of this tragedy, significantly, occurs at the moment when Zarathustra the hermit decides to rejoin the community of which he is a part. This decision involves a juxtaposition of the perspectives that are inherent to tragedy as Nietzsche understands it. For Zarathustra gazes beyond the limited but secure view of himself which he has experienced in his cave and considers his role in the less secure context of the larger human world.

A similar juxtaposition of perspectives is suggested in the movement of the narrative. Zarathustra confronts the failure imposed by his individual limitations and concludes that his life is made meaningful through his work as a teacher, a vocation in which he understands himself to be participating in a project much larger than himself. In this, Zarathustra moves to an increasingly Dionysian perspective on his life. And this movement conforms to Nietzsche's recommendations regarding our modern need for a tragic vision. Since Socrates, the Western world has been one-sidedly rational, privileging a truncated Apollonianism as the correct way of interpreting the world. Zarathustra's recognition of his position in the flux of a larger world is a step away from this imbalanced perspective and toward the healthy vision of individuality afforded by Greek tragedy.

Admittedly, Zarathustra's situation does not sound very much like a scenario from Greek tragedy. The book's justification of individual and communal perspectives, which I have been calling tragic, has a decidedly modern flavor. Nietzsche uses this juxtaposition to consider problems of communication in their modern cultural form; and the individual that Zarathustra exemplifies is a modern individual, given to spells of introspection that do not at all remind us of the ancient Greeks.

Nonetheless, Zarathustra does resemble Greek tragic heroes and their situations in a salient, if general, respect: he fails. He fails early on in his effort to communicate to the circus crowd. And things do not get better. Although Zarathustra's objective from the beginning of the book is to communicate with others, we rarely see even a glimmer of success. And at the end of the book Zarathustra fails to communicate even with the few disciples in whom he still had confidence.

Zarathustra's failures reveal an aspect of human existence that Nietzsche takes to be essential to the tragic vision; they suggest that the individual cannot count on the rest of life—whether in the form of natural forces or of other human beings—to conform to his or her plans. And perhaps Zarathustra's failures make this suggestion most forcefully when the causes of his failure seem rather silly, as in his encounter with the circus crowd. The precariousness of the individual in the world is underscored here because it appears that the individual—in this case Zarathustra—cannot count on the rest of life even to support his sense of personal dignity.

Zarathustra's response to failure also corresponds to Nietzsche's tragic vision, as one of his speeches to his dinner guests indicates:

> You higher men here, have you not all failed?
> Be of good cheer, what does it matter? How much is still possible! Learn to laugh at yourself as one must laugh!
>
> . . . Man's greatest distance and depth and what in him is lofty to the stars, his tremendous strength—are not all these frothing against each other in your pot? Is it any wonder that many a pot breaks? Learn to laugh at yourselves as one must laugh . . . [5]

Given the fragile status of the individual, failure is natural, particularly for individuals who pursue grand ambitions. The only meaningful response to such failure, says Zarathustra, is to say, "So what?" and laugh at oneself. This laughter, although it may not seem so, is a tragic response; for by laughing at one's failure one takes joy even in the aspects of life that cause one's figurative destruction. Zarathustra's speech continues with a reminder that human beings need to restore themselves with what *The Birth of Tragedy* calls the Apollonian—images of perfection, orderliness, and beauty.

> You higher men, how much is still possible!
> And verily, how much has always succeeded! How rich is the earth in little good perfect things, in what has turned out well!
> Place little good perfect things around you, O higher men! Their golden ripeness heals the heart. What is perfect teaches hope. [6]

Zarathustra's Story

Zarathustra's complex role as tragic hero and parodic counterpart to Christ and Socrates would seem to require a complicated story line. But this is not what we discover. The surrealistic tour de force in the prologue gives way to no plot at all in the immediately following section, which is a parable. At times we are simply given texts of Zarathustra's speeches; at other times we hear elaborate reports of his adventures, sometimes as they are happening, sometimes in the past tense.

The variability of the story line is undeniable; but this may not be an unambiguous fault. Even if it makes the book a bit hard to follow, the scrapbook effect of what we read in *Zarathustra* is not without literary precedent. The New Testament consists of a similar wide variety of things—reports of Christ's adventures, transcripts of his sermons and encounters, narrative that continues without interruption for several chapters. In *Zarathustra's* format, therefore, we can again recognize Nietzsche's project of parodying Scripture. Moreover, Zarathustra's story, like Christ's, does have a kind of developmental structure. In Zarathustra's case, the story from the prologue traces his recognition of his mistakes and his efforts to learn from them. His understanding of his own teachings becomes more mature over time, as I will argue in the third section, in large part as a result of his learning from error.

The absence of a strong plotline makes more prominent Nietzsche's tactic of juxtaposing and superimposing diverse materials. We have already observed that Nietzsche occasionally superimposes parodies of Christ and parodies of Socrates; but these parodies are only the most systematic patterns of allusion. Nietzsche regularly alludes to Goethe, Shakespeare, Schopenhauer, Greek mythology, Apuleius, and the Old Testament as well. The multiple allusions make many demands on our attentiveness, and when we are attentive we find ourselves in the dreamlike world of images and suggestions.

The reflection that *Zarathustra* is dreamlike can perhaps help us interpretively, particularly because Freud has accustomed us to the idea that dream symbols are overdetermined. We are likely to find the imagistic character of the book burdensome if we see the images and parables as colorful ways of making definite points. But if we read *Zarathustra's* images as meaning multiple things in the way that dream images mean multiple things, we are likely to see them as enjoyably suggestive. The imagistic character of *Zarathustra* makes the work's content rich and interpretively demanding. By focusing on certain prominent themes, however, we can gain the beginning of an interpretive orientation.

Zarathustra's Gospel

The Meaning of Life

If *Zarathustra* is a kind of narrative dream, it is nonetheless a dream about something. What is *Thus Spoke Zarathustra* all about? I have suggested that the book deals with the meaning of individual human life. And by invoking an expression like "the meaning of life" I have probably directed us back to a view that sees *Thus Spoke Zarathustra* as a handbook of platitudes which we would, in general, do best to avoid.

I would point out, however, that even Monty Python uses the expression "the meaning of life"; and this observation is not the irreverent irrelevance that it might seem. Monty Python's movie *The Meaning of Life*, though comically stylized, focuses on the absurd character of human behavior, the laughable pettiness that simultaneously calls the meaning of life into question and makes questions of cosmic significance seem hopelessly out of touch with life. Monty Python's view of human life is, while hilarious, seriously satiric. I want to suggest that Nietzsche is serious in a similar way in *Zarathustra*. Even when Zarathustra's formulations sound absurdly abstract and cosmic, Nietzsche makes a point of directing our forces back to the details of mundane existence.

Nietzsche emphasizes his concern that questions of meaning be grounded in day-to-day living in *Ecce Homo*. There he attributes his cleverness to such things as his dietary habits and his ingenious choices of recreation. After analyzing such matters in considerable detail, he rhetorically pauses and says,

> One will ask me why on earth I've been relating all these small things which are generally considered matters of complete indifference: I only harm myself, the more so if I am destined to represent great tasks. Answer: these small things—nutrition, place, climate, recreation, the whole casuistry of selfishness—are inconceivably more important than everything one has taken to be important so far. Precisely here one must begin to *relearn*. What mankind has so far considered seriously have not even been realities but mere imaginings—more strictly speaking, *lies* prompted by the bad instincts of sick natures that were harmful in the most profound sense—all these concepts, "God," "soul," "virtue," "sin," "beyond," "truth," "eternal life." . . . All the problems of politics, of social organization, and of education have been falsified through and through because one mistook the most harmful men for great men—because one learned to despise "little" things, which means the basic concerns of life itself.[7]

Although this statement is made later in a very different context, I think it reveals much about Nietzsche's attitude toward meaning in human life, an attitude that is evident throughout *Thus Spoke Zarathustra*.

Zarathustra's concept of "the meaning of the earth," central in his first speech, is consistent with the vision of life Nietzsche presents in *Ecco Homo*. God is dead, says Zarathustra in that speech, and human beings should remain true to the meaning of the earth. He introduces the image of the overman at this juncture, calling the overman the meaning of the earth—an image which might make us conclude that Zarathustra has soared into a romantic never-neverland, never to return to *our* earth again. More needs to be said about the overman, certainly; for the relationship between this nebulous concept and the nitty-gritty of our reality is not immediately clear. But in the narrative context of Zarathustra's speech, we see that he is immediately confronted with nitty-gritty: no one understands him. And, furthermore, he doesn't get the opportunity to dwell on this for very long. He witnesses a tightrope walker's fatal accident, provoked by a jester who startles the performer too much for him to maintain his balance. It is the image of this accident that directs Zarathustra's reflections through the rest of the prologue. "Human existence is uncanny and still without meaning: a jester can become man's fatality . . . ," he thinks to himself.[8]

We see that Nietzsche juxtaposes Zarathustra's abstract sermons and the debris of his practical situation already in the prologue; this demonstrates that he has no aspiration to keep Zarathustra's "wisdom" hermetically sealed from the practical details of life that might threaten it. And, during the course of the book, we find a pattern of interplay between Zarathustra's insight and his sometimes messy situation. Sometimes an insight seems to help Zarathustra in a practical situation. But at other times Zarathustra's insight seems to provide no practical help at all, as is the case in the first part of the section called "The Convalescent." There Zarathustra has a major tantrum because he is nauseated by the thought that petty people will recur throughout human history, infecting the whole with their attitude. In this case, Zarathustra is motivated by this moment of nausea to rearticulate his worldview, although this accomplishment takes both time and a lot of prodding from Zarathustra's animals. Zarathustra's chronicle continually depicts the interplay between thought and practical experience and Zarathustra's effort to bring the two into balance, thus reflecting a basic feature of the human "earth" in which any meaning must be grounded. Thinking and living are not perfectly attuned in human experience. And any honest attempt to find meaning in life must contend with this fact.

Thus Spoke Zarathustra contends with this fact by reflecting it. So far I have emphasized how the practicalities of living can frustrate both thought and a sense of life as meaningful for Zarathustra. Yet, the negativity of this emphasis is inappropriate. Two of Zarathustra's central ideas demonstrate the positive side of his tragic vision: the idea of the overman and the doctrine of eternal recurrence.

The Overman

The overman, says Zarathustra, is the meaning of the earth. But what does that mean? Neither Nietzsche nor Zarathustra offers much of a characterization of the overman. The overman is a kind of goal, a goal that stands as far from present humanity as humanity stands from the ape. And the meaning of the earth seems, from Zarathustra's first speech, to be found in striving toward the overman's mode of being. Still, Zarathustra spends more time discussing the details of this striving than he does explaining what the overman is.

I think Nietzsche intends this vagueness in his image of the overman. The overman is a kind of place-holder for the aim of human aspiration toward greatness. The particular form of such aspiration varies from individual life to individual life. The overman's lack of defining characteristics makes it possible for this image to accommodate the full range of great striving as it appears in all individual cases.

But what is so important about having the general concept of the goal of all great human striving? We can understand the importance of having such a general concept only if we recognize the role of self-transcendence in the kind of aspiration Zarathustra is calling for. The person who strives toward the overman, according to Zarathustra, is a person who is willing to perish in his efforts. He is prompted by the conviction that some goal is so much worth attaining that any expense to himself is justified.

That the overman has been identified by some as a social Darwinian evolutionary goal is unfortunate; but there is a modicum of truth in the evolutionary model. The overman is the ultimate concern of humanity because he is to be our descendent. When Zarathustra calls for self-sacrifice in the name of the overman he is speaking of the kind of self-sacrifice that parents would make for their children. The images of parent-child relationships that run through the book—striking when one considers that Zarathustra is a part-time hermit—function to suggest the same idea. The human life that is true to the meaning of the earth involves, in one form or another, the emotional self-transcendence that is involved in commitment to one's child. The overman symbolizes the object of this commitment, an object that one must recognize externally because the object is outside oneself.

The Doctrine of Eternal Recurrence

The overman is essential to the vision of the meaningful life that Nietzsche develops. Consistent with the tragic view of individuality suggested by *The Birth of Tragedy*, this vision suggests that meaning in individual life depends on one's ability to see beyond a perspective that is preoccupied with one's own well-being and satisfaction. The doctrine of eternal recurrence fortifies Zarathustra's tragic vision of meaning. This doctrine holds that the entire flux of life is a causal nexus which cyclically repeats itself over and over again. Interpreters disagree on what one should make of this doctrine. I accept Magnus's view that "recurrence . . . is a visual and conceptual representation of a particular attitude toward life," specifically an attitude of life-affirmation.[9]

But how does this doctrine of time and causality emblemize life-affirmation? A full answer to this question is complicated; nevertheless, we can get an idea of the connection by considering the alternative view of time and causality involved in the Christian interpretation of the world. Christianity, according to Nietzsche, sees time on a linear model. Our lives in time involve a linear progression toward a finish line, after which we will be rewarded or punished on the basis of whether our souls are in a state of grace or a state of sin.

According to Nietzsche, this view is life-negating, for it suggests that the real significance of any particular action has nothing to do with its connections to other parts of the causal scheme of life. The real significance of any action is a matter of how it is evaluated from a perspective that lies outside of time. The effect of this is more pernicious than it may sound. If we succeed in interpreting the events of our lives according to the atemporal Christian ledger, we divorce ourselves from a sense of real interaction with the larger world.

Worse yet, the Christian interpretation almost inevitably leads the individual to a negative perspective on his or her own life, which is also a consequence of the Christian understanding of time and causality. The causality that Christianity is concerned with is not a part of the natural order; it is a supernatural kind of causality, in which behavior in the natural order that is deemed sinful has damaging, supernatural effects on the soul. Another kind of supernatural agency must be called in to undo the effects of sin; sin needs to be redeemed.

From the earthly perspective that Nietzsche and Zarathustra endorse, the effects of the doctrine of sin on one's ability to affirm life are tremendously harmful. As a consequence of one particular event in a life of events, the individual's entire perspective on himself or herself can change. A serious sin (for example, a single act of adultery) ruins one's life. And no further interaction with the rest of the world is sufficient to undo sin. One can only turn to God with the hope of unconditional forgiveness. Built into this model of interpreting the bad moments of life is the demand for absolute reassurance. Sin makes life absolutely bad, and only absolute reassurance can make life good again. The condition for obtaining absolute reassurance from God is that one absolutely repudiate one's objectionable, sinful actions. And so the doctrine of sin and divine forgiveness demands that the individual disassociate himself from parts of his past in order to feel good about anything in his present.

The doctrine of eternal recurrence, by contrast, considers these moments of failure as subsidiary to the present. Every part of life is causally bound together; the present moment is a configuration of all the tendencies that the past has contributed to it. The present individual is who he (or she) is as a consequence of the convergence of his (or her) entire past, including, to some extent, his (or her) ancestry.

The cyclical aspect of the doctrine's model of time gives every moment equal prominence. At every moment the currents of life are equally in flux. Every aspect of the present is causally conditioned by the past, according to the doctrine of eternal recurrence. But instead of interpreting the present reactively, as burdened by the legacy of the past, the doctrine of eternal recurrence interprets it actively. Each of us, as the definite individual each of us is at the present moment, creatively forms the materials that the past has tossed up into some design. This is the nature of life-affirming human activity. And this activity is most life-affirming when one directs the accumulation of one's life's moments toward some definite end. Zarathustra expresses this vision of his own activity:

> . . . "I walk among men as among the fragments of the future—that future which I envisage. And this is all my creating and striving, that I create and carry together into One what is fragment and riddle and dreadful accident. . . .
>
> "To redeem those who lived in the past and to recreate all 'it was' into a 'thus I willed it'—that alone should I call redemption."[10]

The doctrine of eternal recurrence uses aesthetic criteria to evaluate the significance of an individual life. The events of one's life gain significance when one approaches them as artistic raw material, appropriated in aspiring toward some individually determined vision of greatness. This vision is symbolized, in Zarathustra's scheme, by the overman.

Magnus has analyzed eternal recurrence as an existential imperative,[11] and this interpretation underscores its normative character. We can find our lives meaningful if we approach their events as aesthetic material; and according to Zarathustra's tragic position we *ought* to do this. If our lives are not given significance by something outside them, and there is no ultimate point of individual satisfaction, the significance of our lives must be judged by immanent criteria.

Nietzsche is not suggesting that we adopt an "aesthetic" lifestyle in which everything is done for some theatrical effect. Nor does he believe that we have ultimate control over whether our guiding project of aspiration succeeds; our lives are not self-contained art projects. But he is suggesting that we can find meaning in our lives by postulating something like an aesthetic goal—a vision of greatness—that we can pursue with our entire effort, arranging our activities in such a way that they contribute to the project.

I have suggested that Nietzsche's basic goal in *Zarathustra* is to explore the question of the meaning of individual human life. The visions of the overman and the eternal recurrence—the major thematic elements— are both parts of Nietzsche's answer to this question. The perspective that renders life meaningful is the tragic perspective, Nietzsche contends. The tragic perspective does not denigrate individual life by urging the individual to associate meaning with notions of survival or perfect contentment. Instead it finds individual life to be meaningful in the way that art is meaningful—meaning emerges from the artist's caring arrangement of limited material.

The Ambivalence of Zarathustra's Doctrines

The Attitudinal Character of Zarathustra's Doctrines

Both the doctrine of eternal recurrence and the ideal of the overman are presented as images of sorts, images that can help us to achieve a life-affirming orientation. Their function, then, is not the traditional function of doctrines of succinctly stating some unalterable point of truth. Zarathustra's doctrines embody ideals that are as hard to pinpoint and as dynamically achieved as Aristotle's Mean.

The difficulty is that these doctrines do not always sound elusive. Zarathustra seems to have some pretty definite ideas about the life he has in mind—and some of these ideas seem to be quite directly presented in his platitudes. Is it really the case that Zarathustra's doctrines are aesthetic ideals that cannot be followed like recipes? Why am I so convinced that their meaning is dynamically developed in the life of one who lives in their spirit, not defined forever in the letter of the doctrines?

I am convinced that Nietzsche intends Zarathustra's doctrines to be seen in this way because of the way he portrays Zarathustra. Zarathustra's glib formulations, pronounced to his disciples with increasing fluency, are only one aspect of Zarathustra's chronicle. Nietzsche also includes a number of scenes in which Zarathustra's composure and eloquence break down. The reports of Zarathustra's nightmare, visions, private emotional outbursts, etc., provide an ironic subtext that comments on Zarathustra's public presentations.

The point of these reports is that the words that articulate Zarathustra's doctrines are understood only when the importance of the attitudinal aspect of his insights is appreciated. In these scenes Zarathustra himself is shown forgetting his doctrines' real significance by losing sight of the spirit that originally inspired them.

"The Soothsayer"

In the section entitled "The Soothsayer," for example, Zarathustra becomes deeply depressed after hearing a "soothsayer" preach that "all is empty, all is the same, all has been."[12] He dreams that he is a nightwatchman who is a "guardian of tombs upon the lonely mountain castle of death." As guardian of tombs, he possesses "the rustiest of all keys" which he is able to use "to open the most creaking of all gates." This appears to be the extent of Zarathustra's movement. His entire life seems to be devoted to guarding memorials to what is dead and opening gateways that are all but dead. The context of this scene is "the brightness of midnight," the moment of the day that most obviously symbolizes the potency of the present. But Zarathustra seems spiritually asleep to this brightness.[13]

He is, however, awakened. Three strokes strike "at the gate like thunder." Zarathustra interprets this as the knock of someone else who is burdened by the past: " 'Alpa!' I cried, 'who is carrying his ashes up the mountain?' " Zarathustra tries to open the gate where the knocks had sounded, but his key can't open it. The gate opens, instead, with a roaring wind that blows a black coffin into the vault where Zarathustra is standing. The coffin bursts open, and out comes a chaotic flurry of living and ephemeral things: the "thousandfold laughter" and "thousand grimaces" of "children, angels, owls, fools, and butterflies as big as children." Zarathustra is terribly frightened.[14]

These beings are scarcely frightening in themselves. Zarathustra must be frightened not of them, but of what is alluded to in their laughter, which he describes as mocking. They mock the way of life that Zarathustra has become immersed in—a life of guarding his teachings, the purpose he announced many sections before when he was seized with terror that his teachings had fallen into the hands of his "enemies." But the dynamic insight that originally provoked these teachings is as dead, for the waking Zarathustra, as are the remains of the dead whose tombs he guards in his dreams. He has forgotten the insight, at the basis of the doctrine of eternal recurrence, that the present moment is not subordinate to any other moment, and that it has a kind of priority in being the point where our activity occurs. He has succumbed to a misinterpretation of his doctrine that is consistent with the letter, though not the spirit, of his word—the view that if time is cyclical, everything has already happened and there is no point in taking an active role in the moment.

In the dream, Zarathustra is so far removed from the dynamic movement of life that the lively beings who pour out of the coffin are terrifying to him. His need at this point of the book is for life to stir him back to activity. He has slumped into a cautious rut from which he cannot extricate himself with the words of his doctrines, the "keys" to insights he has had previously. He can only emerge from this "tomb" of his own making by becoming open again to the lively spirit that moved him in the first place.

Zarathustra, *Part IV*

Nietzsche's tactic of portraying Zarathustra's turbulent relationship to his own insights is particularly evident in "The Fourth and Last Part" of the book. The received view has been to downplay part IV as an unfortunate afterthought to a work that would have been better without it. Part IV, it is true, shows Zarathustra repeating many of his previously enunciated doctrines, and it fails to depict any major breakthroughs along theoretical or doctrinal lines. But part IV is much more of a coherent story than the previous parts. Its achievement, consistently, is more literary than theoretical. Part IV is rather slapstick, satirizing Zarathustra's temptation to lapse into the mental habits of the Christian tradition he verbally renounces. In this way, it serves to remind the sympathetic reader of his or her own similar temptations.[16]

One of Zarathustra's foibles that part IV brings into focus is his continuing tendency to take a rigidly protective stance toward his doctrines. When he discovers his dinner guests, the "higher men," holding a service to worship an ass, Zarathustra responds like Moses returning from Mount Sinai.

> At this point of the litany Zarathustra could no longer control himself and himself shouted Yea-Yuh, even louder than the ass, and he jumped right into the middle of his guests, who had gone mad. "But what are you doing there, children of men?" he cried as he pulled the praying men up from the floor. "Alas, if someone other than Zarathustra had watched you: Everyone would judge that with your new faith you were the worst blasphemers or the most foolish of all little old women."[17]

Everyone might judge as well that Zarathustra's behavior is that of the most defensive true believer, insisting that the behavior of others conform to his own belief. And some of the higher men point this out. The ugliest man, for instance, reminds Zarathustra that he least of anyone has any right to demand that others adhere to his gospel of atheism.

> "O Zarathustra," replied the ugliest man, "you are a rogue! Whether that one *still* lives or lives again or is thoroughly dead—which of the two of us knows that best? I ask you. But one thing I do know; it was from you yourself that I learned it once, O Zarathustra: whoever would kill most thoroughly, *laughs*."[18]

Nietzsche's portrait of Zarathustra as something of an ass is not intended as a vindication of the resurgence of religious belief among those who have rejected it. But it is an indication that Zarathustra is as vulnerable as his disciples to the mental habits that his gospel is pitted against. Again we see Zarathustra forgetting the vital insight that spawned his teachings and remembering only their conceptual remains.

But the movement of part IV is toward Zarathustra's recovery of his vital insight. At the end he laughs at having committed a "final sin"— ironically the "sin" of acting on the Christian virtue of pity in response to the higher men. After a moment of guilt at having done something contrary to his doctrine, he recognizes that he has slipped into the old habit of judging his mistake "sinful" and feeling guilty about it.

What Zarathustra puts behind him at the end of the book is the conceptual scheme of judging behavior in terms of sinfulness. We don't know how enduring the change is. But we are reminded, as is Zarathustra, of something important: that inner orientation is more difficult to transform than verbal platitudes, and that Zarathustra himself is still struggling to achieve the former transformation. We are also, and perhaps more importantly, reminded that to see through these old habits is itself to regain a stance beyond them. Zarathustra may slip into his old habits again in the future, but he can also learn to laugh at them again, and in this way most effectively put even habituated folly to rest.

Conclusion

In one of his many speeches attacking the Christian worldview, Zarathustra claims, "They would have to sing better songs for me to learn to have faith in their Redeemer; and his disciples would have to look more redeemed!"[19] Perhaps we can turn this *ad hominem* against Zarathustra himself. By the end of the book he may not look very redeemed to us. He has overcome an inconsistent attitude, but this may be temporary. And his mission has failed. We have little reason to believe that he is about to fare better in the future. Zarathustra himself obviously does not expect his renewed mission to lead to satisfaction; one of his parting comments is, "Am I concerned with *happiness*? I am concerned with my *work*."[20]

In the end, Nietzsche offers us a vision of life that we can take or leave. To use the terminology of his subtitle, he has written a book for no one, in the sense that he has not packaged his worldview to ensure that we will find it attractive. And we may well find Zarathustra's final plight quite undesirable, particularly if we are attached to our tradition's high appraisal of success and satisfaction.

Nietzsche offers his tragic vision as an alternative to our traditional view of human life, however, and Zarathustra's portrait at the end remains consonant with the tragic vision. He has failed as a result of his individual limitations and the world's noncooperation; but his transformed perspective on life is light-hearted anyway. He has no grounds for confidence that his project will succeed, but he has the buoyancy of someone who enjoys the unpredictability of life and is open to whatever might happen. *Amor fati.*

Appropriately, the book ends in midair. Zarathustra is not at a resting point. Instead, we see him glide mirthfully forward, despite his discouraging circumstances. At the end, he embodies the side of the tragic vision that he articulates in the claim, "We should consider every day lost on which we have not danced at least once. And we should call every truth false which was not accompanied by at least one laugh."[21]

Notes

1. *Z*, p. 124/*KGW* VI:1, p. 8.
2. *EH*, p. 259/*KGW* VI:3, pp. 296–97.
3. *Z*, p. 121/*KGW* VI:1, p. 5.
4. *GS*, p. 203/*KGW* V:2, p. 251.
5. *Z*, p. 404/*KGW* VI:1, p. 360.
6. *Z*, p. 405/*KGW* VI: p. 360.
7. *EH*, p. 256/*KGW* VI:3, pp. 293–94.
8. *Z*, p. 132/*KGW* VI:1, p. 17.
9. Bernd Magnus, *Nietzsche's Existential Imperative* (Bloomington: Indiana University Press, 1978), p. 142.
10. *Z*, p. 251/*KGW* VI:1, p. 175.
11. See Magnus, pp. 142–43.
12. *Z*, p. 245/*KGW* VI:1, p. 168.
13. *Z*, p. 246/*KGW* VI:1, pp. 169–70.
14. *Z*, p. 247/*KGW* VI:1, p. 170.
15. See, for example, R. J. Hollingdale, *Nietzsche: The Man and His Philosophy* (Baton Rouge: Louisiana State University Press, 1965), p. 190.
16. For a detailed analysis of part IV and an account of its relationship to Menippean satire, see chap. 7 of my *Nietzsche's Zarathustra* (Philadelphia: Temple University Press, 1987).
17. *Z*, p. 425/*KGW* VI:1, p. 386.
18. *Z*, p. 427/*KGW* VI:1, p. 388.
19. *Z*, p. 204/*KGW* VI:1, p. 114.
20. *Z*, p. 439/*KGW* VI:1, p. 404.
21. *Z*, p. 322/*KGW* VI:1, p. 260.

The Deification of the Commonplace: *Twilight of the Idols*[1]

BERND MAGNUS

I

If Nietzsche was right in saying that there are no immaculate perceptions and that there is only a perspective knowing, as he says in *GM* III 12, and elsewhere[2]; moreover, if in asserting these claims their very iteration does not undermine their cognitive force,[3] then it follows that there are no immaculate perceptions of a text either, or a knowledge of its contents, which is not perspectival.

Perspectivism derives some of its intuitive force from the emerging popularity of the still-picture camera in Nietzsche's time and can be understood as a generalization of its point. Imagine, if you would, a physical object with a camera circling 360° about it in equidistant orbits, orbits which eventually traverse the object as if it were encased in an invisible globe. Imagine further that this camera constantly took pictures of the object in question as it moved in its relentless spherical orbits. In terms of this crude image, a nonperspectival view of the object would amount to a simultaneous rather than successive picture from all the orbital points traversed by our camera. In fact, to press this analogy further, nonperspectival representation would in this case amount not only to a simultaneous picturing of the object from all equidistant orbital points, but may require that our camera traverse an infinite number of such concentric orbits, each one of which satisfies only the requirement that it be at every point equidistant from its object's center.

The purpose of this illustration is twofold: first, to help to motivate

152

Nietzsche's claim that knowing, like seeing and representing, is always from some point of view or other, and second, to bring to the surface an ambiguity in the very perspectivism metaphor itself. For perspectivism has been interpreted to mean at least two seemingly different things. First, it has been taken to assert that the notion of a unique, final, canonical account of an object or state-of-affairs—an absolute standpoint—is not possible. The force of this claim is primarily epistemic. It suggests that, if there are only perspectives, there is no point in asking which one is the correct one *without reference to further specifying conditions.*[4] It suggests that there is no one true or privileged perspective *simpliciter*, no absolute standpoint. If there were to be such an unconditionally true perspective, such an account would perhaps require what Hilary Putnam recently has called a God's-eye-view,[5] a view from no point whatsoever save all the possible perspectives simultaneously, a notion which may well be incoherent.[6] Second, perspectivism has been taken to mean that the very notion of a thing-in-itself is incoherent.[7] The force of this claim is primarily ontological. It may amount to no more than the suggestion that my camera illustration only makes sense because a God's-eye-view is presupposed, is smuggled in as it were, because one assumes in my illustration that apart from and independent of any single perspective there exists an object only partially revealed from any given, single perspective. But one never has the object in view save from a perspective, and one never has anything other than the perspective.

Appearances to the contrary notwithstanding, my topic is *not* perspectivism. Rather, what frames and informs my reading of *Twilight of the Idols*—the primary topic of this paper—is that this reading is itself an enactment, illustration, and embodiment of Nietzsche's perspectivist point; it is a token of its type; for there are inevitably many different possible ways to read Nietzsche's texts if Nietzsche's perspective claim is right. The reading I shall be pursuing will be contentious in that it takes seriously not only the commonplace view that how a reader approaches *Twilight of the Idols*—and Nietzsche's other texts as well—shall shape what one takes Nietzsche to mean, but, less obviously, that Nietzsche invites a self-transformation on the part of the reader who is related to Nietzsche's texts in a certain way. Put crudely and in a sloganeering way, I shall read Nietzsche in this paper as a therapeutic philosopher and his texts as self-referentially illuminating diagnostic tools, when focused in the appropriate way or ways. The "therapeutic philosopher" label can also mislead. It may, for example, be construed in the medical sense in which Danto reads *Toward the Genealogy of*

Morals (in his paper in this volume). "Therapy" understood in that way provides either prophylaxis or medicine, as Danto argues. In Nietzsche's case such "therapy" may include a dependence on the part of the physician upon certain physiologizing assumptions, including a sort of residual Darwinism—to which Danto's paper seems to commit Nietzsche. The sense of "therapy" I have in mind is different. It is more psychoanalytic than prophylactic. Reading Nietzsche in this way assumes that his reader is already ill, that he is not likely to understand the nature of his illness—indeed that his illness may mask *itself* as health—that he came to his "physician" for reasons other than those he believes have motivated him, and that, finally, he will resist treatment by persistently misinterpreting and misrepresenting his own motivation and condition. The difference, then, reduces to this: I do not commit Nietzsche to any final substantive, first-order generalizations. Each book becomes for me an exercise in perspectivism, an invitation to look at the data from a given, altered perspective. Hence, on my reading, the subtitle of *Toward the Genealogy of Morals* is as important as its title: *A Polemic*. What this interpretation entails, among other things, is an implicit rejection of the view that one's task is to find the literal philosophy beneath or behind Nietzsche's figurative prose. On the view I shall pursue, searching out Nietzsche's literal "philosophy" resembles offering a plot summary of Tolstoy's *War and Peace* or Dostoevsky's *The Brothers Karamazov* and mistaking those summaries for the *point* in reading either author's novel; or to vary the analogy, to read the Bible or the Koran entirely and exclusively as imaginative literature. What is at issue in such cases is the failure to see or to acknowledge that some persons read such texts not merely to be informed but to be enlightened by them and sometimes even to be transformed. To read Nietzsche in the way I shall propose, then, is to attend not only to *what* is said but to the mode of address as well; indeed it may be to argue implicitly that an intrinsic feature of what Nietzsche has to say to us just *is* the manner in which he addresses us.

One final preliminary point: It has sometimes been said that perspectivism commits one to the view that there is no way to choose among perspectives. This does not seem right to me. As in the case of interpretations, one may merely mean that no definitive perspective, no final, canonical commentary is possible. It is just to say that no single interpretation of a text (or perhaps even any object) is *the* unique interpretation which that text (or object) would offer concerning itself—if it could. It is a rejection of the view that we play the role of Charlie McCarthy to the text's or object's Edgar Bergen. It does not follow from this concession that we cannot choose between good and bad perspectives, useful and unhelpful ones, simplistic and informed ones, thoughtful and superficial ones, well-argued and badly argued ones, intelligent and stupid ones, subtle and crude ones, deep and shallow ones.

II

Nietzsche insists in *Ecce Homo* and elsewhere that readers authentically his own must read him forwards and backwards. Each book was to be read prospectively and retrospectively. This self-indulgent, self-referential quality of Nietzsche's writing is vividly in evidence in the quartet of books he composed in 1888—*The Wagner Case, Twilight of the Idols, The Antichrist*, and *Ecce Homo*—and, of course, in his own slender selections from his previous writings on Wagner gathered on Christmas Day, 1888 in Turin, under the title *Nietzsche contra Wagner*. This self-referential quality is in turn quite complex. Sometimes Nietzsche explicitly mentions his other works in a given book, sometimes he refers only to ideas present elsewhere in them; sometimes he comments on his own books, as in *Ecce Homo* where his commentary becomes a sort of arch and closure; sometimes he comments on the trajectory and progress of his work; and occasionally his work is itself a commentary on commentary about his work—including his own commentary. Nietzsche is a subtle writer, in brief. Even his bombast, which forces us to recoil at his excess and arrogance, may be read as a strategy of "honesty" designed to contrast with Socratic-Platonic "dishonesty." In Plato's texts disembodied reason speaks; Nietzsche, in contrast, never leaves in doubt who is speaking. Occasionally, perhaps always, his books are masks. Ideas referred to self-referentially but *not* discussed, such as the *übermensch* in *Twilight of the Idols*, occasionally frame the discourse, a sort of controlling absence. Finally, having abandoned traditional discursive philosophical procedures (procedures of the sort in which an author frequently tells his reader where he is headed and how he proposes to get there), Nietzsche favors an accumulation of self-sufficient insights, epigrams, maxims, aphorisms, fragments, and notes, which require of the reader that he *himself* provide the missing ligature which unifies his books. In consequence, the reader's constructed ligature both establishes and, paradoxically, dissolves authorial identity and intention. "Nietzsche" becomes Nietzsche-as-read-by-*x*-on-occasion-*y*.[8]

Many, perhaps all, of these self-referential characteristics are evident in *Twilight of the Idols*. The very title itself is a complex verbal icon, referring as it does internally not only to Nietzsche's contemporary idols but to his critiques of Western philosophy, morality, and religion: As he says in the preface to that book, "This little essay is a great declaration of war . . . not just idols of the age, but eternal idols . . . are here touched with a hammer as with a tuninǵ fork"[9]; and the title of the book also reminds the reader of Nietzsche's distance from Wagner, whose *Götterdämmerung*, *Twilight of the Gods*, is subsumed and consumed in the pun which constitutes the book's title: *Götzendämmerung*. This internal self-referentiality does double duty here, too, referring *to* but not naming the book Nietzsche had just completed—*The Wagner Case*—and referring *to* but not mentioning the subject of that book, Richard Wagner.

If the title's complexity is largely if not entirely self-referring, in contrast the subtitle of *Twilight of the Idols* is an invitation to misconstruction: *or How One Philosophizes with a Hammer*. Much Nietzsche commentary consists of invoking this metaphor of the hammer for destructive, sometimes sinister purposes, bludgeoning its victims, smashing its target. But, as Walter Kaufmann[10] pointed out long ago, and as the above quotation from the preface shows, "idols . . . are here touched with a hammer *as with a tuning fork*." And Nietzsche adds immediately: "there are altogether no older, no more convinced, no more puffed-up idols—and none more hollow. That does not prevent them from being those in which people have the most faith."[11] One frequent characteristic of Nietzsche's compressed, terse style—which is the presentation of contradictory metaphors in a single pithy sentence, phrase, or paragraph—surfaces in the very subtitle and, when wrenched out of context, invites mischief. For how many of us are able without effort to assimilate the image of a hammer to that of a tuning fork which sounds out hollow idols, and, moreover, in the very sounding out of their hollowness, their emptiness, destroys them in the sense of deconstructing them without overt violence?

Nietzsche referred to *Twilight of the Idols* as a "Zusammenfassung wesentlichen philosophischen Heterodoxien" [a "summary of (my) essential philosophical heterodoxies"] in letters to Peter Gast on September 12 and to Franz Overbeck on September 16, 1888. In his notes he simultaneously refers to it as an *Auszug*, a point of departure, a starting point. And one way of reading *Twilight of the Idols* is to read this synopsis and point of departure as summarizing his philosophical intention not only in substance but in form as well. *Twilight of the Idols* is Nietzsche's alembic in the double sense that one finds there Nietzsche's philosophy as such, distilled, purified, while finding it expressed in aphoristic alembic at the same time.

Thus this book begins, just as one would expect, with aphorisms which Nietzsche calls "maxims and arrows" (*Sprüche und Pfeile*). For, indeed, Nietzsche has often been called the archtypal aphorist—and these pithy forty-four aphorisms remind us that aphorisms are meant to atomize rather than provide unity, connection, totality, and closure. Aphorisms divide, mark off.[12] Or, put differently, the aphorism, epigram, or maxim requires a special effort on the reader's part to provide the connective tissue, the logical ligature, which transforms glistening shards into a single organic whole which subtends them. And this, too, is an exercise in perspectivism, one in which the reader is the unindicted coconspirator who blames or praises Nietzsche for his own results. And maxims, like arrows which are perfectly poised to strike their target, can inscribe themselves upon or sear our psyches long after the details of another philosopher's argument have been forgotten. Two illustrations from *Twilight of the Idols* should suffice to make this point plain: "*Out of life's school of war*: What does not destroy me strengthens me"[13] and "I mistrust all systematizers and I avoid them. The will to a system is a lack of integrity."[14]

Having reminded this reader of the role and limits of aphorisms, Nietzsche turns immediately to a series of essays in miniature, each with its own subject—a genre for which the term "aphorism" may merely suggest our own impoverished vocabulary. The subjects of these essays—or essays-turned-aphorisms—are Socrates (in the section titled "The Problem of Socrates"); the history of philosophy (in the section " 'Reason' in Philosophy" and in "How the 'True World' Finally Became a Fable"); morality, with special attention to its religious sanction (in the section titled "Morality as Anti-Nature"); four sustaining errors which have inseminated much of Western religion, morality, and philosophy (in the section "The Four Great Errors"); morality again, with special attention to its will to improve humankind (in the section "The 'Improvers' of Humankind"); nationalism, with special attention to Germany (in the section "What the Germans Lack"); the longest section—fifty-one entries which range primarily over contemporary idols—with revealing Nietzschean critiques in the bargain (in the section "Skirmishes of an Untimely Man"); his debt to and distance from classical antiquity (in the section "What I Owe to the Ancients"), and—as if to goad the reader back to the book *Thus Spoke Zarathustra*—the concluding section of *Twilight of the Idols* is a verbatim presentation of *Thus Spoke Zar-*

athustra's part III, section 29, from "On Old and New Tablets," here reprinted by Nietzsche under the title "The Hammer Speaks."

None of us has the time, inclination, or patience to read an account of what I think is going on in each of these rich sections of *Twilight of the Idols*. I do want to remark on the sense in which they summarize his philosophy, however indirectly, especially the ones concerning Socrates, reason in philosophy, morality, and religion.

My point of entry into Nietzsche and *Twilight of the Idols* is oblique. One could say, without too much exaggeration, that I am trying to connect, make sense of, and then apply to *the act of reading* Nietzsche himself four notions he mentions in *Towards the Genealogy of Morals* III 10–13, in the essay "What is the Meaning of Ascetic Ideals?"

> For man is more sick, uncertain, changeable, indeterminate than any other animal, there is no doubt of that—he is *the* sick animal: how has that come about? ... (*GM* III 13).

> Read from a distant star, the majuscule script of our earthly existence would perhaps lead to the conclusion that the earth was the distinctively *ascetic planet*, a nook of disgruntled, arrogant, and offensive creatures filled with a profound disgust at themselves, at the earth, at all life, who inflict as much pain on themselves as they possibly can out of pleasure in inflicting pain—which is probably their only pleasure. For consider how regularly and universally the ascetic priest appears in almost every age; he belongs to no one race; he prospers everywhere; he emerges from every class of society. Nor does he breed and propagate his mode of valuation through heredity ... It must be a necessity of the first order that again and again promotes the growth and prosperity of this *life-inimical* species—it must indeed be in the *interest of life itself* that such a self-contradictory type does not die out. For an ascetic life is a self-contradiction ... (*GM* III 11).

> ... *the ascetic ideal springs from the protective instinct of a degenerating life* which tries by all means to sustain itself and to fight for its existence; ... life wrestles in it and through it with death and *against* death; the ascetic ideal is an artifice for the *preservation* of life ... (*GM* III 13).

> ... for the longest time philosophy would not have been *possible at all* on earth without ascetic wraps and cloak, without an ascetic self-misunderstanding. To put it vividly: the *ascetic priest* provided until the most modern times the repulsive and gloomy caterpillar form in which alone the philosopher could live and creep about ... (*GM* III 10).

One way of reading Nietzsche's *Twilight of the Idols* and connecting it with the four quoted passages above is to see it telling a story about how we in the West became who we are.[15] It will have to be a sweeping tale, to be sure, centering on our philosophical, religious, and moral heritage. The use of the singular "heritage" already begs the question in Nietzsche's favor; for it suggests that, deep down, there is a family resemblance among the many things that have been called "philosophy" which is more interesting than their differences, that there has been a resemblance within the Judeo-Christian tradition as interesting as its internecine strife, that there are more and different things to be said about moral philosophy than are captured in the consequential-ist/deontological debate, for instance. For Nietzsche's story to succeed two further assumptions must be added. The first is that there are important points of intersection between the history of "philosophy," "religion," and "morality," motivational intersections which make it possible to speak of all three simultaneously as expressing a single ascetic ideal motivated by the will to power[16]; the second assumption is that of all the complex historical factors which have shaped Western civilization and character,—social, economic, political, demographic, and ethnocentric—none is as important as the first-mentioned trio in telling us how we in the West became who we are—philosophy, religion, and morality.

Nietzsche appears to have been persuaded early on that what philosophers today call essentialism and realism are mistaken, so to speak, that there is no indwelling structure of the universe which it is reason's task to unveil. Even some of our most basic stock-in-trade distinctions—subject/object, mind/world, consciousness/reality, and their successors, such as transcendental unity of apperception/constituted object, language/referent, conceptual scheme/content of scheme, signifier/signified—would appear to be optional products of natural languages. This is because, as Nietzsche says in *BGE* 3:

> The singular family resemblance between all Indian, Greek and German philosophizing is easy enough to explain. Where there exists a language affinity it is quite impossible, thanks to the common philosophy of grammar—I mean thanks to unconscious domination and directing by similar grammatical functions—to avoid everything being prepared in advance for a similar evolution and succession of philosophical systems . . .[17]

The domination of thought by the tyranny of common grammatical functions is not some lamentable fact which is to be overcome. Rather, Nietzsche seems to offer a thoroughly naturalistic and instrumentalist account of the origins of consciousness and language, as he does in *GS* 354.

> [C]onsciousness evolved at all only under the pressure of need for com-
> munication—it was from the very first necessary and useful only between
> man and man . . . and also evolved only in proportion to the degree of this
> usefulness. Consciousness is really only a connecting network between
> man and man—only as such did it have to evolve. . . . —My idea, as one
> can see, is that consciousness does not really belong to the existence of
> man as an individual but rather to that in him which is community and
> herd.[18]

Rather than understanding language and thought as communication
instruments with which to cope, however, humanity's genius for self-
deceptive self-descriptions did not take long to evolve either.

> The significance of language for the evolution of culture lies in this, that
> mankind set up in language a separate world beside the other world, a
> place it took to be so firmly set that, standing upon it, it could lift the
> rest of the world off its hinges and make itself master of it. (HH 11)[19]

So the significance of language for our history lies not only in the di-
chotomy of mind and world which it supplied for Indo-European vocabularies, but in presenting the dominating metaphor of the mind as
the faculty for accurate representations of the world as it is in itself.
This in turn helps to explain the later denigration of the apparent world
in favor of some other "true" world: " 'Reason' is the cause of our
falsification of the testimony of the senses . . . The 'apparent' world is
the only one: the 'true world' is merely added by a lie," Nietzsche says
in *Twilight of the Idols.*[20] And Nietzsche further suggests that because
"the prejudice of reason forces us to posit unity, identity, permanence,
substance, cause, thinghood, being, we see ourselves somehow caught
in error, compelled into error."[21] So Nietzsche suggests that there are
no fixed standpoints, no common measure between representation and
represented—no common measure between "language," "consciousness," "idea," "transcendental ego," "conceptual scheme," "signifier"
on the one hand, and "world," "object," "thing," "phenomenon," and
"signified," on the other hand. But he also adds in *GS* 354:

> You will guess that it is not the opposition of subject and object that
> concerns me here: This distinction I leave to the epistemologists who have
> become entangled in the snares of grammar (the metaphysics of the peo-
> ple). It is even less the opposition of 'thing-in-itself' and appearance; for
> we do not 'know' nearly enough to be entitled to any such distinction.
> We simply lack any organ for knowledge, for 'truth': we 'know' (or believe
> or imagine) just as much as may be *useful* in the interests of the human
> herd, the species.

And what follows from these considerations is that

> Henceforth, my dear philosophers, let us be on guard against the dan-
> gerous old conceptual fiction that posited a "pure, will-less, painless,
> timeless knowing subject . . . There is *only* a perspective "knowing"; and
> the *more* affects we allow to speak about one thing, the *more* eyes, dif-
> ferent eyes, we can use to observe one thing, the more complete will our
> "concept" of this thing, our "objectivity," be. (*GM* III 12)[22]

The claim that there is only a "perspective 'knowing' " is formulated
in various ways in Nietzsche's published and unpublished writings of his
mature period. Sometimes he connects this thesis with phenomenalism
and perspectivism and argues that our "animal consciousness" as such
grasps the world only in terms of its lowest common denominator. At
other times he offers his perspectivism to counter prevailing philosophic
orientations, positivism for example. At still other times Nietzsche
seemed simply to believe that his perspectivism permits a collapse in
distinctions between the definition of truth, criteria for truth claims, and
the justification for truth claims, as when he suggests boldly in dustbin
manuscripts, "there is no truth,"[23] "truth is error,"[24] and "truth is the
kind of error without which a certain species of life could not live. The
value for *life* is ultimately decisive."[25]

From considerations of this sort, and others I have not mentioned, it
follows for Nietzsche that language systematically "falsifies" the world.
Language interprets the world according to a scheme we cannot throw
off. Categories ossify and congeal, but the imposition of language, of
categories which congeal, is not a contingent fact about ourselves.
Rather, language schemes seem to be based upon our psychological
need to find meaning, order, and stability in the world. This also helps
to account for other putative facts, for instance that we tend to seek
permanence where there is none, that we seek nonhistorically grounded
starting points for inquiry where there are none, that we seek an order
in everything. For, on this view, we *need* coherence, purpose, unity,
and meaning. The metanarrative of the ascetic ideal appears to be at
work here, too. All this is summed up nicely in a single famous, terse
sentence in *Twilight of the Idols*: "I am afraid we are not rid of God
because we still have faith in grammar."[26]

Such views, of course, require enormous adjustments in our conception of the role of philosophy, science, religion, and morality in our
lives. Indeed they require an adjustment in our conception of culture
itself, for it too must now appear as the imposition of form upon chaos,
masks worn by the ascetic ideal. What holds for individuals is meant to

hold for cultures as well. On this view, each culture copes with its world, imposes its order upon an indeterminate continuum.

As a result, says Nietzsche in *Ecce Homo*, "I learned to view the origins of moralizing and idealizing very differently from what might be desirable: the *hidden* history of philosophers, the psychology of their great names came to light for me."[27] And then Nietzsche announces a theme of his thinking for which, at first, he became notorious:

> Gradually it has become clear to me what every great philosophy so far has been: namely, the personal confession of its author and a kind of involuntary and unconscious memoir. . . . Accordingly, I do not believe that a "drive to knowledge" is the father of philosophy; but rather that another drive has, here as elsewhere, employed understanding (and mis-understanding) as a mere instrument . . . (*BGE* 6)

The drive which is expressed in philosophy is the will to power self-deceptively exhibited as the dispassionate will to truth: "Their 'knowing' is *creating*, is a lawgiving, their will to truth is—*will to power*" (*BGE* 6). And so the family resemblance of all philosophy hitherto is that it carves up world and discourse into two unequal chunks. There is the "true world," reality as it is in itself. Only philosophers have access to this domain, not the *hoi polloi*. This reality is captured in philosophic vocabularies which contrast with slippery, transitory, second-rate discourse directed at the merely "apparent" world, stained by the tincture of history. And so Nietzsche asks in *Twilight of the Idols*, "You ask me which of the philosophers' traits are really idiosyncrasies? For example, their lack of historical sense, their hatred of the very idea of becoming, their Egypticism."[28] And he answers that

> They think that they show their *respect* for a subject when they de-his-toricize it, *sub specie aeterni*—when they turn it into a mummy . . . they threaten the life of everything they worship. Death, change, old age, as well as procreation and growth, are to their minds objections—even re-futations . . . And above all, away with the body, this wretched *idée fixe* of the senses, disfigured by all the fallacies of logic, refuted, even impossible, although it is impudent enough to behave as if it were real![29]

This is scarcely a flattering picture of the role of philosophy and philosophers in culture, but it follows from Nietzsche's allegation in *Twilight of the Idols* that

> Judgments, judgments of value, concerning life, for it or against it, can, in the end, never be true: they have value only as symptoms, they are worthy of consideration only as symptoms; in themselves such judgments are stupidities. One must by all means stretch out one's fingers and make

the attempt to grasp this amazing finesse, *that the value of life cannot be estimated.*[30]

If the value of life cannot be estimated, then the world-denigrating pronouncements of traditional philosophers, their preference for binary oppositions, for dualisms of all sorts, may usefully be viewed in a self-referring light. If "the wisest men of all ages have judged alike" concerning life that "*it is no good,*"[31] then such views must be read, at least in part, as symptoms of those who offer such appraisals.

If the history of metaphysics can be read as at bottom a disguised power game, born of *ressentiment*, for Nietzsche, then morality and religion are easier to construe as parallel developments. On this view, religion, like philosophy, is ultimately a disguised power game, even if the power is directed at oneself—and morality is the intersection of both.

> Life itself is to my mind the instinct for growth, for durability, for an accumulation of forces, for *power*: where the will to power is lacking there is decline. It is my contention that all the supreme values of mankind *lack* this will—that the values which are symptomatic of decline, *nihilistic* values, are lording it under the holiest names.[32]

Nietzsche identifies corruption with decadence, and identifies both with humankind's highest, supreme values; the sustaining and informing values of humankind have all been decadence-values, Nietzsche asserts here. The history of our highest aspirations is the history of nihilism. And one should not take lightly Nietzsche's identification in the quoted aphorism of nihilism with a sublimated instinct of self-destruction, as well as his conclusion that the loss of an instinctual vitality reappears as a counterfeit "under the holiest names." On this view, the highest values hitherto—identified by Nietzsche as "the ascetic ideal"—have been thanatological values dressed up in life-affirming disguise. This is an interesting sense in which the ascetic ideal—intensional suffering—which is life-preserving, can be and become inimical to life, can generate extensional suffering.

Even Jesus of Nazareth, often depicted by Nietzsche as an apostolic anticleric, had to be transvaluated if "Christianity would become master over *beasts of prey*: its method is to make them *sick*; enfeeblement is the Christian recipe for *taming*, for 'civilizing.' " (*A* 15). And in a clever series of steps Nietzsche argues that the notion of a "moral world order" had to be invented to reinstate priestly authority. But the most powerful instruments for the reascendancy of the priest are the notions of sin and guilt: "the priest rules through the invention of sin" (*A* 49). As Nietzsche reads post-Nazarene Christianity, the entire scaffolding of its ideology, the entire redemptive drama, is designed to retain the power of the priestly class, born of *ressentiment*: " 'Last Judgment,' 'immortality of the soul,' and 'soul' itself are instruments of torture, systems of cruelties by virtue of which the priest became master, remained master" (*A* 38). So the history of Christianity, Nietzsche seems to argue, is the history of an error, a misunderstanding in which the original symbolism of Jesus becomes transvaluated into a crass ecclesiastical tale, a tale which becomes as vulgar as the slave's mentality which seeks power and revenge in and through it.

> The destiny of Christianity lies in the necessity that its faith had to become as diseased, as base and vulgar, as the needs it was meant to satisfy were diseased, base, and vulgar. In the church, finally, *diseased barbarism* itself gains power. (*A* 20)

The figure most responsible for the emergence and triumph of Christianity as "diseased barbarism" is Paul, of course; and "Paul was the greatest of all apostles of vengeance," says Nietzsche in *A* 42.

Jesus, as Nietzsche depicts him in *The Antichrist*, had set aside notions of guilt, sin, and atonement; but the ludicrous image of Jesus crucified required, step by step, notions of sin and atonement once again, of the doctrine of resurrection above all. And Paul seizes precisely on this resurrection requirement. Thus, through Paul, Jesus the evangel is transvaluated, becoming the Redeemer, the dysangel.

> Nothing remained untouched, nothing remained even similar to the reality. Paul simply transposed the center of gravity of that whole existence *after* this existence—in the *lie* of the "resurrected" Jesus. At bottom, he had no use at all for the life of the Redeemer—he needed the death on the cross *and* a little more. (*A* 43)

The "little more" Paul needs to gain supremacy is the notion of the potential immortality of each and every soul, ultimate democratization of and through the spiritual realm.

> That everyone as an "immortal soul" has equal rank with everyone else, that in the totality of living beings the "salvation" of *every* single individual may claim eternal significance . . . cannot be branded with too much contempt. And yet Christianity owes its triumph to this miserable flattery of personal vanity: it was precisely all the failures, all the rebellious-minded, all the less favored, the whole scum and refuse of humanity who were thus won over to it. The "salvation of the soul"—in plain language: "the world revolves around *me*." (*A* 43)

Many commentators have observed, quite rightly, that for Nietzsche democracy and socialism—as well as nationalism and world wars—would have a different etiology without the triumph of Christianity as a Pauline invention, if they had indeed been possible at all. And throughout *The Antichrist* Nietzsche remarks repeatedly on the political consequences of the triumphal slave's morality, as for example,

> The aristocratic outlook was undermined from the deepest underworld through the lie of the equality of souls; and if faith in the "perogative as the majority" makes and *will make* revolutions—it is Christianity, beyond a doubt, it is *Christian* value judgments, that every revolution simply translates into blood and crime. (*A* 43)

Further, Christianity ultimately undermines any distinction in rank, merit, through a "tarantula" morality in which the base inveigh against nobility. "Christianity is a rebellion of everything that crawls on the ground against that which has *height*: the evangel of the 'lowly' *makes* low" (*A* 43). Flattered, self-congratulatory conceit borne in and nurtured by resentment finds expression in Pauline Christianity, on this view, mocks noble values, and converts the "noble" into the "evil" ones. But this self-congratulatory conceit veils itself as modesty, as humility, argues Nietzsche.

> What really happens here is that the most conscious *conceit of being chosen* plays modesty: once and for all one has placed *oneself*, the "community," the "good and the just," on one side, on the side of "truth"—and the rest, "the world," on the other. (*A* 44)

In *The Antichrist* the distinction between life-affirming and life-denying values is couched in the language of a contrast between aristocratic and chandala moralities. This contrast, in substance and form, parallels Nietzsche's earlier contrast between "base" and "noble" moralities.

Nietzsche's account began with two types, in *GM*, the aristocratic master, the servile slave. The master is, and his morality extols, health, competition, beauty, independence, power, self-control, pride, spontaneity, and sensuality. The self-directed master derives his values not from the community, not from "the herd," but presumably from the abundance of his own life and strength. The slave, however, fears the strength and power of the master; and he despises him. He is dependent, powerless, without self-direction, discipline, or self-control. To seize control over his own psychic destiny the slave must curb and tame his master. He must displace him in a sense. And the method of "overcoming" the master and his morality, the means to his displacement, is to render the values of the herd absolute and universal. This revolt of the slaves in moral matters is both creative and resentful. Powerless to effect a fundamental change in his condition, he wreaks vengeance against the master by converting the master's attributes into vices. And while master morality sanctions coexistence with differing types and morals, the resentment of the slave yearns for universality. Nothing is to escape its moral clutches alive. Nietzsche does not mean to suggest, of course, that the slave's resentment of and revenge against the master is either direct or conscious.

It is in this context, the context of moral-psychological imperialism, that the slave's resentment is to be understood.[33] Since the slave cannot displace the master in reality, he avenges himself symbolically, mythically. Hence the triumph of the religion of the slave—Christianity (and Judaism). Christianity is above all the ideology of slave morality for Nietzsche. It expresses the slave's resentment against the attributes of master morality by vilifying them. The virtues of the master become "sin." In place of power, it is said that the meek shall inherit the earth. Pride is sin. Humility is virtue. Charity, chastity, and humility replace competition, sensuality, and autonomy.

Finally, the innocence of existence, its topic neutrality, too, is abolished in the triumph of slave morality *qua* Christianity. On this view, Christianity is the fruit of resentment. As a product of weakness it represents the decline of life, decadence, degeneracy, in contrast to the exuberant ascent of life which seeks expression in master morality. And so it also follows for Nietzsche that Christianity, like Platonic philosophy, severs body and soul, that it deprecates the human body, impulse, instinct, passion, beauty, the intellect, as well as aesthetic values generally.

We may now be in a slightly better position to appreciate the force of Nietzsche's claim that democracy and socialism are to be understood as growing on the soil of Christianity; for we now need to see the state as the supplanting deity in the lives of Europeans. The state is a secular surrogate deity. The nation-state retains a transcendent value and mission, a providential role, which history expresses and seeks to realize. "Bismarckphobia" and virulent "nationalism" may generally be read as interchangeable expressions in Nietzsche's *Twilight of the Idols* without any loss of sense. And again it is the herd instinct, the morality of the slavish, which seeks expression here. Dreams of universality now attach to the nation and its state with missionary fervor and zeal. The slaughter of rivals and the conquest of the earth proceed under the banner of universal brotherhood. But that is merely symptomatic of "the tyrannomania of impotence." Again, the herd instinct, the need to be in it *together*, collective *ressentiment* is what runs rampant in nationalism. And just as the God of Christianity represented life at ebb tide, at bottom, just as God represented a force essentially hostile to life, so the nation-state, too, represents the aspirations of the "base," the "despicable," the "slave," on this view.

If Western humankind has been dominated by and has come to depend upon moral values which have been associated with Platonism and Christianity, it will be difficult to wean it from those values without a cultural transvaluation of staggering proportions. When the death of God informs our lives, when the "true world" has been abolished with it, loss of faith in values *per se* accompanies loss of faith in those values specifically nurtured by Christianity. With the collapse of the Platonic and theological foundations and sanctions for "morality," only a pervasive sense of ultimate purposelessness, meaninglessness, remains. And the triumph of meaninglessness, of the Absurd, is at the same time the triumph of nihilism. When the highest values become devalued, nihilism is a danger not because there are no other possible values, but because most of Western humanity knows no other values than those associated with an asymmetrically hierarchically dualistic, binary ascetic ideal.

One way of reading Nietzsche's famous conclusion in the section of *Twilight of the Idols* called "How the 'True World' Finally Became a Fable," then, is to argue that the cheerful acceptance of the collapse of the appearance/reality binary hierarchical opposition is phony, incomplete, and self-deceptive. It is to argue that the asymmetrical binary oppositions which are deeply characteristic of Western intellectual history, morality, and culture do not evaporate or collapse; rather the terms of the binary opposition merely change, offices are vacated and new incumbents take their place. Read in this way, Nietzsche's powerful insight that the modern nation-state would become the supplanting deity in the lives of Western humankind became prophetic; and it also helps to explain why a vivisection and attack on German nationalism would occupy such a prominent place in the synopticon of Nietzsche's views which *Twilight of the Idols* is supposed to represent. Incomplete nihilism, passive nihilism triumphs with the devaluation of the highest values; for as long as Western humankind has become accustomed to regarding life as something to atone or repent for, to surmount or to justify, it will take more than positivism to transform our deepest hopes, yearnings, and expectations. *Incipit Zarathustra.*

III

One persistent theme in *Twilight of the Idols* and in Nietzsche's philosophy generally is the need to overcome hierarchically asymmetrical binary oppositions of all sorts; but it is never suggested by Nietzsche that his own most dominant binary opposition—disease and health—ought to be surmounted. Indeed, one reasonably natural reading of Nietzsche has been to interpret his critique—that traditional philosophy, religion, and morality were masks the ascetic ideal has worn—as itself parasitic upon a prior paradigm of health. And the quintessential metaphor for health in Nietzsche's works is that of superhumanity, the *übermensch*.[34] If this natural interpretive line is followed, the section of *Twilight of the Idols* which speaks of Goethe illustrates the *übermensch* and the concluding and penultimate sections of that book describe the hermeneutic arc back to the book *Thus Spoke Zarathustra* and thus lead us back to the thought of eternal return, which, Nietzsche tells us, is Zarathustra's most important notion.

Let me motivate this discussion of Nietzsche's paradigm of psychic health, his *übermensch*, by suggesting a contrast in ways of reading the *übermensch* which—if I am right—may help to explain why there is so little said after *Thus Spoke Zarathustra* about the *übermensch*. For the sake of brevity I shall simply assert that most Nietzsche commentators have tended to argue quite naturally that *Übermenschlichkeit*, what it is like to be a superhuman being, endorses some more or less specific set of character traits, some specific "virtues" or blessings. To be an *übermensch*, on this quite natural ideal-type view of health, is to possess or exhibit certain traits of character, traits which in the typical case are associated with notions of self-overcoming, sublimation, creativity, and self-perfection. An *übermensch*, construed in this way, expresses Nietzsche's vision of a higher, more noble, healthier human ideal, of what human beings should or might be like if they were to overcome decadence, spiritual disease. On this ideal-type view, Nietzsche seems to be continuing the ancient project of articulating a human ideal, a conception of human perfection. For the late Walter Kaufmann, for example, the *übermensch* is the Goethe-like Dionysian mentioned in *Twilight of the Idols*, one who has overcome his animal nature, has sublimated his impulses, has organized the chaos of his passions, and has given style to his character.[35] In Arthur Danto's influential study, the *übermensch* is a free human being, joyous, the master of instinctual drives which do not overpower him. For my cosymposiast Richard Schacht, the *übermensch* is the essence of "the higher man"; he is vital, healthy, self-controlled, refined, spiritual, well-mannered, independent, just, honest, undaunted by suffering and disillusionment, and he is creative.[36]

I have argued elsewhere in contrast to the ideal-type interpretation—

which I myself once supported[37]—that an *übermensch* is instead the representation only of a particular *attitude* toward life, that it articulates a certain form of life. The attitude toward life which is captured is that of a person who would have *nothing* more fervently than the eternal recurrence of each and every moment of his or her life. This radical notion is suggested in Nietzsche's first published aphorism concerning eternal recurrence and thereafter; and I take the notion of eternal recurrence to be essential to explaining *übermenschlichkeit*, just as Nietzsche himself did:

> *The greatest stress.* What if one day or night a demon were to sneak after you into your loneliest loneliness and say to you, "This life as you now live it and have lived it, you will have to live once more and innumerable times more; and there will be nothing new in it, but every pain and every joy and every thought and sigh and everything immeasurably small or great in your life must return to you—all in the same succession and sequence—even this spider and this moonlight between the trees, and even this moment and I myself. The eternal hourglass of existence is turned over and over, and you with it, a dust grain of dust." Would you not throw yourself down and gnash your teeth and curse the demon who spoke thus? Or have you once experienced a tremendous moment when you would have answered him, "You are a god, and never have I heard anything more godly." If this thought were to gain possession of you, it would transform you, as you are, or perhaps crush you. The question in each and every thing, "Do you want this once more and innumerable times more?" would weigh upon your actions as the greatest stress. Or how well disposed would you have to become to yourself and to life to *crave nothing more fervently [um nach nichts mehr zu verlangen]* than this ultimate eternal confirmation and seal?[38]

Nietzsche refers to this very aphorism in *Ecce Homo* when he writes "my *Gaya Scienza* . . . contains hundreds of signs of the proximity to something incomparable; in the end it even offers the beginning of *Zarathustra*, and in the penultimate section of the fourth book the basic idea of *Zarathustra*."[39] So the aphorism cited above, "The Greatest Stress," "the penultimate section of the fourth book," is "the basic idea of *Zarathustra*", a book Nietzsche characterized with predictable hyperbole in *Twilight of the Idols* as "the most profound book [mankind] possesses."[40]

It is easy to see from the hypothetical diction of "The Greatest Stress" why the ideal-type interpretation of Nietzsche's thought of eternal recurrence should have gained widespread currency. From the modified perspective I am proposing, however, one needs primarily to emphasize the *conclusion* of this aphorism rather than its hypothetical form. The conclusion asks: How well disposed would we have to *become*, have to *be*, toward life, toward our lives and the world, in order to affirm eternal recurrence? How life-affirming indeed would one have to be to crave *nothing* more fervently than eternal recurrence?[41]

On a superficial level, of course, it may be easy to say Yes to Nietzsche's demon. After all, given Nietzsche's alternative—death with no afterlife—who would hesitate? I think the right answer is that it would or should give virtually all of us pause. For how many persons can assert without self-deception that they crave nothing more fervently than the eternal recurrence of each and every moment of their lives? Moreover, to affirm, to internalize the thought of eternal recurrence would require not only a nonselective affirmation of one's existence— past and present—but by implication would commit its affirmer to pre- ferring his or her life *to any and all other possible lives*. To crave *nothing*, absolutely nothing, more fervently than the ultimate confirmation and seal of eternal recurrence for one's life seems to exclude preferring the life of another. And my suspicion is that just as each of us would affirm the eternal recurrence of our lives only selectively—omitting this or that illness, loss, pain, regret or humiliation—virtually none of us would fervently prefer our lives to all other possible lives.[42] Who, for example, would not prefer to be God, if he were still alive?

The point of these remarks may now be clearer. An *übermensch*, and perhaps only an *übermensch*, would be so well disposed to himself and the world that he would crave *nothing* more fervently than the eternal repetition of his life, not even the life of God or the gods. What it would be like sincerely, nonpathologically, and without self-deception to have such an attitude as one's defining disposition only *übermenschen*, Nietzsche, and other paragons of psychic health may know.

Before concluding this section on the *übermensch* as the paradigm of health, I should like to enter three further observations concerning the *übermensch* and then make a few comments about each one. My first observation is that *übermenschlichkeit* is the closest approximation to God in a posttheistic age. On my reading, an *übermensch* is a secular god equivalent, the inverted embodiment of the God of the world-weary. The second observation is that *übermenschlichkeit* need not be construed as a normative ideal at all—not merely because one would not know how to begin to realize it or because of its banality,[43] but because it seems, on the surface at least, to entail no specifiable behavioral norms at all. My third and final observation is that, appearances to the contrary notwithstanding, the normative ideal-type view and the diagnostic view of the *übermensch* I have been proposing recently[44] need not be incompatible.

Concerning the first observation—that the *übermensch* is a sort of god—consider again the defining disposition of an *übermensch*, the person who would crave nothing more fervently than the repetition of each and every moment of his or her life. Thought through carefully, it seems to me that this means that an *übermensch* cannot live or imagine her life "under erasure," edited, emended in this way or that. Rather an *übermensch* must love each and every moment of life unconditionally. As Nietzsche puts it in *Ecce Homo*,

> My formula for greatness in a human being is *amor fati*: that one wants nothing to be different, not forward, not backward, not in all eternity. Not merely to bear what is necessary, still less conceal it . . . but to love it.[45]

And this unconditional love of each and every moment of her life and the world's life must *not* be because she views each moment holistically, so to speak, as a necessary blemish in the telos, the scenario of her total life. She must instead love each moment *simpliciter*, be willing to reaffirm it and will it again for its *own* sake, not as a cop-out on the way to a Neil Simon happy ending. She must not merely bear what is necessary. She must love it instead, Nietzsche tells us. When Aristotle argues—as he is said to do in the *Nicomachean Ethics*, for example—that happiness is the highest good, he argues that it alone is wanted unconditionally, is wanted for its own sake. On this view, health and medicine are not wanted for their own sakes but because they promote happiness, they are desired *in order to* achieve happiness. Even pleasure is not the highest good for Aristotle, just because it is pursued not only for its own sake but as a means of achieving happiness. It is not wanted simply and only for its own sake. On the reading of Nietzsche's eternal recurrence I am proposing, each moment must be wanted sheerly for its own sake, as Aristotle thought happiness was wanted, neither because of something else nor as a means to something else.

To make this point more vivid, imagine or recall for a moment the most entirely satisfactory sexual experience of your life, the moment in which you preferred your beloved to any possible alternative beloveds, a moment in which you also urgently preferred to be the lover you were just then. Imagine further, upon reflection, that you would welcome the eternal recurrence of that experience, just as it is, without addition, subtraction, or remainder. Let us say of this unconditionally cherished sexual ecstasy—real or imagined—that you desired it for its own sake.

Now also imagine, in contrast, the moment of your deepest despair, or the searing pain of your most unfulfilled longing, or the shattering blow of your most ruinous humiliation, or the self-deceptive acid of your most secret envy. Finally, imagine—if you can—having just the same attitude towards the cataloged moments of your greatest anguish that you were asked to imagine of your most cherished sexual ecstasy. Just *that* is what Nietzsche's eternal recurrence requires of each and every moment wanted for its own sake, it seems to me, and just *that* is what turns this requirement into a self-consuming human impossibility.

Who could live, as some of us have had to do, in the midst of extermination camps and love *that* unconditionally? And who among us would not will the recurrence of our lives *minus* the assassinations of John and Robert Kennedy, Martin Luther King and others, minus Apartheid, minus the deaths of millions of innocent children who died and still are dying brutal deaths in Ethiopia, South Africa, El Salvador and elsewhere throughout the Third World—and not only there? Who among us, in brief, would not prefer some other possible life and world, no matter how content we may be with our present lot? The point is that no matter how content I may be with my life I can always imagine a better one, for example, my life plus a reduction in the total sum of the world's misery and suffering, or a universe in which *everyone* wished for nothing more fervently than the eternal unaltered repetition of their lives. But there is more. The *übermensch* must not only affirm unconditionally each and every moment but must, as a sign of her responsive self-love, be willing to eternalize each moment. To love each moment unconditionally, for the *übermensch*, just *is* to will its eternal return. And there is more still. The *übermensch* alone, like the God whose death Nietzsche announces, wants *nothing* more fervently than the eternity of each and every moment of her life. What I am suggesting, therefore, can be put crudely but succinctly: if the God of the Judeo-Christian tradition could be said to have had an attitude toward his own life and his world it would have coincided with the attitude of an *übermensch*. *Only gods and übermenschen love each moment unconditionally, want nothing to be different, not forward, not backward, not in all eternity. Only for God, Leibniz and übermenschen is this the best of all possible worlds.* And Nietzsche was right to characterize this as his most abysmal thought; for me at least, the thought *is* abysmal!

The second observation—that *übermenschlichkeit* need not be construed as a normative ideal—would seem to follow from my characterization of it. The *übermensch* alone loves her own life unconditionally, without evasion, on my reading. We mortals can always imagine a better possible life and world, if we allow our imaginations free rein.[46] But that is just to say that Nietzsche's famous injunction, "become who you are," may be far more difficult than simply coming to terms with one's own life and destiny. On my reading, *only* an *übermensch* sincerely wills her *own* life. The rest of us will our life and the world's in an edited version, if we are honest with ourselves. And it is difficult to see why wishing most fervently the repetition of each and every moment of one's life yields anything like Kaufmann's injunctions to sublimate one's impulses, consecrate one's passions, or Danto's joyous, guiltless, free human being, or Schacht's injunctions to be vital or healthy, well-mannered or self-controlled, refined, spiritual, just, independent, or creative. Yet precisely these sorts of virtues would seem to be required if the *übermensch* is to function as a normative ideal of health. Put differently, one can certainly ask the question, "Is it possible to crave nothing more fervently than the eternal recurrence of each and every moment of one's life and yet *not* be vital or healthy, well-mannered or refined, spiritual or just?" As discomfiting as this conclusion may be, I see no easy way of avoiding an answer other than "Yes." Nietzsche himself, for instance, lacked good health at a minimum. No neat or easy tablet of virtues or blessings appears to be inherent in the notion of *übermenschlichkeit.* Like Kierkegaard's knight of faith—who would be impossible to distinguish from the rest of the congregation by any external sign—the *übermensch* does not appear to wear her defining disposition on her sleeve either, if I am right.

My third and final point concerning the *übermensch* can be stated briefly: Despite the suggestion that a distinction between higher humanity and *übermensch* ought to be maintained, the suggestion that the ideal type and the diagnostic interpretation ought to be distinguished, they are not necessarily incompatible. Rather, what I have cited as the laundry list of virtues characteristic of ideal type interpretations may more appropriately belong to the preparatory "higher man," who reflects Nietzsche's preferred virtues, virtues which do not necessarily follow from the notion of *übermenschlichkeit.* Remember that Nietzsche's Zarathustra expresses contempt for and indifference to the plight of his higher man throughout part IV of *Thus Spoke Zarathustra*: "what are your many small short miseries to me? You do not yet suffer enough to suit me . . . You all do not suffer from what *I* have suffered,"[47] he says, reserving the most abysmal thought—eternal recurrence—for himself. Remember also that the so-called higher men are cocelebrants at the Ass Festival, Zarathustra's parody of the Last Supper. If, as Nietzsche has Zarathustra say in the prologue, "man is a rope tied between beast and *übermensch*" then higher men still appear all-too-human when the rope-bridge is crossed across the abyss of Nietzsche's most abysmal thought.

The normative interpretation, the natural construal of Nietzsche's paradigm of health, the interpretive line which runs from Kaufmann through Danto to Schacht may well be right, therefore, in delineating a set of features one praises and admires, but mistaken in thinking that their articulation and summation yields an *übermensch*. It yields an all-too-human higher humanity instead. As usual, Nietzsche made this point more forcefully and economically in his published writings than I could ever hope to do, in "The Convalescent": "Naked had I once seen both, the greatest person and the smallest person; all-too-similar to one another, even the greatest all-too-human. All-too-small the greatest! *That* was my disgust with humankind!"[48]

IV. Concluding Nonexpository Postscript

I began this paper by suggesting that reading Nietzsche is itself an enactment of perspectivism and that his texts can be a reader's illuminating self-referential diagnostic tool when approached in an appropriate way or ways. So it may not be entirely inappropriate for me to insert a confession here. I had always in the past had difficulty understanding the fourth and concluding part of *Thus Spoke Zarathustra* (as has every other commentator) until I realized that "higher humanity" can be read as the interstices, the middle term, between man and *übermensch*, just as "man" is characterized by Nietzsche as the bridge, the interstices, the middle term, between beast and *übermensch*.

Recall that the entire drama of Nietzsche's *Thus Spoke Zarathustra*, his inverse Gospel, up to its concluding part, seems to be a voyage of self-discovery and self-overcoming on Zarathustra's part. It is as if the goal of this book "for everyone and no one" was for the reader to accompany Zarathustra's transfiguration to a figure capable of consecrating his passions, sublimating his impulses, and giving style to his character. But suddenly part IV seems virtually to satirize, to mock this very trajectory itself, this effortful striving to be rid of vestiges of "the last man" within each of us, as in the section "The Ass Festival" I cited earlier, but especially in the puzzling concluding section of the book as a whole. Here, in the concluding section after "The Drunken Song"—a section called "The Sign"[49]—Nietzsche parts company from his higher humanity altogether and realizes his own final sin—pity for "the higher man"—as having dominated his own spiritual quest.

The aphorism begins the morning after the drunken song's jubilant refrain is stilled—"all joy wants eternity—wants deep, wants deep eternity." Zarathustra leaves his cave "glowing and strong as a morning sun that comes out of dark mountains," and he immediately separates himself from his higher humanity.

> . . . "Well then, they still sleep, these higher men, while *I* am awake: *these* are not my proper companions. It is not for them that I wait here in my mountains. I want to go to my work, to my day: but they do not understand the signs of my morning; my stride is for them no summons to awaken. They still sleep in my cave, their dream still drinks of my drunken songs. The ear that listens for *me*, the *heedful* ear is lacking in their limbs."

After acknowledging his eagle, the symbol of pride, Zarathustra is at once surrounded by a host of swarming, fluttering birds and is then caressed by his lion. Zarathustra then calls this legion his own children; they in turn recoil as Nietzsche's higher humanity awakens, and this higher humanity in turn retreats into Zarathustra's cave as the lion roars. Baffled, Zarathustra says:

> . . . "Here is the stone, where I sat yesterday morning; and here the soothsayer came to me, and here I first heard the cry which I heard just now, the great cry of distress.
>
> "O you higher men, it was *your* distress that this old soothsayer prophesied to me yesterday morning; to your distress he wanted to seduce and tempt me. O Zarathustra, he said to me, I come to seduce you to your final sin.
>
> "To my final sin?" shouted Zarathustra, and he laughed angrily at his own words; "*what* was it that was saved up for me as my final sin?"
>
> And once more Zarathustra became absorbed in himself, and he sat down again on the big stone and reflected. Suddenly he jumped up. "Pity! Pity for the higher man!" he cried out, and his face changed to bronze. "Well then, *that* has had its time! My suffering and my pity for suffering—what does it matter? Am I concerned with *happiness*? I am concerned with my *work*.
>
> "Well then! The lion came, my children are near, Zarathustra has ripened, my hour has come: this is *my* morning, *my* day is breaking: *rise now, rise, thou great noon!*"
>
> Thus spoke Zarathustra, and he left his cave, glowing and strong as a morning sun that comes out of dark mountains.

At this point the book breaks off, reminding us that, as Nietzsche will later say in *Twilight of the Idols*, the great noon is the moment of the briefest shadow, end of the longest error, final escape from a shadowy platonic cave, escape from meaning-mongering without nostalgia or regret.

On the interpretation I have offered, it is plain that the *übermensch* cannot be the essence of higher humanity, any more than God can be the essence of humanity at its best. And when I first became aware of this I tried—as Zarathustra's pity tried—to read the virtues of "the higher man" as *effects* of the attitude, effects of the defining disposition of the *übermensch*. I deeply *wanted* to be reassured that those who wish nothing more fervently than the eternal recurrence of each of life's moments surely must have overcome their animal nature—despite the lion's mocking roar—surely must consecrate their passions, surely must be vital, healthy, self-controlled, spiritual, well-mannered, independent, and just. But try as I might I could not see my way clear to surfacing a connection, textually or conceptually. And then I realized that my own keen sense of disappointment may well be a consequence of my own masked salvific yearnings, this animal's own sickness, the mask the ascetic ideal wears in me, my own need for ultimate reassurance. I wanted the *übermensch* to be some realizable goal or other, achievable by human effort, perhaps an "improved" version of humankind. And I could not bear the thought at first that *nothing* followed from my characterization of *übermenschlichkeit*, save perhaps a sense of what Yea-saying, genuine health, genuine life-affirmation and celebration would be like, would *feel* like for Nietzsche. And the thought behind that thought was the realization that my felt need to conflate higher humanity and *übermensch* was itself probably an expression of *ressentiment*, just another mask worn by the ascetic ideal, a deeply disguised need to find some purpose served by suffering, investing life with meaning, humanity with a goal. It slowly dawned on me that—as in psychotherapy—the cure for my own *ressentiment* and asceticism consisted in becoming aware of how deeply they had come to dominate the structure of my life and thought.

At that moment it seemed to me that the character Zarathustra and his reader had reached much the same conclusion. "Higher men" still experience life as a struggle, a fight whose meaning must be revealed in its highest specimen, its most creative instances. And this reader's sin was either to pity such persons as Zarathustra did or more often to yield instead to the temptation to place life itself under the yoke of a secular redemptive explanation.

In either case Nietzsche's self-consuming gospel, *Thus Spoke Zarathustra*, which seeks to expose the need for gospels itself as not only a living need, but a fraud and offense against the living remains a "book for everyone and no one"—which is what its subtitle declares. This subtitle itself has typically been taken to mean that *Zarathustra* is a book which everyone will read believing it has been understood, but that it will not be understood by anyone. On the reading I have tried out, the perspective I have brought to bear on it today, it shall also mean, in addition, that *Thus Spoke Zarathustra* is a book to which many readers are drawn in search of *ersatz* salvation, secular salvation to help invest their lives with ultimate meaning; or to give them a recipe for achieving greatness, some glimpse of how disaffected persons with an urgent need to feel superior and unique might conduct their lives. It shall be a book for "no one," however, because salvation, liberation, health, consists in seeing that "no one" *can* be an *übermensch* in that sense and that *that* just *is* Nietzsche's mocking point; *that there are no glad tidings*, religious or philosophical, that those *are* the glad tidings, and that we will be made glad when we truly come to understand that the glad tidings consist in the fact that there is not now nor ever was a need for them. Reader, heal thyself!

Notes

1. The title of my paper is a variant of the title of Arthur Danto's remarkable book, *The Transfiguration of the Commonplace*, a title he himself derives from Muriel Spark's novel *The Prime of Miss Jean Brodie*—a case of life (or philosophy) truly imitating art. (See Danto's preface on this point.) By transfiguring Danto's and Spark's titles I mean to prefigure what I take to be one of the central motifs of Nietzsche's writings: to stamp the quality of "being" upon "becoming", which—as Nietzsche once put it—is the most extreme approximation of a world of "becoming" to that of "being." *The commonplace is deified in the alembic of eternal recurrence.*

2. Perhaps the paradigmatic expression of this point, in Nietzsche's published work of the "mature" period, occurs in *GM* III 12: "Henceforth, my dear philosophers, let us be on guard against the dangerous old conceptual fiction that posited a 'pure, will-less, painless, timeless knowing subject'; let us guard against the snares of such contradictory concepts as 'pure reason,' 'absolute spirituality,' 'knowledge in itself': these always demand that we should think of an eye that is completely unthinkable, an eye turned in no particular direction, in which the active and interpreting forces, through which alone seeing becomes seeing *something*, are supposed to be lacking; these always demand of the eye an absurdity and a nonsense. There is *only* a perspective seeing, *only* a perspective 'knowing'; and the *more* affects we allow to speak about one thing, the

178   READING NIETZSCHE

more eyes, different eyes, we can use to observe one thing, the more complete will our 'concept' of this thing, our 'objectivity,' be."

3. The difficulty which threatens to undermine the cognitive force of the perspectivist's claim is the often treated self-reference problem. If the claim that "there is only a perspective knowing" is itself a knowledge claim, then it is either an instance of perspectival knowledge—in which case it is robbed of its unconditional force, it leaves open the possibility of nonperspectival knowledge—or it is meant to apply unconditionally to all knowledge claims. In that case perspectivism is unconditionally true, is true from no perspective whatsoever—hence undermining itself.

4. For discussions of this point, see especially Arthur Danto's *Nietzsche as Philospher*, John T. Wilcox's *Truth and Value in Nietzsche*, Alexander Nehamas's *Nietzsche: Life as Literature*, Bernd Magnus's *Nietzsche's Existential Imperative*, and Richard Schacht's *Nietzsche*.

5. See his *Reason, Truth and History* (Cambridge: Cambridge University Press, 1981).

6. The suggestion is that superimposing frames (pictures) upon one another from all equidistant orbital points would result in a lapse dissolve (or black "picture") effect rather than the object seen from an absolute, nonperspectival point of view.

7. Perhaps the clearest account of this point is to be found in Maudemarie Clark's "Nietzsche's Perspectivist Rhetoric", *International Studies in Philosophy* 12 (1986).

8. Since the task is to give an account of what Nietzsche is up to in his many notes, genres, and styles, their connection—"his" theses—are always provided by his reader: "provided" in the strong sense that the difference between making and finding, creating and discovering is out of place here. In answer to the question, "Is this what Nietzsche meant?" the answer is always both yes and no. Yes, because we really cannot in practice separate what is said in a text from what is meant by it; no, because what is meant only becomes explicit in the reader's construction of the text's meaning. "Reading" is interpretation.

9. *TI*, preface.

10. See his *Nietzsche: Philosopher, Psychologist, Antichrist* and the editor's notes to his many editions of *TI*.

11. *TI*, preface.

12. Consider *aphorizein*: to divide or mark off; *apo*—from; *horizein*—to bound; horos a boundary.

13. *TI*, "Maxims and Arrows," 8.

14. *Ibid.*, 26.

15. Some of the paragraphs which follow first appeared in revised form in the *Journal of the British Society for Phenomenology* 14, (October 1983).

16. The ascetic ideal, put crudely, arises when suffering is endowed with ultimate significance. Suffering existence thus requires explanation, justification,

or expiation. The ascetic ideal thus becomes the metanarrative, in this reading, which frames Nietzsche's narrative.

17. *BGE* entry numbers appear hereafter in the body of the text.

18. *GS* entry numbers appear hereafter in the body of the text.

19. *HH* entry numbers appear hereafter in the body of the text.

20. *TI*, " 'Reason' in Philosophy," 2.

21. *Ibid.*, 5.

22. *GM* entry numbers appear hereafter in the body of the text.

23. *WP* 540. Nietzsche was right to reject the hyperbole of this remark—as well as the others he discarded. For a discussion of the textual problems and implications of *The Will to Power* see my "Nietzsche's Philosophy in 1888: *The Will to Power* and *Übermensch*" in *The Journal of the History of Philosophy* (January 1986).

24. *WP* 454.

25. *WP* 493.

26. *TI*, " 'Reason' in Philosophy," 5.

27. *EH*, preface, 3.

28. *TI*, " 'Reason' in Philosophy," 1.

29. *Ibid.*

30. *TI*, "The Problem of Socrates," 2.

31. *Ibid.*, 1.

32. *A* 6.

33. For a similar treatment, that absolutism of moral doctrine is Nietzsche's target, see Nehamas's *Nietzsche: Life as Literature*, esp. chap. 4.

34. I use the term *übermensch* and its surrogates rather than "overman" and "superman" for reasons I have explained in "Perfectibility and Attitude in Nietzsche's *Übermensch*," *The Review of Metaphysics* 36 (March 1983), pp. 635–636.

35. See his *Nietzsche* (4th ed.), pp. 312, 316.

36. See his *Nietzsche*, p. 340.

37. I seem to embrace a version of what I am here calling the "ideal-type" interpretation in *Nietzsche's Existential Imperative*, primarily in the opening "Overview" chapter. The point, however, was to argue for the diagnostic force of the doctrine of eternal recurrence. This connection is made more explicit in my "Perfectibility and Attitude."

38. *GS* 341. This is the penultimate aphorism of Book Four.

39. *EH*, "Thus Spoke Zarathustra: A Book for Everyone and No One," 1.

40. *TI*, "Skirmishes of an Untimely Man," 51.

41. My insistence on the force of this conclusion runs counter to the received view which reads the doctrine of eternal recurrence as a litmus test for one's life as a whole, in a sense meant to exclude imagining alternative possibilities. I think this underestimates the seriousness of the greatest stress (or weight: *Schwergewicht*) and rests on dubious doctrines from *The Will to Power* which Nietzsche had discarded, including the views that to change anything is to change

everything, for any X, and that a thing is the sum of its effects. Note that the above aphorism does *not* say that the thought of eternal recurrence either transforms or crushes its conceiver. It "would transform you as you are or *perhaps* (*vielleicht*: my italics) crush you." Nietzsche recognized that there was nothing automatic in this, if I am right, and that there are more options than have been dreamt of in Nietzsche commentary.

42. There is a common tendency to commit Nietzsche to a view of personal identity such that to reject any feature of one's life is to reject all of it, to affirm (any of?) it is to affirm all of it. This is connected to the view that to change anything is to change everything. Sometimes (see Nehamas, for example) this view is connected to the view that a thing is the sum of its effects. However, such nonperspectivist theses can be sustained only by turning Nietzsche's discarded manuscripts (e.g., *The Will to Power*) into primary source materials, a practice I find unsupportable. See my "Nietzsche's Philosophy in 1888." The upshot of these remarks is that it is *not* the case that Nietzsche's published remarks divide humanity into life-affirmers, biophiles, and life-deniers, biophobes—*übermenschen* and "last men." On the thesis argued here and elsewhere, we are probably all self-deceived biophobes. On this construal, the ascetic ideal lurks concealed behind our puny "affirmations."

43. How to act on a maxim or precept is not the same difficulty as the banality of maxims. "Consecrate your passions," "sublimate your impulses," "give style to your character" are impotent maxims in that it is hard to know how and where to begin. Which passions am I to consecrate, and how? And what does that mean? Which impulses am I to sublimate, and how? Like injunctions to "be creative" or "be yourself," one scarcely knows how or where to begin. But the difficulty of such injunctions noted, their banality does not follow. Some people regard such directives as powerful reminders (e.g. "know yourself"), even though what they enjoin is unclear. For others—e.g., Nehamas, Danto, and I—such maxims are banal as well. This is an honest difference of opinion among commentators about what does and does not matter, what is and what is not interesting and important. I know of nothing that would count as settling this difference of opinion.

44. See my "Perfectibility and Attitude" and "Nietzsche's Philosophy in 1888."

45. *EH*, "Why I Am so Clever," 10.

46. Many Nietzschephiles will have to find this conclusion unattractive, if my interpretation is at all plausible. For, as I will suggest below, Nietzsche's potential "higher men"—perhaps his philosophically intoxicated reader or his adolescent self-seeker—will want to embrace his own existence without evasion. And this, too, shall be a piece of evasive self-deception, the ascetic ideal's muted incarnation, if I am right. Moreover, on my view, Nietzsche probably knew *that* about his audience too!

47. *Z*, "On the Higher Man," 6.

48. *Z*, "The Convalescent," 2.

49. It follows from the interpretation for which I have been arguing that part IV of *Z* is bound to disappoint the reader, Nietzsche's would-be "higher man." For such readers the book's conclusion is even more baffling than a psycho-therapist's silence is for a patient in the grip of a neurosis. Nietzsche's rhetoric of self-overcoming, with which he baits the book in the first three parts of *Z*, tears our own yearnings to bursting in part IV. Who can breathe such air?

Dr. Nietzsche's Office Hours Are Between 10 and 12 A.M.

LARS GUSTAFSSON

It is hard to project oneself into one's work. And still philosophers and writers love to do that. Not to speak about painters like Velasquez in "Las Meninas." They constantly return to this experiment. Charles Baudelaire does it, for example in "Le Jeu," when he places himself at the corner of the gambling hall. This is an unusual room, hall and belly at the same time time, populated by unreal gamblers, where the faces are dry and the ladies' jewellery produces metallic sounds:

> Voila le noir tableau qu'en un rêve nocturne
> Je vis se derouler sous mon oeil clairvoyant.
> Moi-même, dans un coin de l'antre taciturne,
> Je me vis accoudé, froid, muet, enviant, [—]
>
> (Here is the dark painting which in a nightly
>   dream I see unfolding itself under my
>   clairvoyant eye.
> I see myself in a corner of the silent cave
>   cornered, cold, mute—envious,")

There is always something very fascinating which takes place at the moment when the artist tries to project himself into his own picture. What attracts our attention by such attempts is, of course, the play with perspective, not unlike that in Baroque painting, the tendency towards infinite regress involved in such enterprises, and last, but not least, their ironic possibilities.

This operation has something adventurous about it, adventurous in the way in which self-referential operations always seem to take us into a special realm of problems.

If I, myself, am visible in my work, who, then, is seeing me? If the world is such as I describe it, then what am I? If it seems to be a true picture of ourselves, we are less inclined to believe that it is we who have created it. If, on the other hand, it seems as if we had created it, we are less inclined to believe in the truth of it. The big beautiful example of this is found, of course, in the opening chapters of Fichte's "Theory of Science" of 1794. Who is actually writing Fichte's philosophy? Is it the transcendental ego or an ordinary German professor?

If Hegel's philosophy is true, that very edge of history where the World Spirit becomes aware of itself is of course Hegel's philosophy. Is it, then, really the case that the World Spirit at least in a certain historical moment could be a German professor? Obviously the subjective element in German idealism tends to give to some German professors a role which is unusual and—one hopes—even embarassing.

In Berlin, in the late 1960s, I was friendly with a very intelligent and very Marxist, I must admit, young lady, who in spite of her intelligence refused to sell her old Volkswagen long after it had become dangerous: not, as some people believed, because the late Georg Lukacs had been driven from a cocktail party to a lecture in it, but because, *ipso facto*, the World Spirit had ridden in that car for fifteen minutes. Many of her friends found this idea rather weird. I also found it weird.

The place in Nietzsche's work where the question—*If the world is such as I describe it, then what am I?*—a question every honest philosopher has to ask himself—for a moment comes to expression is that part of the "Genealogy of Morals" where Nietzsche speaks of philosophy as a special case of the ascetic ideal. With some right it could actually be said that Nietzsche is the only philosopher who gives us his office hours in his work. This takes place in Chapter Eight of the book, where Nietzsche speaks about the means at the disposal of the present-day ascetic, that is, the philosopher, when he wants to turn his back on the world. Deserts, real old theatrical Syrian deserts, certainly not. A small room, a small job, small everyday pleasures—all this does the job as well as the desert once did it.

But there *are* no longer temples like the huge one in Ephesus where once Heracleitus used to spend his time in the labyrinths of the sanctuary of Artemis. Or are there?

—sie fehlen uns vielleicht nicht: eben gedenke ich meines schönsten Studierzimmers, der piazza di San Marco, Frühling vorausgesetzt, insgleichen Vormittag, die Zeit zwischen zehn und zwölf).

(—maybe we do *not* miss them: I am thinking of my most beautiful study, the Piazza San Marco, of course in the spring, the time between ten and twelve.)

It almost sounds like an invitation to come and see him. What a pity he is dead!

And doesn't this ironical and ambiguous self-referential approach beautifully contrast with that of the professor of philosophy who claims to have found truth?

Philosophy itself poses a profound philosophical problem. The self-referential situation is a test which makes that problem visible. At the turn of the eighteenth century, Fichte, Schelling, and Hegel all expressed the same conviction in their letters and introductory remarks: after a somewhat shaky beginning of a few thousand years, philosophy has now entered its phase of systematic science; it has become *Wissenschaftslehre*. At the turn of the nineteenth century the letters between positivists in Vienna, logicians in Warsaw, and logical empirists in Cambridge, show the same conviction, a conviction which does not quite fade away before Quine's later works.

There is an *escatological* tendency in a lot of philosophy, implicit rather in the activity itself than in the temperaments of the individual thinkers; the ultimate goal of the activity is to end itself. This goes on in Fichte's *Theory of Science* as much as in Wittgenstein's *Philosophical Investigations*. Just as many wars are said to be carried out in order to prevent all further wars, quite a number of philosophies contain the implicit claim to put an immediate or almost immediate end to further philosophizing. (Even in a work by such a humble and genial man as A. J. Ayer, his *Language, Truth and Logic*, the solemn wingbeats of the apocalyptic eagles are heard over the ruins of Metaphysics.)

Thus, evidently, something in the situation of philosophy itself—if you permit the expression—in its *pathology*—coerces philosophers whose ambitions go beyond mere commentary and interpretation to want to become the last of their sort. The pathological in this situation becomes clearer if you try to imagine a mathematician who wants to put an end to mathematics. And exactly this fact makes philosophers look bizarre at just the very moment when their projection takes place and their own work is turned into an autoreferential mirror of themselves.

The contrast between the escatalogical ambition to be the last abstract fact (Transcendental ego, *Weltgeist*, Primary Science as opposed to Secondary science, ideal language as opposed to ordinary language; there are indeed many disguises for the transcendental ego) which ends a system of questions and the empirical fact of a professor asserting that same claim has something about it which is deeply provocative to our sense of irony.

Why is it that Nietzsche, on the other hand, looks completely natural and not at all ridiculous on his beautiful piazza? We are as perfectly willing to accept him there as we are unwilling to accept the *Weltgeist* in a Volkswagen.

Is that because he does not have the ambition to be the last of his sort? That he realizes that there will be many more philosophers without anybody's being able to end the game? Perhaps it is so.

People prefer to want *nothing* than to not-want anything at all. That is the observation which opens Nietzsche's reflections on the ascetic ideal. With the artist, and especially Richard Wagner, this ascetic ideal means very little, merely to turn against one's own *libido*. The philosopher seems to want to get rid of much more. This is described in a sort of *crescendo*, which starts in the sixth paragraph of the chapter on ascetic ideals and culminates somewhere between ten and eleven, where a new actor, "the ascetic priest," is brought up on the stage.

Philosophy, in order to survive, had for most of its history to appear disguised as *priest*. Is it possible to get out of that disguise? The philosopher-priest, the guardian of serenity, a species endemic to life, obviously still is of some use to life as he insists on returning to the historical stage time after time.

Obviously he is a contradiction because he wants power and at the same time wants to abstain from the ordinary world in its multitude and contingency. Where our rich senses tell us that there is a realm of truth and existence, and our reason is excluded from it, the philosopher tries to talk us into the opposite, unreasonable opinion. To sum up the well-known point of the chapter: philosophy is one among many activities by which life, which has lost its ability to maintain life in the normal way, pathologically strives to preserve itself.

This might be right or wrong. But if Nietzsche is right, the philosophical problem which philosophy itself poses can of course never be solved by philosophical means. Or, in other words, Friedrich Nietzsche approaches the problem in a spirit which, instead of being—like almost all major philosophical problems—*escatological*, simply is *ironical*.

That is probably why we find it absolutely normal and probable to find this professor at his coffeehouse table on a beautiful spring morning in Venice between ten and twelve, while the idea of a World Spirit which can be driven around by a redhaired young Prussian woman in a Volkswagen is such an absolutely ridiculous idea.

Nietzsche's *Daybreak: Thoughts on the Prejudices of Morality*

ARTHUR C. DANTO

It was Peter Gast, Nietzsche's copyist, claque, practical nurse, and constant correspondent, who gave this book its epigraph from the *Rig Veda*: "There are so many days that have not yet broken." It may have been a fateful ornament, since *Rig Veda* I, 113 (To Dawn) chants "She, first of endless morns to come hereafter, follows the path of morns that have departed," and the doctrine of eternal recurrence struck Nietzsche with the force of a revelation later that year—1881. But it in any case suggested the title *Eine Morgenröte* to Nietzsche. "There are so many gay and particularly red colors in it!" he wrote Gast in February, but the "*Eine*" was dropped in proof, on grounds of pretentiousness. Gast regarded the new title as pretentious, preferring the original *Die Pflugschar*—"The Ploughshare"—whose vivid connotations perhaps better suited his, and for that matter Nietzsche's, perception of the kind of book it was: turning over the caked and stubborn crust of moral custom, preparatory to fresh growth. In a late preface, Nietzsche writes "In this book you will discover a subterranean man at work, one who tunnels and mines and undermines." This metaphor was with him from the beginning: "I go on digging in my moral mine," he wrote to Gast in 1880, "and sometimes seem to myself wholly subterranean." And in the pages devoted to *Morgenröte* in his strident and exclamatory apologia, *Ecce Homo*, ploughing and mining give way to fishing: "Almost every sentence in the book was first thought, *caught*, among that jumble of rocks near Genoa, when I was alone and still had secrets from the sea."

Bringing something unsuspected out of the depths may characterize the *labor* of the book, but *Morgenröte*—felicitously translated by R. J. Hollingdale as *Daybreak* rather than *Dawn*, or than the redundant and vapid *Dawn of Day* of the first English translation in the Oscar Levy edition—expresses Nietzsche's hope for the historical position of the book. "This book is what one calls a 'decisive step,' " he wrote his dour publisher Ernst Schmeitzner on February 23: "More a destiny than a book." To his mother he wrote "I have brought forth one of the boldest, loftiest, and most self-possessed books ever born from human heart and brain." To his friend and colleague Franz Overbeck he says on March 18 that "This is the book on which my name will probably depend," and, in August, claiming that the effect of his book will be like that of the strongest spiritual drink, he writes "It is the beginning of my beginning." "With this book," he wrote again in *Ecce Homo*, "my campaign against morality began." *Morgenröte* was published in July 1881, without anyone much noticing it. A cautious acknowledgement came from Jacob Burkhardt, who only had had time to leaf through it. The predictable epistolary handshake came from Overbeck. "It's all very decent and well-intended, what they write me," he laments to Gast on August 14, "but distant, distant, distant." Mostly it was silence. Crazed that summer with physical pain—"Five times I have called for Doctor Death!"—the most original mind in Europe, the best philosopher of his time, the finest writer of his own language, led a crank's life. He walked, watched his diet, eked out his pennies, moved restlessly from pension to pension, sought a possible climate, maintaining throughout an adorable cheerfulness and an incredible literary energy. By 1882 he was sending a new book to Schmeitzner. And book after book followed until his breakdown in 1889 and his almost simultaneous global fame.

The book is composed—or compiled—of 575 short "thoughts," some no more than a single line, none much more than three pages, grouped into five "books." Each component piece has a title of its own, but none of the five books do, so it is unclear what, if any, principle of organization may have applied. The "thoughts" of one book seldom relate more closely to the other thoughts in it than they do to those in other books, though on occasion we get a suite of thoughts on the same topic, e.g., pity. Many of the later thoughts, on the other hand, are aphoristic rephrasings of thoughts treated more expansively in early pages, as though a constant process of distillation were taking place. Though less sharply structured than *The Genealogy of Morals* or *Beyond Good and Evil*, for which it is a precursor, it is considerably less sprawling than

Human, All Too Human, which preceded it by three years, which suggests that he was beginning to find his way to a somewhat more architectonic exposition, and that he wanted something more than tiny bits, however striking and bright. The pieces treat of The Artist, The Lover, The Philosopher, The Christian, The Jew, The Greek, The Roman, and The German—and of women, animals, death, marriage, genius, feelings, morals, and the structure of the mind. "A book such as this is not for reading straight through or reading aloud," Nietzsche says in thought 454, "but for dipping into, especially when out walking or on a journey." So the absence of headings from the five books, the small format of the individual components, as well as the abrupt shift from topic to topic, *could* be devices for slowing the reader down. But 454 could also be a lame effort at making a virtue of the fact that he had not yet found himself able to work with larger forms, and even was not yet clear on where he was heading. "I feel that I may have found the main gallery," he told Gast in 1880, "but that is a belief one can form and reject a hundred times." *One* price of being subterranean is that one is in the dark. And in any case Nietzsche then lacked what we now possess, namely his own later works, in the light of which we can discern the deeper themes already sounded in *Morgenröte*, but too softly yet to hint at the systematic structures which were at last to emerge. The great Nietzschean formulations lay ahead: Eternal Recurrence, Will to Power, Superman, Antichrist, Master and Slave Morality, the Death of God, Nihilism, and the Transvaluation of Value. Without the structural benefits of the whole system, it would be difficult, as it would then have been impossible, to appreciate the book as a contribution to moral theory rather than to moralistic literature, though of an uncommonly high order, or to see a great philosophy being born. One could not, for instance, have read 501—"On Mortal Souls"—as presaging a consequence of accepting eternal recurrence, or 502 as an anticipatory gloss on the *übermensch*.

The stance of the moralist, all the more so the stance of the moralist who insists on aphorisms, is commonly to hold the human all-too-human delinquencies up against a background of received moral notions. His aim is to describe moral weakness, expose hypocrisy, and depict, like Hogarth, the varieties and degrees of vice. He is reminding his readers of what they already believe, and in a way seeking to deepen that belief. There is a strain of moralism in Nietzsche, but mainly it is the very principles moralists take as givens that *he* terms moral "prejudices" and puts in question. So his attitude to deviants from these principles is somewhat complex: they really are, so to speak, sinners, even though the dogmas which define them as such are in fact merely prejudices. What makes the work profound, however, is that he is beginning to impose onto moral codes as a class a structure of interpretation which is quite original with him. He is at least as original as those other interpretative strategists of the nineteenth century, Marx and Freud, with whose thought his shares a kind of logic. They sought to reveal both the choices men make and the patterns of justification they use to validate those choices, as expressing a set of underlying material causes of which agents are in general unaware—are explicitly unconscious on Freud's analysis. These I call "deep interpretations" and they are more and more the form of what pass for theories in the so-called human sciences. Nietzsche in this sense is giving deep interpretations of moral conduct and moral reasoning together: his question is what are we *deeply* doing which shows up on the surface as moral existence.

Deep interpreters typically claim that their theories are ultimately liberating. Once we understand the underlying dynamisms, we shall be in a position at last to make our own history, in the case of Marx; and once we see what underlying conflicts get transformed into irrational behavior we shall be freed from the latter and at liberty to work and love, in the case of Freud. Nietzsche too believes his theory to be liberating, not so much from morality as such, but from misperceiving the function of morality through not understanding the subsocial forces which express themselves in the medium of moral codes, and so putting us in a position to choose the values we want to live by. "In us there is accomplished—supposing you want a formula—the *self-sublimation of morality*." The German phrase is *die Selbstaufhebung der Moral*. "Self-sublimation" will pass as a bare translation of *Selbstaufhebung*, but *aufheben* is one of the legendary terms of German, especially Hegelian philosophical vocabulary, meaning: to negate, to preserve, and to transcend—*all at once*; and a translator or editor ought to give a warning footnote to this effect. "It goes without saying," he writes in 103, "that I do not deny—unless I am a fool—that many actions called immoral ought to be avoided and resisted, or that many called moral ought to be done and encouraged—but I think the one should be encouraged and the other avoided *for other reasons than hitherto*."

What morality as morality deeply expresses, I suppose, is the power—he will later say the will to power—of a group, internalized as a kind of form through which the individual perceives others and perceives himself, so that a distorting screen of self-interpretation interposes itself between our awareness of ourselves and ourselves. Diagnostics to one side, it is here that Nietzsche sounds most contemporary, philosophically speaking, since his moral psychology is so resolutely anti-Cartesian. It *had* to be anti-Cartesian, since his critique of morality entailed the view that we do not really know what we are, and Cartesianism is precisely the view that what we essentially are is something immediately present to consciousness, so that nothing is true of us psychologically of which we are not directly and noninferentially aware. The connection between his philosophy of morals and his philosophical psychology is but one example of how his work is finally systematic, the system only revealing itself late in the course of his working itself out through his book, and only dimly discriminable here. It is as though the book itself exemplifies its teaching that with regard to what goes on in our minds we are typically out of cognitive touch. The psychology in the book is dazzling and precocious, and it is fair to say that after several decades of intense analytical work, the discipline of philosophical psychology has only begun to pull abreast of Nietzsche's thought.

In the great prime of his literary prowess, Nietzsche's prose suggests the performative assurance of a marvelously gifted and intuitive lover. The text of *Morgenröte*, with its sudden shifts of rhythym and of tone, at one moment lyrical and at the next moment earthy, its mock distance and its sudden intimacy, its sweeping playfulness, its jeers, sneers, jokes, and whispers—and its abrupt unanticipated kills—is a kind of eroticism of writing, and requires of its reader a partnership in pleasure and intelligence. Nietzsche's voice has lost the professorial authority of the early writing and has not yet acquired the strident conviction of a prophet unheeded. And in none of his books, I feel, is there a more palpable sense of spiritual well-being. *Morgenröte* was put together at an especially quiet moment in Nietzsche's life. "The whole book," he wrote later, "contains no negative word, no attack, no spite—it lies in the sun, sound, happy, like some sea animal basking on the rocks." For something finally so incendiary, it is a sunny book, and Nietzsche describes it that way at 553: "Whither does this whole philosophy, with all its circuitous paths, want to go? Does it do more than translate as it were into reason a strong and constant drive, a drive for gentle sunlight, bright and buoyant air, southern vegetation, the breath of the sea . . . ?" It was a time when the ideas he was mothering were still tender, did not yet show the savage power that would tear him along with them towards their terrible destiny, not loosing him from their grip till madness intervened just when history was about to take them up and put them to uses undreamt of as he clambered, half-blind, over the sea-rocks near Genoa on his endless hopeful walks—when he still could write to Gast "Nothing has happened to anyone because of me; no one's given me any thought."

An earlier version of this essay appeared as a review of R. J. Hollingdale's translation of *Daybreak* (Cambridge: Cambridge University Press, 1982) in the *Times Literary Supplement*, 4148 (1982), p. 1074, with the title "Thoughts of a Subterranean Man."

The Writing on the Wall:
The Antichrist and the Semiotics
of History

GARY SHAPIRO

Even those writers who have good things to say about Nietzsche usually do not have good things to say about his penultimate book, *The Antichrist*. Like *Ecce Homo* it is often described as at least prefiguring Nietzsche's madness if not (as is sometimes the case) said to be part of that desperate glide itself. Those inclined to reject the book may be encouraged in this view by Nietzsche's statement to Brandes, in November 1888, that *The Antichrist* is the whole of *The Transvaluation of All Values* (originally announced as a series of four books) and that *Ecce Homo* is its necessary prelude. The reader will have already discerned my intention of retrieving this exorbitant text for the Nietzschean canon. Such operations of retrieval are standard enough moves within a certain kind of philological discourse that privileges the book as an expressive or cognitive totality. But Nietzsche, the arch philogoist, is today often regarded as having undercut the grounds of such moves: first, by challenging their hermeneutic presuppositions and, second, by exemplifying in a paradigmatic fashion the discontinuous, fragmentary, or porous text. The second view of Nietzsche's writings is a very traditional one; it is a commonplace among Nietzsche's earlier readers that his writing is distressingly wanting in order and style, despite the brilliance for his thought. Such has continued to be the assumption of Anglo-American readers like Walter Kaufmann and Arthur Danto, who have aimed at articulating the internal order of Nietzsche's thought which the stylistic fireworks of the texts obscure. Recent French readers, most notably Jacques Derrida, have tried to show that fragmentation and undecidability are not merely secondary features of Nietzsche's writing but its very element. Derrida outrageously suggests that the jotting "I forgot my umbrella" is typical of *all* Nietzsche's writing in its ambiguity and undecidability of meaning and in its systematic evasion of all contextual explication. One might wonder whether such a strategy of reading is indebted to Nietzsche's own hermeneutic strategy in *The Antichrist*. There Nietzsche anticipates Heidegger and Derrida by relying on the figure of *erasure* to designate his own relation to Christianity, its textual traditions, and its central figure, Jesus. Following the nineteenth century philogoical and historical methods to their extreme, and thereby overturning and transvaluing (*umkehren* and *umwerten*) both the methods and Christianity, Nietzsche tries to restore the blank page which is Jesus' life to its pristine purity of white paper, *tabula rasa*, although we know that such a project can approach its goal only asymptotically. In this respect Nietzsche's project is very much like Robert Rauschenberg's erased De Kooning painting and like Derrida's attempt to shatter any determinate meaning in Nietzsche himself by revealing the irreducible plurality of woman in the apparently masculine ambitions of order and control in Nietzsche's style. All of these efforts nevertheless remain marked with the *signatures* of their authors; the negation of a negation cannot be negation itself. At the end there is Rauschenberg's art, Derrida's project of deconstruction, Nietzsche's graffito scrawled on the Christian text. This, however, is to anticipate the results of my project of retrieval.

Just as erasure is always an act that leaves its own mark, so retrieval is possible but need not produce that totalizing organic unity that has been the constant phantom of aesthetic thought. If retrieval is always partial, it is also easier, because the excess of Nietzsche's readers here have been egregious. Consider, for example, Eugen Fink's Heideggerean book on Nietzsche which discounts any philosophical value the book might have by means of a brief analysis of *The Antichrist*:

> In the text *The Antichrist* (*Attempt at a Critique of Christianity*) Nietzsche battles against the Christian religion with an unparalleled fervor of hatred, and with a flood of invectives and accusations. Here the virtuosity of his attack, leaving no stone unturned, reverses itself. The lack of measure destroys the intended effect; one can't convince while foaming at the mouth. Essentially the text offers nothing new; Nietzsche collects what he has already said about the morality of pity and the psychology of the priest—but now he gives his thoughts an exorbitant, violent edge and wants to insult, to strike the tradition in the face, to "transvalue" by valuing in an anti-Christian way.[1]

Fink's comment suggests that his reasons for thinking that "the text offers nothing new" may be just the stylistic excesses and rhetorical fallings of which he accuses it. Certainly his judgment on the book follows well-established opinion about its place in the Nietzschean canon. Even when the book is regarded as a culminating work (applying a dubious schema of linear development), it is usually employed to demonstrate the tragedy of Nietzsche's career as author and thinker. Karl Löwith calls it the "logical conclusion" of the critique of Christianity begun in the untimely meditation on D. F. Strauss, author of the nineteenth century's first great life of Jesus. Yet according to Löwith even this late work shows that Nietzsche has not escaped his obsession with Christianity. From this perspective we would have to say that Nietzsche the philosopher is not free of the bad blood of German theology which he denounces so vehemently:

> Among Germans one will understand immediately when I say that philosophy has been corrupted by theologian blood. The Protestant pastor is the grandfather of German philosophy, Protestantism itself is *peccatum originale*. (*A* 10)[2]

It could then be argued that the growth and intensity of the obsession is part of the madness that prevented Nietzsche from seeing the book through to publication and which led him to consider it, alternatively, as the first part of the *Transvaluation*, as the entire *Transvaluation*, and then as the *Curse on Christendom* which required *Ecce Homo* as a balance.[3] Yet even the last self-interpretation permits another construction: *Ecce Homo* balances *The Antichrist* by showing that the great curser and destroyer is one who lives in the halcyon element of the "perfect day when everything is ripening and not only the grape turns brown" and asks, *"How could I fail to be grateful to my whole life?"*[4]

What Arthur Danto calls the "unrelievedly vituperative" tone of the book is everywhere evident. At the conclusion of the book Nietzsche says of the Christian church that "to me, it is the extremest thinkable form of corruption, it has had the will to the ultimate corruption conceivably possible. The Christian church has left nothing untouched by its depravity . . . " (*A* 62). And Nietzsche pushes the rhetorical contrast to the extreme by defending the Roman Empire against Christianity, inverting the usual belief in the civilizing virtue or necessity of the latter's conversion of the former:

> Christianity was the vampire of the *Imperium Romanum* . . . this most admirable of all works of art in the grand style was a beginning, its structure was calculated to prove itself by millennia. . . . But it was not firm enough

to endure the *corruptest* form of corruption, to endure the *Christian*. . . .
These stealthy vermin which, shrouded in night, fog and ambiguity crept
up to every individual and sucked seriousness for *real* things, the instinct
for *realities* of any kind, this cowardly, womanish and honeyed crew gradually alienated the "souls" of this trememdous structure . . . (*A* 58)

It is this tone which might be taken to justify the reduction of Nietzsche's
thought to the first-liner of a graffito sometimes found in modern cells
and catacombs:

God is dead—NIETZSCHE

Nietzsche is dead—GOD

This reduction could appear to be the creative interpretation of a mas-
terful will to power—if Nietzsche's thought and style are as uncontrolled
as the critics suggest. Yet there are some signs at the beginning and end
of the book that might lead us to hesitate. Nietzsche himself anticipates
the strife of revengeful graffiti at the conclusion of his text:

Wherever there are walls I shall inscribe this eternal accusation against
Christianity upon them—I can write in letters which make even the blind
see . . . (*A* 62)

At the same time Nietzsche says in his preface that his readers must
have a "predestination for the labyrinth" and "new ears for new music"
if they are to understand this difficult writing. So, like all of Nietzsche's
books, *The Antichrist* is self-referential. It is concerned with those very
questions of how it is to be read and how it exists as a piece of writing
which we are supposed to think of as the derivative and external interests
of the critic and historian. The words which can be written on the wall
are also directed by a powerful thought and a complex rhetorical
strategy.

In *Ecce Homo* Nietzsche imagines "a perfect reader" who would be
"a monster of courage and curiosity; moreover, supple, cunning, cautious; a born adventurer and discoverer" (*EH* 3). *The Antichrist* is in
search of such readers and its need is compounded and complicated by
the fact that it offers a Nietzschean account of what might variously be
called interpretation, hermeneutics, or semiotics. To see this point it is
necessary to contest an expressivist or emotivist reading of the text. That
is, we must question the assumption that because of the emotional
intensity of its utterance we must read the book primarily as an outburst
of rage or hostility. The rage and hostility are there in abundance; but
we should not assume that their very presence excludes a significant

structure of thought, or that a writing with such a tone could not possibly contain any new thoughts.

As both the inscription and the quotation from Nietzsche suggest, a graffito, whatever its peculiarly individual and private aspects, is inscribed in a public space, often in reply to others and inviting its own challenges and defacements. Like other texts, but in a self-conscious way, *The Antichrist* makes sense only in relation to other texts. It is a book that recalls a number of similar genres (lives of Christ, polemical histories of religion) which were an important part of nineteenth century thought. Even its title is one which had been used before, for somewhat different purposes (in 1873) by Ernest Renan, in a book which Nietzsche read a year before writing his own *Antichrist*. It is worth pointing out that Renan is a frequent antagonist both in *The Antichrist* and in other texts of the same period. In Renan's *Antichrist*, the Antichrist is Nero; not Nero merely as a savage persecutor but as the anxious parodic artist whose terrible and genuine aesthetic accomplishment is the theater of cruelty. Renan credits Nero with the discovery of a new form of beauty in which the defenseless virgin torn by the wild beast replaces the classic beauty of the integral and well-formed sculpture. Did Nietzsche, whose justaposition of Rome and Christianity is a constant theme of *The Antichrist* and *The Genealogy of Morals*, identify himself with Nero? Perhaps only later when, mad, he entertains fantasies of imperial or divine power and writes "I'm am all the names of history." Renan notes that Nero's histrionic ambitions led him to imitate or parody all of the great poetry of the classical world.[5]

These resonances are meant to suggest that *The Antichrist* is not simply immediate expression, but a book which refers us back to other books, and that the processes of writing, interpreting, reading, censoring, and defacing are so far from being taken for granted that they form the chief means of elucidating Nietzsche's attack on Christianity. Nietzsche's *Antichrist* is full of references to the texts of the Old and New Testaments, to their textual histories, to the priestly fraudulence which produced them, to the texts of the liberal apologists for religion of the nineteenth century, to the textual sophistication of philogists and to the possible text, better and more accurate than all the others, which Dostoyevsky or his like would have written if alive at the time of Jesus. Within this context *The Antichrist* offers, at its heart, one more narrative of the life of Jesus and one of the choicest examples of what Paul Ricouer has called the hermeneutics of suspicion.

All of the book either leads up to or proceeds Nietzsche's concern with the textual politics of Judaism and Christianity. That Nietzsche should focus so much of his attention on the way in which the Bible was successively produced, edited, re-edited, interpreted, and criticized could be justified simply in terms of the Jewish and Christian claims to be religions of the book. But Nietzsche has more specific reasons for this concern. All morality is a semiotic interpretation of the body and society; if there is to be a transvaluation of values it must proceed by offering a new reading of that which has been misread. So we find, as in *The Genealogy of Morals*, that the great hermeneutical conflict in *The Antichrist* is between the priest and the philologist. Nietzsche's great enemy is Paul, whom he credits with a genius for lying which was immediately taken up by the church; in doing so he and they declare war on the philologists:

> Paul *wants* to confound the "wisdom of the world": his enemies are the *good* philologists and physicians of the Alexandrian School—upon them he makes war. In fact, one is not philologist and physician without also being at the same time *Anti-Christian*. For as philologist one sees *behind* the "sacred books", as physician *behind* the physiological depravity of the typical Christian. The physician says "incurable", the philologist "fraud" . . . (*A* 47)

The paradigm of priestly misreading and fraud is to be found in the editing of the Old Testament. Nietzsche accepts the general results of the higher criticism here, although his tone is completely different from the scholarly objectivity at which the professional philologists aimed. Just ten years before the writing of *The Antichrist*, Julius Wellhausen had written his *Prolegomena to the History of Ancient Israel*, in which he argued that the law could not be the basis of the histories and prophetic writings but must have been composed at a later date.[6] More specifically he attempted to show that it was only during the exile, following the Assyrian victory in the sixth century, that the shift occurred from Israel—a land of warriors, kings, and prophets—to Judaism, a religion of extensive law and ritual reserving a special place of power for the priests. It was the priests who attempted to preserve the life of their people even at the cost of exchanging a vital life for ritualistic constraint; and part of the price to be paid for this change would be a trememdous enhancement of the power of the priests within Judaism. In order to consolidate their power they edited the sacred writings which already existed and added new ones of their own which radically displaced priestly law and the political supremacy of the priest much further back into the past, providing them with divine and traditional sanction. The work of Wellhausen and others like him is not at all Nietzschean in tone; it is not only firmly grounded in contemporary philology but offers a brilliant example of how that philology could be employed with methodical precision to produce works of the greatest scope. Nietzsche alludes to this scholarly tradition although he never explicitly mentions Wellhausen. Certainly the five-stage history which Nietzsche offers of Judaism and which he declares to be "invaluable as a typical history of the *denaturalizing* of natural values" is a radicalization of Wellhausen's method of distinguishing exilic and pre-exilic Judaism; here it is filtered through the opposition of "good and bad," "good and evil," and the psychology of the priest. This capsule history may bear some comparison with that which Nietzsche had written concerning ontological inversion in his previous book, *Twilight of the Idols*: "How the 'True World' Finally Became an Error." According to Nietzsche the strata of Jewish history are: (1) "in the period of the Kingdom, Israel too stood in a *correct*, that is to say natural relationship to all things. Their Yahweh was the expression of their consciousness of power, of their delight in the expression of their consciousness of power, of their delight in themselves, their hopes of themselves"; (2) after internal anarchy and external oppression have destroyed this natural state, it remains as an ideal—expressed by the prophets; (3) when the ideal fails an an ideal, Yahweh becomes *only* a god of justice "in the hands of priestly agitators" who establish that most mendacious mode of interpretation of a supposed "moral world-order"; (4) the priests, who have seized power within Judaism, rewrite history in order to disparage the earlier great age in which the priest counted for almost nothing; (5) the rise of Christianity extends priestly *ressentiment* to all hierarchy and rank by attacking the conception of the Jewish people (the chosen people) as such. For Nietzsche this is not a new narrative analysis except insofar as it extends and intensifies his philological conception of history as a forceful reading and rereading of texts. When Nietzsche says that there are only interpretations he must be understood not as licensing all logically possible interpretations whatsoever but as indicating that each and every meaning or change of meaning is an exercise of power. To the extent that we accept this principle, we are being prepared both for the content of Nietzsche's erasure of Jesus and for an understanding of how such an operation is possible. What Nietzsche objects to in priestly reading is hardly forceful interpretation as such, but that specific interpretation of "the moral world-order" which is incapable of recognizing itself as interpretation.

Consider the following observation on priestly reading from Nietzsche's history of the five stages:

the "will of God" (that is to say the conditions for preserving the power of the priest) has to be *known*—to this end a "revelation" is required. In plain words a great literary forgery becomes necessary, a "sacred book" is discovered—it is made public with all hieratic pomp, with days of repentance and with lamentation over the long years of "sinfulness" . . . the whole evil lay in the nation's having become estranged from the "sacred book." (*A* 26)

The passage is noteworthy for several reasons, not the least of which is a typographical one. The extensive use of quotation marks is a philosophical device for quite literally *bracketing* the ideas and expressions with which Nietzsche is dealing. Unlike Husserlian bracketing, Nietzsche's use of quotation is not so much intended to put the ontological status of its objects into doubt, but to suggest that we are dealing here with what has been said by specific people on specific occasions, perhaps gathering force through being repeated or reprinted. As opposed to conceptual analysis, it refuses to grant that its objects are part of an impersonal world of ideas to be assessed on their own merits. Instead they are texts which issue from and are signs of power; to put them into quotation marks is to show that the method employed here is that of textual politics. In analyzing the Bible and the culture of the Bible this synthesis of philology and the hermeneutics of power finds its most important and most inexhaustible subject. That which is quoted is often provided with a translation: "sacrifice" as food for the priests, and " 'God forgives him who repents'—in German: *who subjects himself to the priest*" (*A* 26). Transvaluation is accomplished by translation. What gives the book its fevered pitch and shrill tone is this *duality*, its constant sense of turning one extreme into another. The duality is introduced by Nietzsche's own catechism of values, defining good and bad in terms of power and weakness (*A* 2); is continued through a declaration of war on theology (*A* 9); and concludes with the antithetical translations of biblical language and antinarrative of the life of Jesus. Within the Christian tradition itself the church has been constructed "out of the antithesis to the Gospel" (*A* 36), and Paul "embodied the antithetical type to the 'bringer of glad tidings' " (*A* 42). What seems at first like stylistic excess is simply a consistent carrying through of the polarity announced by the book's title. In a letter to Georg Brandes, Nietzsche himself indicates that such an analysis is appropriate when he calls the *Umwertung* a trope.[7] It is not just a deflection from the imagined normal path of thought but a movement of inversion and upending.

In this sharp play of oppositions there are also some surprising continuities. Christianity is simply a continuation of Judaism, and the New

Testament employs a falsification similar to that of the Old. At the same time things which seemed to belong together turn out to be opposed: the real contrast is not Judaism and Christianity but early Israel, with its heroism and passion, and the late development of both religions; Jesus is not the origin of the church but its opposite. More radically, Jesus is the antithesis of Christianity because the real " 'glad tidings' are precisely that there are not more opposites" (*A* 32), while Christianity is committed to the antithetical "good and evil" mode of value which Nietzsche analyzed in *The Genealogy of Morals*.

Jesus is the center of *The Antichrist*, but it is possible to reach him only by decoding and restoring the false oppositions of the gospels and the Church. The Church led by Paul is said to have falsified the life of Jesus just as the priests of Judaism falsified the early history of Israel. The more modern and more secular quest for the historical Jesus (Nietzsche refers explicitly to the work of D. F. Strauss and Renan and shows a familiarlity with other toilers in this philological vineyard) does not arrive at its object, for it is vitiated by the same assumption that structured the earliest accounts. That assumption is that the truth about Jesus must take the form of a story or narrative. Whether the principles are the miraculous history which begins with a remarkable birth and is punctuated by incursions of the supernatural, or whether we are presented with a demythologized Jesus, there is a common presupposition that there is a significant temporal sequence of events which will illuminate Jesus' life. Nietzsche proposes an ahistorical and nonnarrative psychology of the redeemer, according to which Jesus was, in our everyday language, "blissed out." Nietzsche's Jesus does not develop from a theological perspective because he is not a supernatural figure; no divine interventions mark off the different stages of his career. But neither does he develop in the secular and biographical sense, because his whole life and teachings consist in the notion that the kingdom of heaven is a present condition of the heart to which we can all have instant access by becoming as children. All that seems to be fixed is melted down into its experiential import. "If I understand anything of this great symbolist," Nietzsche says, "it is that he took for realities, for 'truths,' only *inner* realities—that he understood the rest, everything pertaining to nature, time, space, history, only as signs, as occasion for metaphor" (*A* 39). In calling Jesus "a symbolist *par excellence*," Nietzsche suggests that Jesus is both the origin of the many interpretations which have accrued to him (or, more accurately, which have been *imposed* on him) and also the refutation of all these interpretations. Jesus is a symbolist in the late nineteenth century sense of an artist seeking to reveal a single great timeless insight through a variety of devices; like Jesus' parables none of these will be perfectly adequate to its subject matter, yet taken collectively they will all point to the ineffable experience that generates them. Symbolism is a nonnarrative and nonrepresentational style; if it uses narrative or representational elements, as Jesus sometimes does, they are employed metaphorically to point beyond themselves. A true symbolist such as the one under analysis "stands outside of all religion, all conceptions of divine worship, all history, all natural science, all experience of the world, all acquirements, all psychology, all books, all art—his 'knowledge' is precisely the *pure folly* of the fact *that* anything of this kind exists" (*A* 32).

The history of Christianity is that of a complex series of signs and interpretations in which each sign points back to an earlier one and is susceptible of interpretation by later ones. Now Christian hermeneutics, from its beginnings in Paul to its sophisticated secular forms, supposes that this sign chain, if followed backwards, is not an infinite regress but terminates in an ultimate meaning which is the life of Jesus. Nietzsche perceives the chain of signs but sees them finally leading back to an absence rather than a fullness of meaning. Bruno Bauer, a young Hegelian whom Nietzsche referred to as one of his few genuine readers, had suggested the same view in a somewhat crude and material fashion by arguing that Jesus never lived and that the literature of the early church was all fabrication or delusion.[8] Nietzsche accepts a historical Jesus who is historically relevant only because his actual presence was that of a radically ambiguous sign capable of indefinite interpretation. As a philologist Nietzsche seems to have asked himself the Kantian question "How is a Christian semiotics possible?" and to have answered it by the transcendental deduction of a man who stands so far outside the usual processes of signification that everything is metaphor and symbol for him. Whereas later Christian semiotics assumes that there is some proper relationship between signs and their referents (or between signified and signifier), the semiotics of Jesus consists in a radical refusal of any such relationship. For Nietzsche, Jesus is an antisign or "floating signifier" who, if he incarnated anything, embodied the absence of meaning. The signs that Jesus uses are always *mere* signs or *only* signs: "Blessedness is not promised, it is not tied to any conditions: it is the only reality—the rest is signs for speaking of it" (*A* 33). In the beginning, then, there is not the word, but the enigmatic indication of the insufficiency of the word. The difference between Jesus and the Church is that Jesus' signs are used with a consciousness of their inadequacy to their subject, while the Church believes that the gospels are divinely inspired and hence adequate signs. The growth of allegorical methods of interpretation within Christianity should not be cited as a counterinstance because its practitioners still tend to believe in a literal level along with the nonliteral modes, and because they suppose that the nonliteral methods of interpretation are capable of elucidating their subject matter. Nietzsche's Jesus could be thought of as the metaphorical or symbolic principle itself; for him there is always such a large discrepancy between experience and its representation that he fails to establish any determinacy of meanings. It is just this indeterminateness which allows Paul and the Church to impose their own meanings on Jesus.

The same result follows from Jesus' lack of a history. If Jesus had a history then the tradition of text and commentary would have been under some constraint, such that even falsifications of Jesus' career would have contained internal evidence pointing back to their origins. This is the case in the Old Testament, "that miracle of falsification the documentation of which lies before us in a good part of the Bible" (*A* 26). It is because there are historical narratives of a sort, based on the history of Israel, in the Old Testament, that scholars like Wellhausen are able to detect internal inconsistencies in the whole and reconstruct a *critical* history of Israel in which the formation of different historical accounts itself plays a role. In dealing with the Christian records, philology has no such role to play because of the radical indeterminacy of its beginnings. Nietzsche throws up his arms in distress at the prospect of a philological study of the gospels. Here D. F. Strauss and others had expended enormous energy. But what was the point of it?

> I confess there are few books which present me with so many difficulties as the Gospels do. These difficulties are quite other than those which the learned curiosity of the German mind celebrated one of its most unforgettable triumphs in pointing out. The time is far distant when I too, like every young scholar and with the clever dullness of a refined philologist, savored the work of the incomparable Strauss. I was then twenty years old: now I am too serious for that. What do I care for the contradictions of "tradition?" How can legends of saints be called "tradition" at all! The stories of saints are the most ambiguous literature in existence: to apply to them scientific procedures *when no other records are extant* seems to me wrong in principle—mere learned idling (*A* 28).

The same holds for the more imaginative attempts to reconstruct the life of Jesus, such as the immensely popular and influential *Life of Jesus* by Ernest Renan; that book serves as a foil for Nietzsche to exhibit the more radical accomplishment of his own antibiography. Renan was himself a philologist specializing in the Semitic languages. His *Life of Jesus* walks a thin line between the philological concerns of Strauss and the Germans and a tendency toward imaginative biography (incipient psychobiography) with a heavy dose of religious liberalism. Aware of the discrepancies in the sources, Renan explains the gospel narratives as the result of confusion, wishful thinking, and the tendency of the disciples and others to read their own idiosyncrasies into Jesus' life. The gospels are neither biographies nor legends but "legendary biographies."[9] Renan's basic hermeneutic principle is borrowed, more or less consciously, from the well-formed nineteenth century novel with its omniscient narrator:

> The essential condition of the creations of art is, that they shall form a living system of which all the parts are mutually dependent and related. In histories such as this, the great test that we have got the truth is, to have succeeded in combining the texts in such a manner that they shall constitute a logical, probable narrative, harmonious throughout. . . . Each trait which departs from the rules of classic narrative ought to warn us to be careful.[10]

The disordered paratactic form of the gospels is to be overcome for the sake of both art and history.[11] Accordingly Renan constructs a biography of Jesus as a child of nature who lived blissfully but briefly ("for some months, perhaps a year") with the consciousness that the kingdom of God was within. Soon he becomes involved with John the Baptist and begins to preach a moral revolution to be produced by men. Meeting with opposition, Jesus proclaims himself the son of God, alienates himself from nature, and preaches that the kingdom of heaven is at hand, although it will be brought about through a divine rather than human agency. Yet this extreme tone, involving as it did a confrontation with established society and religion, could be maintained only briefly; at this point Jesus' death was a necessity, and Renan seems to mean that it was an aesthetic and narrative necessity.

It is worth noting that Renan encapsulates in Jesus' life that same distinction between a blissful inwardness and the spirit of opposition and revenge which is, from Nietzsche's perspective, the difference between Jesus and the early church. By this move Renan makes Jesus' more or less unconscious barbarization of his own message the pattern and the basis for the rancorous element within the whole Christian tradition. A continuous life serves as the model of an intelligible history. In this respect, Renan, despite the Church's opposition to his book, is a reformer rather than a revolutionary; he just wants to purge the intelligible history of Jesus and the Church of legendary and supernatural elements. This motive of Renan's work appears even more clearly when it is realized that the *Life* is only one of seven parts of his comprehensive series, *The Origins of Christianity*. Nietzsche was acquainted with this ambitious historical project. A year before writing *The Antichrist* he wrote in a letter to Overbeck, himself a church historian,

> This winter I have also read Renan's *Origines*, with much spite and—little profit. . . . At root, my distrust goes so far as to question whether history is really *possible*. What is it that people want to establish—something which was not itself established at the moment it occurred?[12]

For Nietzsche, Renan represents the modern attempt to salvage the values of religion by means of history and science. He must have been particularly angered by Renan's use of his philological credentials to interpolate a continuity into discontinuous materials. In *The Antichrist*, Renan is mentioned repeatedly, and always as another example of one who has constructed a false narrative. There is too great a "contradiction between the mountain, lake and field preacher, whose appearance strikes one as that of a Buddha on a soil very little like that of India, and the aggressive fanatic, the mortal enemy of theologian and priest, which Renan has wickedly glorified as '*le grande maître en ironie*' " (*A* 31). Given this discontinuity, Nietzsche argues that it is more plausible to see it as the radical break between Jesus and those who invoke his name. This is also a critique of Renan in his own terms; for the attempt to impose a narrative form on his materials causes him to violate his own canons of organic unity.

Renan also errs in importing the narrative and character types of the hero and the genius into his story. But "to speak with the precision of the physiologist a quite different word would rather be in place here: the world 'idiot' " (*A* 29). Such a character ought not to be portrayed as if he were the hero of a narrative; rather "one has to regret that no Dostoyevsky lived in the neighborhood of this more interesting *décadent*; I mean someone who could feel the thrilling fascination of such a combination of the sublime, the sick and the childish" (*A* 31). Nietzsche may very well have had *The Idiot* in mind as a literary model for his own analysis of Jesus.[13] That book exemplifies and solves the narrative problem that is essential to Nietzsche's account. It has long been thought that the portrayal of a thoroughly good main character in the novel must be problematic; for one who is thoroughly good will not exhibit the tensions and contradictions which lend themselves to action and development. The problem goes back to Plato, who objected to the traditional stories of the gods on the grounds that they represented that which was perfect as changing; such change was, strictly speaking, impossible, but to imagine it as occurring is to imagine the perfect becoming worse, or as having a defect which must be repaired through growth. Now Dostoyevsky's Prince Myshkin is the still point of a narrative which is constituted by the feverishly spiraling reactions of those around him to such a mixture of "the sublime, the sick and the childish." Just because he does not act and does not desire, he exists as a kind of empty space upon which the other characters can impose their own acts, desires, and fantasies. In citing these parallels and contrasts with the work of Renan and Dostoyevsky I mean to indicate more than influences and thematic correspondences. Nietzsche's polemic against Christianity is concerned with the falsifications of Christian narrative. Only by considering a variety of literary models can we begin to work our way back to the event at the heart of Christian semiotics. There is a kind of Platonic correspondence for Nietzsche between the large texts, which are the body and the instincts, and the smaller ones, which are actual written documents; unlike Plato, however, he will use the smaller in order to read the larger. An even more striking difference, however, is that both texts stand in need of extensive emendation; like graffiti, they do not have the permanent existence of the forms, but are always in danger of corruption and effacement by any who are powerful enough to wield an actual or a metaphorical pen.

To understand Christianity is to understand the blank wall which must be presupposed as the support of all of the inscriptions of history. In this respect Nietzsche's view of semiotic history, or at least of this portion of it, more closely resembles that of C. S. Peirce than it does that of Jacques Derrida. Derrida frequently cites Nietzsche in behalf of his idea that all writing refers back to an earlier writing and so on *ad infinitum*; he believes that an infinite regress of writings implies that in following back the chain of texts and interpretations we will never reach a point prior to the writing process itself.[14] Peirce on the other hand makes a crucial distinction between the continuity of the sign-process and its indefinite or infinite exension. According to him, the sign-process is continuous in that it has no absolute first or last term. But there are many cases of continuous series which are not indefinitely or infinitely extended—such as a line segment. We can consistently conceive of a sign-process beginning (or ending) at some point in time, even though it makes no sense to talk of the absolutely first (or last) sign in the series.[15]

The difference between Peirce and Derrida here is like that between

Aristotle and Zeno on the possibility of motion. Aristotle showed that the infinite density and intensive continuity of the interval, however short, between Achilles and the tortoise ought not to be mistaken for an infinitely extended line. Motion is impossible, argues Zeno, because movement across any given interval requires an infinite number of steps, each taking a finite bit of time. Therefore, not even the first step is possible. But (as Peirce points out) motion is a continuous process in which there is no unique first step or movement. Yet motion has a beginning despite its lack of a unique first or final term. Derrida is a skeptic about meaning who thinks that if there were to be any meaning at all it would require the inclusion of an infinite number of moments at the "beginning" and the "end" of the process of meaning. But all intervals here are too dense to be traversed, and all presumed ends or beginnings dissolve into endless ranges or prior and posterior nodes of meaning. Anything with such indeterminate boundaries can hardly be that full, present, and defined thing which we are wont to think of as meaning. Therefore there is no meaning, although there is, in its place, an ultimately plural and diffuse web of *écriture*. From a Peircean point of view this is to confuse intensive and extensive infinity. It is to suppose that that which has an internal complexity of the highest degree must necessarily lack all definition and boundary. What Nietzsche adds to this account is an explanation of the setting and dissolution of bounds by acts of force. What is variously designated as will to power by Nietzsche, as secondness by Peirce, and as simply power by Foucault is what gives contour and integrity to meaning. Such power is exercised variously in the different modes of writing, interpreting, rewriting, censoring, defacing, and erasing. Both Peirce and Derrida see the impossibility of a Cartesian account which would found all meaning on the intuitive presence of clear and distinct ideas, a first sign. Every sign is also an interpretation, as Nietzsche and Peirce would agree. But it does not follow that the process is without beginnings, ends, or limits.[16]

For Nietzsche, Jesus is not the first sign in the series (corresponding to a Cartesian intuition), as he is for Christian tradition, but neither is he caught up, as he would be on Derrida's reading, in a chain of signs which extends back indefinitely behind him. He is rather a break or rupture in semiotic history which is the ground of a new branch of that history; like the *tabula rasa* he is the empty presupposition of a history of signs, or, like the wall on which the graffiti are inscribed, he is the now invisible background of all that is visible. The significant difference between Nietzsche and Peirce here is that Nietzsche rejects the Peircean eschatology of the last sign as well as the first sign of Christianity. Peirce's vision of the "ultimate interpretant" has posed a major problem for his commentators, who should have noted earlier than they did that the "ultimate interpretant" can only be attained by the Christian virtues of faith, hope, and charity.[17]

At this point there may appear to be a tension between Nietzsche's psychological reconstruction of Jesus and his semiotic use of him. According to the latter, the entire quest for the historical Jesus is misguided, whether carried out along orthodox, philological or Hegelian-aesthetic lines (the last being Renan's case). Yet Nietzsche does seem at times in *The Antichrist* to be writing one more life of Jesus to add to the pile he is simultaneously rejecting in principle. If Jesus is properly a blank page in semiotic history then why does Nietzsche provide us with his vivid sketch of a blissful naif? The case may appear even more difficult when it is noticed that, despite Nietzsche's polemic against Renan, the two—read from a certain modern perspective and juxtaposed either with orthodox Christian predecessors, thorough philologists (such as Strauss and Wellhausen), or the form criticism of the last fifty years—appear to share a number of distinctive theses concerning Jesus' life. Yet this would be a truncated reading of Nietzsche's argument. It is the semiotic rather than the biographical thematic which takes priority in *The Antichrist*. The blankness of the semiotic account, the project of erasure, is not one which can be accomplished by a simple pronouncement that "Jesus had no meaning, no life, no history"; the biographical obsession, the urge to find intelligible development and character, is not so easily suppressed. In order to approximate a sense of semiotic blankness, erasure is an activity to be ever renewed. So to write of the blissed out Palestinian is to approximate such blankness within the framework of the biographical project. Like Socrates attempting to give his young men a sense of that which is "beyond Being" by a series of analogies, Nietzsche suggests the series formed by accounts of the orthodox, the philologists, the historical aesthetes, his own reconstruction—all suggesting the erasure, the break, the motivated but powerfully instituted boundary.[18] When Nietzsche talks of Jesus he is careful to suggest the many *different* narratives which might be written to replace the standard ones. The wish to have a Dostoyevskian novel of Jesus must not be understood on the assumption that *The Idiot* (or any narrative, in Nietzsche's view) is to be seen as mimetic or referential. This becomes clear when Nietzsche invokes the Amphitryon story, the philologists, and the aestheticians. Such methodological reflexivity distinguishes

Nietzsche's approach from Renan's: Renan shows no awareness of the possible divergence between the demands of the bildungsroman and those of historical truth.

Nietzsche undertakes to tell "the real history of Christianity" (*A* 39), by showing how the church's narrative distortions of Jesus are intertwined with the untold narrative of its own depredations of culture. Even where Jesus may plausibly be believed to have used narrative expressions himself, they must be construed in terms of his timeless experience; yet the church has not only misconstrued them as narratives but has written a poor and hackneyed story. Jesus speaks of himself as the Son in relation to the Father. What is the semiotic analysis of these expressions?

> It is patently obvious what is alluded to in the signs (*Zeichen*), "Father" and "Son"—not patently obvious to everyone, I grant: in the word "Son" is expressed the *entry* into the collective feeling of the transfiguration of all things (blessedness), in the word "Father" *this feeling itself*, the feeling of perfection and eternity. I am ashamed to recall what the church has made of this symbolism: has it not set an Amphitryon story at the threshold of Christian faith? (*A* 34)

As Giradoux's title for his modern version of that story, *Amphitryon 38*, indicates, the story has been told many times of a god (Zeus) having impregnated a mortal woman (Alcmeme) who then gives birth to an extraordinary son (Herakles). Surely one could have discovered a better model than this, which is more suitable for comedy than sacred narrative; this is the sort of thing that Nietzsche may have meant when he remarked that it was very strange of God to write Greek and then to write it so badly (*BGE* 121). "Dionysus vs. the crucified" (the last words of *Ecce Homo*) can refer to the opposition between the true and false gods of tragedy and comedy—among other things. Yet what is most appalling is the generation of such stories, whose early believers, if not their fabricators, may be presumed to have been naive ("I take care not to make mankind responsible for its insanities"), but the modern man and the modern church who *know* the falsity of the tradition while continuing to reaffirm it. Now these signs are used and "recognized for what they are: the most malicious false-coinage there is for the purpose of disvaluing nature and natural values" (*A* 38). Like Hegel, Nietzsche believes that history has produced a self-consciousness about the irrelevance of the narrative and mythological forms in which religious doctrines are presented; but this self-consciousness has the effect of keeping the spirit entangled in ever more hypocritical deceptions rather than liberating it. To tell the "real history of Christianity," then, is to tell it *critically* (in the sense of critical history developed in *The Use and Abuse of History*) in order to explode the ruling falsities of the day.

The plan of Nietzsche's critical history of Christianity has three stages. He begins *The Antichrist* by reiterating those theses about power and the distinction between a morality of self-affirmation and one of *ressentiment* which are familiar from his earlier writings. He proceeds to show how, in the case of Judaism, the priest's distortion of texts is both the product of *ressentiment* and a philological clue to its reconstruction. Given this general understanding of the politics of misreading and miswriting, Nietzsche analyzes the central case of Jesus himself, a man so opposed to the narrative mode that he had no defenses against those who would inscribe their own messages on his body. The final part of the book traces the history of these wicked writers whose imaginary narratives mask the real story of their own envy of the healthy and their subterranean pursuit of power. To reconstruct what they have done we need to know not only their own motives, instincts, and bodily condition, but something of the more or less instinctive hermeneutics and semiotics which such people will employ in constructing their narratives. Now an intelligible narrative will have as its skeleton a sequence of causes and effects. Because of its hostility to the healthy body, however, Christianity refuses to recognize the natural, physiological causes of human experience. Therefore it constructs a world of imaginary causes and effects (such as the soul and redemption) which is also populated by imaginary beings; consequently "this entire fictional world has its roots in hatred of the natural" (*A* 15, cf. *A* 49). Much of Nietzsche's semiotics, like Freud's, is based on the dream; it is a natural part of the dream-work to construct an imaginary narrative to explain some experience after the fact, as when on the verge of awaking because of a loud noise we invent some dream story which culminates in a cannon-shot.[19] We do the same thing in waking life, however, in seeking reasons for feeling well or poorly; never satisfied with experiences by themselves we feel compelled to produce some narrative account of them. Ordinary narrative thus tends to be confused enough, but this confusion will be heightened immeasurably when the typical terms of the narrative are Christianity's sin and repentance, the flesh and the spirit, and so on.

Nietzsche's account of the history of the church after Jesus can be encapsulated rather briefly. Jesus' followers were in revolt against the Jewish establishment and so naturally sought even greater revenge upon that order; thus the early church shows itself to be a continuation of Judaism by other means, extending the Jewish attack on the "world" to institutional Judaism itself. Yet since God permitted Jesus' death, it must be interpreted as a sacrifice for the sake of sins. Paul, who sought power above all things, employed the instincts of *ressentiment* to shift attention away from this life by the fiction of the resurrected Christ. Only then are the Gospels written with their willful distortions and their "seduction by means of morality" (*A* 44). The text itself is dirty: "one does well to put gloves on when reading the New Testament" (*A* 46). These dirty graffiti are also symptoms of the defacing or rewriting of some of mankind's cleaner texts, the ancient world, Islam, and the Renaissance (*A* 59–61). Nietzsche's account of these naughtiest writings on the cultural wall is always bound up with his analysis of the book which justifies them and reveals their psychological principles. The New Testament is a bad dream constructed on the principle of *ressentiment*. After giving an extensive account of its alleged falsifications of Jesus' sayings (*A* 45), Nietzsche says that "every book becomes clean if one has just read the New Testament: to give an example . . . Petronius" (*A* 46). This *Umwertung* of the idea of the dirty book is a characteristic strategy in *The Antichrist*. I suggest that we read the admittedly feverish imagery of dirt and cleanliness, body, blood, and poison, which becomes more and more pronounced as one reaches the end of the book, as intrinsic to the strategies and economy of the text rather than as symptoms of a loss of control. Nietzsche's transvaluation is meant to be an affirmation of the body in opposition to Christianity's denial of it. Therefore it must openly be a text of the body and must describe its pretext as a desecration of the body.

It is striking that Nietzsche invokes Zarathustra in the midst of his narrative (*A* 53–54), for what unites Zarathustra and Nietzsche's Jesus is a break with that metanarrativist style of thought that requires a notion of first and last things. For both, the totality of experience is sufficient unto itself and stands in no need of external explanations. Jesus' opposition to narrative is instinctive and naive, while Zarathustra's living of the eternal return is postnarrative and achieved only with great difficulty. The eternal recurrence is opposed to traditional narrative thought because it knows no isolated agents in the sequence of all events, but only the interconnection of events; it knows no beginning, middle, and end of the narrative but simply the continuous fabric of becoming; and it tends to dissolve the mainstay of conventional narrative, the individual agent, into the ring of becoming. Carefully distinguishing himself from Zarathustra, Nietzsche indicates that he has not attained such a radically antinarrative stance himself, or if he did experience the eternal recurrence he also forgot it from time to time. In constructing his own narratives such as *The Genealogy of Morals* and *The Antichrist*, Nietzsche attempts to incorporate an awareness of the fallibility and perspectival character of conventional narrative which is rejected by the dogmatic, priestly variety. We might think of the distinction between these two narrative modalities as somewhat like the distinction that Marx would make between ideology and science. Ideological accounts of history are dogmatic and uncritical of their own principles of interpretation, while scientific accounts are distinguished not only by knowing where to look for causes (in the relations of production or in the condition of the body) but by their knowledge that they too are products of these causes and therefore subject to explanation and correction from a more comprehensive standpoint. So it would be in the spirit of Marxism to regard Marxist science as itself tied to the material conditions of capitalism and subject to revision when capitalism is overcome. Of course Marx does not envision a nonhistorical science; Nietzsche's pluralizing narratives are even more provisional in that they anticipate the erosion of the narrative principle itself. Or one might point out that, just as the eternal recurrence will bring back the last man, so it will, even though opposed to the narrative principle, bring back that principle as well.

Nietzsche recalls Zarathustra in *The Antichrist* both for his opposition to priestly writing in blood and for his skepticism. As in the passage chosen for *Auslegung* in *The Genealogy of Morals*, Nietzsche chooses a section explicitly touching on the activities of reading and writing. Zarathustra speaks twice of the connection between blood and writing, once to announce "I love only that which is written in blood" (*Z* 67) and then, in the passage quoted in *The Antichrist*, to criticize the priests for writing in blood:

> They wrote letters of blood on the path they followed, and their folly taught that truth is proved by blood.
> But blood is the worst witness of truth. (*Z* 116)

Both passages seem to apply to the *Antichrist*, but only one of them is quoted. In part, their difference has to do with the polyphonic or polytropic character of *Zarathustra*. But beyond that there is still the problem of the bloody tone of *The Antichrist* in addition to its bloody subject matter. In fact, the conclusion of the passage makes a distinction between two sorts of bloody writing:

> And if someone goes through fire for his teaching—what does that prove?
> Truly, it is more when one's own teaching comes out of one's burning.

One kind of writing in blood is that of the ascetic; he deliberately spills his blood and then imagines that whatever he writes with it must be

true. He has too much of an investment, through self-sacrifice, to allow
him to question his own writing. The other sort is that which flows out
of powerful and healthy impulses which cannot be suppressed; it is thus
that Nietzsche describes his own composition of *Zarathustra*. *The Antichrist* would like to be bloody, presumably in the second sense, not
the first. Only this second kind of bloodiness is compatible with the
skepticism which Nietzsche here attributes to Zarathustra and to Pilate,
whose "What is truth?" makes him the "*one* solitary figure one is obliged
to respect" in the New Testament (*A* 46). Writing in blood, like that in
The Antichrist or *Zarathustra*, can be skeptical if it combines intensity
with an awareness of the perspectival character of all discourse ema-
nating from the body. The antithesis to the Christian set of sacred
writings, beliefs, and values is not a new sacred text and alternative
beliefs to be held with the same force; it is the *Umwertung* of all those
things, not simply a change in their content. *The Antichrist* aims at being
the antithesis of Christian graffiti by opening up a space for playful
writings like Nietzsche's own; it is meant to clear the walls for an exuberant profusion of inscriptions which will break out of the narrow
circle of revenge in which writing under the sway of Christianity and
morality has moved.

After completing the manuscript of *The Antichrist*, Nietzsche added a
short section entitled "Decree Against Christianity" ("Gesetz Wider
Christentum"). This page seems to have been removed by his literary
executors and has been restored, somewhat tentatively, in the definitive
Colli-Montinari edition of Nietzsche's works. Since this text does not
(so far as I know) appear elsewhere in English, I take the liberty of
presenting it here. It should be read with special attention to its date
and signature:

Decree Against Christianity
   Proclaimed on the first day of the year one (on September 30, 1888 of
the false time scheme)
   War to the death against depravity: depravity is Christianity

   First Proposition: Every form of anti-nature is depraved. The most
depraved type of man is the priest: he *teaches* anti-nature. Against the
priest one doesn't use arguments, but prison.
   Second proposition: Every participation in a religious service is an attack
on public morality. One should be more severe toward Protestants than
toward Catholics and more severe toward liberal Protestants than toward
those of strict belief. The criminality of being a Christian increases in so

far as the Christian approaches science. The criminal of criminals is consequently the *philosopher*.

Third proposition: The accursed places in which Christianity has hatched its basilisk eggs should be flattened to the ground and be regarded as *vile* places of the earth, to the terror of all posterity. Poisonous snakes should be bred there.

Fourth proposition: The preaching of chastity is a public incitement to anti-nature. Every condemnation of sexual love, and evey dirtying of it through the concept "dirty" (*unrein*) is original sin against the holy spirit of life.

Fifth proposition: Eating at a table with a priest is forbidden: in doing so one excommunicates himself from honest society. The priest is *our* chandala—he should be condemned, starved and driven into every kind of desert.

Sixth proposition: The "holy" story (*Geschichte*) should be called by the name it has earned, the *accursed* story; the words "God," "Saviour," "redeemer," "saint" should be used as terms of abuse and as criminal insignia.

Seventh proposition: the rest follows from the above.

The Antichrist

One can see why Nietzsche's editors did not publish this "Decree," which was eventually classified along with the materials for *Ecce Homo*. The general form of the section confirms and intensifies his announced intention of "writing in letters so large that even the blind can see" or of "writing on the walls, wherever there are walls" (*A* 62). The decree itself could be printed in large letters as a wall poster, like those used by military authorities during their occupation of a conquered territory or in a period of martial law. Such a use would be at most a slight exaggeration of Nietzsche's plan that *The Transvaluation of All Values* (which he came to identify with *The Antichrist*) be presented as a broadside attack on Christianity, appearing simultaneously in seven languages, in editions of one million copies. The wall poster of the Antichrist's army of occupation gives a concrete sense of what Nietzsche may have had in mind when he spoke of "splitting the history of mankind into two" by means of *The Transvaluation*. Consider the passage of *The Antichrist* before the "Decree" (the words that we supposed, before the Colli-Montinari edition, were its last words):

And one calculates *time* from the *dies nefastus* on which this fatality arose—from the *first* day of Christianity!—*Why not rather from its last?*— . *From today?*—Transvaluation of all values! (*A* 62)

Just as Nietzsche supposes that Jesus' entrance into history marked a radical break that made possible the inscription of Christianity, so he now aims at closing the parenthesis and bracketing the Christian era once and for all. The idea of a new time and a new history which are to be marked by the adoption of a new calendar has a history and tradition of its own; the French Revolution, which Nietzsche despised, had promulgated a new calendar, for example. Of course the effort at bracketing or erasing past time cannot succeed in wiping clean the slate of history. The "Decree" itself refers to the sites of former churches and supposes that there will for some time be priests whom it will be one's duty to shun. At most, we might say, Christianity and its history could be placed under erasure. Yet the assumption of continuity that reinforces the Christian-Hegelian view of history as a natural development would be shaken or put into question. The very signature at the bottom of the decree shows how ineluctable is the reference to the Christian tradition. In a letter to Brandes (dated "Anfang Dezember, 1888"), Nietzsche describes *The Antichrist* as the beginning of a war against Christianity and writes that he hopes this war will gain the support of the Jews and "*Grosscaptial.*" He quotes from the "Decree Against Christianity" to demonstrate that the war is in earnest. Like the substance of the decree, the letter suggests that the new time announced by its date must be understood not as an absolute beginning but as one dimension of what could be called an agonistic temporality, a time that is envisioned without absolutes, and with neither first or last things. The noneschatological time is related to Christian temporality not as an alternative or mirror image but by way of irony and parody. Even should Nietzsche's battle cry be successful in "splitting the history of mankind into two," there is no sense that the history that would emerge from the split could be described in nonagonistic terms. The apparent crudity and brutality of the "Decree" confirms and even exacerbates the conventional reading of *The Antichrist* as a work of at least incipient madness; yet if we take seriously the ways in which the book challenges some of our traditional narrative categories we must also be wary of assuming such a biographical reduction and placement of this exorbitant text. What we might learn finally from *The Antichrist* is that temporality and history can be *other* than the continuous eschatological development of Christianity and its philosophical allies. The time of *The Antichrist* is not only bellicose, but fractured and pluralized; it offers not only another name, the antiname under which the tradition aimed to conquer, but a name which suggests that all signs and names are multiple and parodic; it offers not simply a different way of emplotting our place in history, but the sense that all emplottings must recognize their indebtedness to the many *different* stories and storytellers that make us the compulsive narrators that we are.

Notes

1. Eugen Fink, *Nietzsches Philosophie* (Stuttgart: Kohlhammer, 1960), p. 34.

2. References to *The Antichrist* are by numbered section, usually following the translation of R. J. Hollingdale in *Twilight of the Idols and Antichrist* (Baltimore: Penguin Books, 1961).

3. The *Antichrist* and *Ecce Homo* are often treated together in this respect. According to Kaufmann, "The ending of *The Antichrist* and much of *Ecce Homo* show so strange a lack of inhibition and contain such extraordinary claims concerning Nietzsche's own importance that, knowing of his later insanity, one cannot help finding here the first signs of it." Walter Kaufmann, *Nietzsche*, 4th ed. (Princeton: Princeton University Press, 1974), p. 66. Arthur Danto's judgment is a measured one: "The *Antichrist* is unrelievedly vituperative and would indeed sound insane were it not informed in its polemic by a structure of analysis and a theory of morality and religion worked out elsewhere and accessible even here to the informed reader." Arthur Danto, *Nietzsche as Philosopher* (New York: Macmillan, 1965), p. 182. Even in Danto's view, the structure of thought which saves the *Antichrist* is one worked out elsewhere; he would apparently agree with Fink that the book offers nothing new.

4. *EH*, page following preface.

5. Nietzsche calls Renan his "antipodes" (*BGE* 48); the sense of opposition is made more precise a year later in a polemic on modern historiography in *GM* III 26: "I know of nothing that excites such a disgust as this kind of 'objective' armchair scholar, this kind of scented voluptuary of history, half person, half satyr, perfume by Renan, who betrays immediately with the high falsetto of his applause what he lacks, *where* he lacks it, *where* in this case the Fates have applied their cruel shears with, also, such surgical skill!" Renan, then, is Nietzsche's antihistorian; it is notable that both *The Genealogy of Morals* and Renan's *Origins of Christianity* are philosophical histories which focus on the transition from Greek and Roman culture to Christianity. Nietzsche not only narrates the events differently but does so, to speak more precisely, in a genealogical rather than a historical manner. For an anarcho-marxist assessment

by a writer sometimes considered a Nietzschean, see Georges Sorel, *Le Système Historique de Renan* (Paris: G. Jacques, 1905). Cf. also my essay "Nietzsche Contra Renan," *History and Theory*, 1982, pp. 193–222.

6. Julius Wellhausen, *Prolegomena to the History of Ancient Israel* (New York: Meridian Books, 1957).

7. Georg Brandes, *Friedrich Nietzsche* (New York: Macmillan, n.d.), p. 85.

8. Nietzsche's admiring references to Bauer (e.g., *EH* V 2) indicate that he may have known Bauer's works on the history of Christianity. Albert Schweitzer's *The Quest of the Historical Jesus* is the most accessible account of Bauer's writing and of other nineteenth century works of this character.

9. Ernest Renan, *The Life of Jesus* (New York: Modern Library, 1927), pp. 45–54.

10. Renan, *The Life of Jesus*, pp. 62–63.

11. Renan, *The Life of Jesus*, p. 64.

12. Letter to Overbeck, February 23, 1887, in *Selected Letters to Friedrich Nietzsche*, ed. and trans. Christopher Middleton (Chicago: University of Chicago Press, 1969), p. 261.

13. For a scholarly account of Nietzsche's knowledge of Dostoyevsky, see the articles by C. A. Miller in *Nietzsche-Studien*, 1973, 1975, and 1978.

14. Jacques Derrida, *Of Grammatology*, trans. G. Spivak (Baltimore: Johns Hopkins University Press, 1974), and other writings. In saying that for Derrida all writing refers back to an earlier writing, the notion of "referring back" must not be understood as implying a linear temporal sequence but as suggesting that writing always occurs within an infinitely dense texture of writing. Derrida associates his view of writing with the Nietzschean and Heideggerian critique of the linear conception of time (*Of Grammatology*, pp. 86–87).

15. In his classical exposition of the theory of signs in 1868, Peirce argues for the impossibility of a "first sign." See *Collected Papers*, (Cambridge, Mass.: Harvard University Press), vol. 5, paras. 213–317 and esp. 263ff. Cf. also my paper "Peirce and Derrida on First and Last Things," *University of Dayton Review* 17 (1984), pp. 33–38.

16. For Derrida's celebration of undecidability see *Spurs*, trans. B. Harlow (Chicago: University of Chicago Press, 1979); for the understanding of such celebrations as sacrificial religious rites see "From Restricted to General Economy: A Hegelianism without Reserve" in *Writing and Difference*, trans. A. Bass (Chicago: University of Chicago Press, 1978). There are discussions of *Spurs* by David Allison and David Hoy in *boundary 2*. See also my review of *Spurs* in *Man and World*, 1981. For Peirce on Zeno in a semiotic context, see *Collected Papers*, vol. 5, paras. 333–34.

17. For Peirce's claim that logic requires faith, hope, and charity, see *Collected Papers*, vol. 2, paras. 264–65 and Josiah Royce's Hegelian extension of Peirce in *The Problem of Christianity*, vol. 2.

18. Derrida explains the asymptotic conception of the deconstructive process in "Structure, Science and Play in the Discourse of the Human Sciences," in *The Structuralist Controversy*, ed. R. Macksey and E. Donato (Baltimore: Johns Hopkins University Press, 1972).

19. *HH*, para. 113.

An earlier version of this essay appeared as "Nietzsche's Graffito," in Daniel O'Hara, ed., *Why Nietzsche Now?* (Bloomington: Indiana University Press, 1985). Reprinted with permission of the author.

The Use and Abuse of
The Will to Power

BERND MAGNUS

I. The Problem Stated

Anyone who has read very much Nietzsche commentary is surely struck by the absence of any semblance of basic agreement about what Nietzsche's philosophy is, whether he really had one, whether he intended to have one—and if so in what sense—or even whether he wished to show that no one ought to have one. To be sure, disagreement surrounds all commentary, literary or "philosophical." Otherwise there would be nothing left for us to say. It does seem to me that disagreement is more basic and more acute in the Nietzsche case, however, than in any other case with which I am well acquainted. Think for a moment of the Nietzsche who leaps from the pen of a Martin Heidegger, a Karl Jaspers, or a Jacques Derrida, all quite different Nietzsches certainly; then compound that difference by comparing and contrasting these Nietzsche portraits with those provided by, say, Arthur Danto or Richard Schacht. It is tempting to think that disagreements about Kant's first *Critique*, for example, disagreements which distinguish Henry Allison's recent commentary from Jonathan Bennett's somewhat less recent one, are more like the quite different renderings of a putatively identical French landscape by Barbizon School or Impressionist painters, while disagreements about Nietzsche are rather more like Rembrandt's, Jackson Pollock's, and Andy Warhol's depictions of the same subject. In the Barbizon and Impressionist works we can still make out the same subject, however faintly. In Rembrandt's, Pollock's, and Warhol's, identity seems to dissolve altogether. Sometimes nothing is recognizable any longer.

I wish I could convince myself that, deep down, this more acute difference in Nietzsche studies reduced to a difference between analytic and nonanalytic treatments, or to the question of situating him within the philosophical tradition as distinct from reading him out of it entirely. Unfortunately, I take the analytic/continental divide to be somewhat artificial and unhelpful generally—Frege and Wittgenstein as well as Carnap and Schlick, for example, were all "continental" Europeans. It seems to me that that parochial distinction based on natural languages could more usefully be replaced—to follow Rorty's lead—by distinguishing familiar paradigms and discourse from unfamiliar ones instead. In addition, Nietzsche's place in the philosophy curriculum appears to be reasonably secure. Few argue any longer, in contrast to three decades ago, that Nietzsche belongs to the history of some discipline *other* than philosophy. When such infrequent debates occur they are typically reducible—in principle at least—either to disagreements about library cataloging recommendations or to debates about which department has "the right" to teach him, or more characteristically to disagreements about what *status* ought to be assigned to Nietzsche in one's favored discipline. Sometimes disagreements about Nietzsche as a philosopher turn unintentionally comical, resembling a state of affairs not unlike the one recently bemoaned by Arthur Danto:

> A lot of what I have read on Plato reads much as though he to whom the whole of subsequent philosophy since is said to be so many footnotes, were in effect a footnote to himself, and being coached to get a paper accepted by *The Philosophical Review*. And a good bit of the writing on Descartes is by way of chivying his argumentation into notations we are certain he would have adopted had he lived to appreciate their advantages, since it is now so clear where he went wrong. But in both cases it might at least have been asked whether what either writer is up to can that easily be separated from forms it may have seemed inevitable to be presented in, so that the dialogue or meditation flattened into conventional periodical prose might not in the process have lost something central to those ways of writing. The form in which the truth as they understood it must be grasped just might require a form of reading, hence a kind of relationship to those texts, altogether different from that appropriate to a paper, or to what we sometimes refer to as a "contribution."[1]

The distinction I wish to begin to focus on in this paper is neither a distinction between analytic and nonanalytic nor between "philosophical" and "literary" accounts of Nietzsche's works. It is, in fact, quite indifferent to these distinctions. Nor is the distinction I wish to focus on very deep, at least not at first glance. It is, instead, a philological distinction primarily, one not unusual in problems of canon formation, a distinction between those who treat Nietzsche's *Nachlass*, his literary estate, as if such materials were unproblematic philologically—those who treat the *Nachlass* as on at least a par with his published writings— and those who do not. I shall for purposes of this paper call commentators "lumpers" who regard the use of Nietzsche's *Nachlass* as unproblematic. That Nietzsche elected neither to publish nor to polish most of the *Nachlass* seldom if ever becomes an issue for an lumper. He or she assumes, as Richard Schacht does in his instructive recent book, for example, that "these unpublished writings... contain much more of his expressed thinking on certain important matters than do his finished work."[2] Lumpers are drawn to Nietzsche's *Nachlass*, to his literary estate, and are especially fond of the nonbook *Der Wille zur Macht*. In Schacht's case, for example, there are 1,718 quotations from Nietzsche in his 546 pages of text. 861 out of 1,718 quotations—more than half—are from the nonbook *Der Wille zur Macht*. Moreover, in his interesting chapter titled "The World and Life" (a chapter which deals with such matters as "Toward a philosophical cosmology," "The world and 'will to power'," "Life and will to power," and "The Eternal Recurrence"), where Schacht quotes Nietzsche 199 times, 152 of the quotations derive from *Der Wille zur Macht*, better than three out of four on the average. *Thus Spoke Zarathustra*, in contrast, frequently poses something of an embarrassment. It is quoted by Schacht, again for example only, a total of 34 times throughout his book in part because "it [i.e., *Thus Spoke Zarathustra*] does not readily lend itself to the sort of analysis undertaken here."[3] The aim of most lumpers—from Jaspers and Heidegger to Danto and Schacht—is to place Nietzsche's writings squarely within the commentator's conception of the philosophical tradition. And that is no small accomplishment! Indeed it can be a major accomplishment, as it is in Heidegger's case in my opinion. It does not matter especially for my purposes either whether the commentator's tradition is regarded as the metaphysics of presence—in which Nietzsche becomes its closure, as in Heidegger's suggestion—or whether Nietzsche's prose is regarded instead as making disguised yet substantive traditional philosophical recommendations, recommendations which can be recast in argument form defined by an antecedent philosophical agenda, such as truth and knowledge, ontological commitments, the nature of the ideal life, and the nature of morality. It is therefore not at all surprising that for many lumpers Nietzsche's style is regarded as an obstacle to understanding his philosophical intentions. Under this rubric the relatively flat and familiar prose of the *Nachlass*, devoid of literary embellishment, is often thought either to be less ambiguous than work Nietzsche chose to publish or authorized for publication or—in the extreme case—to *be* his real philosophy. To quote Heidegger:

> But Nietzsche's philosophy proper, the fundamental position on the basis of which he speaks in these and in all the writings he himself published, did not assume a final form and was not itself published in any book. . . . What Nietzsche himself published during his creative life was always foreground . . . *His philosophy proper was left behind as posthumous, unpublished work.*[4]

Lumpers come in all shapes and traditions. Heidegger, Jaspers, Deleuze, Müller-Lauter, Danto, and Schacht are paradigmatic lumpers, for my purposes.

In contrast to lumpers there are what I shall call "splitters." Hollingdale, Alderman, Montinari, and Strong tend to be splitters, as I am when I am not incautious. (The late Walter Kaufmann was a special case in this taxonomy. He generally claimed to be a splitter but in practice was frequently a lumper.[5])

Splitters, in contrast to lumpers, tend to distinguish sharply between published and unpublished writings in Nietzsche's case. Moreover, such commentators occasionally read Nietzsche as struggling in his published writings to set aside the felt need to offer canonical ontological descriptions, theories of knowledge, theories of morality and theories of the ideal life.[6]

This methodological difference between lumpers and splitters—this difference of opinion about the use and value of Nietzsche's literary estate—can sometimes become substantive, as could be illustrated in discussions of eternal recurrence, perspectivism, and will to power.

Lumpers frequently tend to argue that eternal recurrence is a normative and/or empirical concept, even when the term "empirical" is equated with "metaphysical." In its normative version, it is argued that eternal recurrence admonishes us to behave as if recurrence were true, because believing it to be true will be the greatest weight upon our actions. In its empirical version, Nietzsche is sometimes thought to propose a "mistaken belief [that] science compels us to accept the [eternal recurrence] hypothesis."[7]

Lumpers tend to construe will to power as an ontology or cosmology, in some sense or other, and have tried to treat his perspectivism as Nietzsche's theory of knowledge.[8]

Splitters typically have views which are more difficult to characterize. Some of them are persuaded that Nietzsche neither had nor wished to offer a theory of knowledge, nor an ontology, nor an ethics. However, they have difficulty explaining why he ought to be taken seriously by philosophers if he had none of these things to offer us. Most splitters will also insist, *contra* lumpers, that Nietzsche's philosophy cannot be divorced from his style, that the mode of expression and what is expressed are in some sense inseparable; yet they have difficulty explaining how this claim is to be understood and why this should be so. For while it may be true that authentic poetry dissolves in paraphrase, it is hard to see why philosophy would or could dissolve in recharacterization.[9]

The uncomfortable upshot for much Nietzsche scholarship to date, particularly in the English-speaking world, seems to me therefore to be this: if splitters are right in their textual claims, and I think that they generally are, the purchase price of their textual probity may be to move Nietzsche out of discursive philosophy altogether or perhaps into its margins. Lumpers, on the other hand, move Nietzsche squarely into the wax museum of the great dead philosophers, but at the price of promoting to primacy and priority many of the very texts and theses Nietzsche seems to have abandoned.

What I propose to do in the pages that follow, therefore, is to sketch briefly the present philological situation in Nietzsche studies as I understand it. The result of that sketch will be the by now familiar suggestion that, in his 1888 manuscripts, Nietzsche performed what I shall call an epistemectomy rather than offering us an epistemology, that he seems also to have abandoned the will to power and eternal recurrence as ontological principles, and that an *übermensch* was perhaps not to be construed as yet another version of the human ideal. Of course, that will leave us with the questions: Is my Nietzsche still a philosopher? And if so in what sense? My conclusion will be disappointingly sketchy and programmatic. I shall suggest that a splitter's Nietzsche—rescued from philological triviality—may usefully situate him as the first full-blooded postmodern, nonrepresentational thinker, the fountainhead of a tradition which flows from him to Heidegger, Derrida, Foucault, Rorty, and much recent literary theory. This shall remain merely a suggestion in this paper, however. I shall not argue this thesis here, leaving it for another occasion and context instead.

II. The Present Philological Situation

The Colli-Montinari[10] editions supersede, expand, and correct all prior Nietzsche editions. The *Nachlass*, for example, is expanded from roughly

3,500 pages in the *Grossoktavausgabe* and *Musarionausgabe* to more than 5,000 pages out of a corpus of circa 8,000 pages. Moreover, the materials are presented in a strictly chronological order as a result of which it has become clear that Nietzsche had not only abandoned his intention to write a book called *Der Wille zur Macht*, but that *even while he was entertaining the notion of writing such a book* its content was *not* to be the pseudo-canonical 1,067 sections gathered under that title by Elisabeth Förster-Nietzsche, Heinrich Köselitz, von Mette, Otto Weiss, *et al.*[11] The book *Der Wille zur Macht*—even in its projected version before Nietzsche conclusively rejected the idea of writing such a book— is probably *not* the one frequently cited. Rather, by February 1888 Nietzsche had settled on 374 previously written entries as raw material for a future book to be titled *Der Wille zur Macht.*[12] Of these entries, 104 never found their way into pre-Montinari editions at all; and only 133 of the remaining 270 fragments are included in unaltered form in the collection of 1,067 sections which appear under the Förster-Nietzsche title *Der Wille zur Macht.* In brief, 934 out of 1,067 entries in the lumpers' favorite book appear to have been intended for no book at all; or, on the most generous construal, 270 notes may have been intended initially for further polishing, only to have been abandoned in the end. The implications of this may be serious, as I will suggest below.

It might be useful at this point to digress and to remind ourselves that Nietzsche's literary estate from roughly 1885 to January 1889 (*The Will to Power* period) was culled by Colli and Montinari from 22 handwritten sources, which consist of 15 very large exercise books, 3 large notebooks, and 4 substantial looseleaf portfolios.[13] These sum collectively to thousands of pages and items. They include materials taken up in previous critical editions as well as materials not included. Over the years I have taken inventory from accounts of the materials from which different critical editions have been culled, an inventory which consists of more than 25 distinguishable categories, including fragments, aphorisms, plans, outlines, titles, prefaces, virtually finished initially unpublished writings such as *Ecce Homo*, *The Antichrist*, and the Basel *Schriften*, memoranda, sketches, drawings, doodles, bills, receipts, fiscal questions, investment information, notices of sales, cost-accounting notes, notices of prices and notices of awards and contests, travel notes and routes, descriptions of walks and paths, snippets of conversations real or imagined, gossip about visits and visitors, weather reports, pages of quoted materials transcribed from other authors and discussions of same; and, of course, there is an endless stream of letters to and from Nietzsche. Sometimes Nietzsche's pages are stained. Some pages are torn. Some are illegible, having been rewritten many times. Some are opaque inscriptions. Sentences set off in quotation marks such as one of Derrida's favorites, "Ich habe meinen Regenschirm vergessen," are not unique. That sentence is to be found for the first time in the Colli-Montinari critical edition, while Nietzsche's quoted laundry lists typically are not to be found in any critical editions.

From 1886 forward—that is for the last three years of Nietzsche's intellectual life—the evidence suggests that he began to review systematically all his published writings and unpublished notes for what seems to have been the first time.[14] He appears to be preoccupied with copyright questions, wishing to have them secured in his behalf, in part because he is eager to revise *Menschliches Allzumenschliches* and perhaps all of his other works as well. Chiefly, however, he is preoccupied with future works, particularly with a book project whose title he changes often, sometimes perhaps to be called *Der Wille zur Macht*.

Space does not permit a thorough chronicle of the fascinating rise, decline, and fall of *Der Wille zur Macht* as a literary project.[15] What merits reiteration, however, is that in mid-February 1888 Nietzsche gathered together and numbered 374 entries himself under the rubric *Der Wille zur Macht*. The mere fact that Nietzsche numbered unpublished entries was unusual. He typically did not do so. His later editors introduced that convention. At any rate, these 374 entries appear in two quarto notebooks—notebooks with 4 leaves per page—and one folio looseleaf notebook. The first quarto notebook is 142 pages long and contains—among other things—Nietzsche's numbering of entries 1–136 for the planned *Der Wille zur Macht*. Nietzsche then numbered serially entries 137–300 in a second 142-page quarto notebook. Sections 301–372 are numbered in a looseleaf folio page book, constituting the first 40 pages among 200 folio sheets.[16] A third quarto notebook then establishes rubrics for all 374 entries for the planned book *Der Wille zur Macht*.

One very interesting contrast between the earlier March 1887 plan on which Elisabeth Förster-Nietzsche based her edition and the February 1888 plan which superseded it may be found in the 1888 outline for *Der Wille zur Macht*, which consists of 12 rubrics for four books:

[zum ersten Buch]
    1. Der Nihilismus, vollkommen zu Ende gedacht.
    2. Cultur, Civilisation, die Zweideutigkeit des "Modernen."

[zum zweiten Buch]
    3. Die Herkunft des Ideals.

4. Kritik des christlichen Ideals.
5. Wie die Tugend zum Siege kommt.
6. Der Heerden-Instinkt.

[zum dritten Buch]

7. Der "Wille zur Wahrheit."
8. Moral als Circe der Philosophen.
9. Psychologie des "Willens zur Macht" (Lust, Wille, Begriff usw.)

[zum vierten Buch]

10. Die "ewige Wiederkunft."
11. Die grosse Politik.
12. Lebens-Recepte für uns.[17]

The most interesting contrast, it seems to me, is between the published 1887 version of Book Three—from the plan Elisabeth followed—and the supervenient 1888 version. The 1887 version, the one which was published and has become an important text for lumpers, remember, has four parts for Book Three of *Der Wille zur Macht*:

1. The Will to Power as Knowledge

2. The Will to Power in Nature

3. The Will to Power in Society

4. The Will to Power as Art

Contrast that with the later 1888 plan for Book Three once again:

1. The "Will to Truth"

2. Morality as Circe of Philosophers

3. Psychology of the "Will to Power" (Pleasure, Will, Concept, etc.)

This 1888 later plan self-consciously supersedes Nietzsche's March 1887 plan, the one on which the pseudo-canonical *Der Wille zur Macht* is based, since Nietzsche had the 1887 outline before him while writing the 1888 plan. Moreover, 104 entries designated by Nietzsche for inclusion in *Der Wille zur Macht* in 1888 never found their way into that nonbook of 1,067 entries, and 137 others are incomplete or are incorrectly cited or incorrectly edited.

More significant, for my purposes, the rubric of the will to power in *nature* silently slips from view in *all* 8 or so post–1887 plans. Equally important perhaps, the 1888 materials I have just described are those Nietzsche took with him to Sils Maria four months later, in June 1888, and some of even these materials he seems to have instructed his landlord, Durisch, to dispose of in September 1888 when he left Sils, having abandoned *Der Wille zur Macht* as a literary project.[18]

Quite apart from the stunning disparity between what Nietzsche had planned to retain and polish in February 1888 but ultimately discarded anyway and what Förster-Nietzsche retrieved and published using earlier, rejected rubrics, there are the equally stunning entries Nietzsche really did *not* plan to publish. These include, for example, the famous last entry, 1,067, of the Förster-Nietzsche edition, an entry Nietzsche jotted down in July 1885 but had set aside by February 1888 as material for which he had no further use.

> And do you know what "the world" is to me? Shall I show it to you in my mirror? This world: a monster of energy, without beginning, without end; a firm, iron magnitude of force that does not grow bigger or smaller, that does not expend itself but only transforms itself as a whole, of unalterable size, a household without expenses or losses, but likewise without increase or income; enclosed by "nothingness" as by a boundary; not something blurry or wasted, not something endlessly extended, but set in a definite space as a definite force, and not a space that might be "empty" here or there, but rather as force throughout, as a play of forces and waves of forces, at the same time one and many, increasing here and at the same time decreasing there; a sea of forces flowing and rushing together, eternally changing, eternally flooding back, with tremendous years of recurrence, with an ebb and a flood of its forms; out of the simplest forms striving toward the most complex, out of the stillest, most rigid, coldest forms toward the hottest, most turbulent, most self-contradictory, and then again returning home to the simple out of this abundance, out of the play of contradictions back to the joy of concord, still affirming itself in this uniformity of its courses and its years, blessing itself as that which must return eternally, as a becoming that knows no satiety, no disgust, no weariness: this, my *Dionysian* world of the eternally self-creating, the eternally self-destroying, this mystery world of the twofold voluptuous delight, my "beyond good and evil," without goal, unless the joy of the circle is itself a goal; without will, unless a ring feels good will toward itself—do you want a *name* for this world? A *solution* for all its riddles? A *light* for you, too, you best-concealed, strongest, most intrepid, most midnightly men?—*This world is the will to power—and nothing besides*! And you yourselves are also this will to power—and nothing besides![19]

My reasons for going on at such length are a bit complex—include the conviction that many lumpers have been elevating the wrong texts, that they can find very little support in Nietzsche's published writings for will to power as a first-order conception—a cosmology, ontology, or what-have-you. Discussions of will to power in larger ontological contexts, in contexts other than the psychological or organic, occur primarily in only *two* entries Nietzsche chose to publish, *Zur Genealogie der Moral* II 12 and *Jenseits von Gut und Böse* 36. The pertinent snippet from a rather lengthy aphorism is typically excised as follows from *GM* II 12:

> I have emphasized this point of historical method all the more strongly because it runs counter to our current instincts and fashions, which would rather come to terms with the absolute haphazardness or the mechanistic meaninglessness of events than with the theory of a will to power mirrored in all process. The democratic bias against anything that dominates or wishes to dominate our modern *misarchism* (to coin an ugly word for an ugly thing) has gradually so sublimated and disguised itself that nowadays it can invade the strictest, most objective sciences without anyone's raising a word of protest.

The other aphorism in question, *BGE* 36, reads, in part:

> Suppose nothing else were "given" as real except our world of desires and passions, and we could not get down, or up, to any other "reality" besides the reality of our drives... Suppose, finally, we succeeded in explaining our entire instinctive life as the development and ramification of *one* basic form of the will—namely, of the will to power, as *my* proposition has it; suppose all organic functions could be traced back to this will to power and one could also find in it the solution of the problem of procreation and nourishment—it is *one* problem—then one would have gained the right to determine *all* efficient force univocally as—*will to power*. The world viewed from inside, the world defined and determined according to its "intelligible character"—it would be "will to power" and nothing else.

The meaning and intention of these two aphorisms is scarcely clear. Even if they were clear they would only constitute two slender reeds out of more than 8,000 pages of text on which to hang an ontology or cosmology of will to power. Similarly, little or no support can be found for eternal recurrence as a cosmology or ontology in works authorized or intended by Nietzsche for publication, as far as I can tell.

But even if one were to take the sensible-sounding route of treating the *Nachlass* as a thought laboratory—as Walter Kaufmann originally suggested when publishing the English translation of *The Will to Power*—the issue is scarcely settled. For which notes are to count as experiments for which published notions? Can such notes not be read with equal justice as *failed* experiments, ideas Nietzsche elected not to follow up, such as *Der Wille zur Macht* 1,067? That is, should the literary estate not be read as one reads rough drafts of papers, plays, novels, or dialogues, as *predecessor* versions, in which the published word just is the last word? And even if one could read the *Nachlass* as Nietzsche's thought laboratory, it is far from clear what that would tell us about any single thought experiment—other than that it was unacceptable in its *Nachlass* form.

An illustration may help here:

1. In the late summer of 1882 Nietzsche wrote a note which reads: " 'But how could you behave that way! a friend said to a very clever person—it was stupidity.' It has become difficult enough for me too, he replied."[20] [*Es ist mir auch schwer genug geworden*]

2. A year later a note strikingly similar to this one appears in the summer 1883 *Nachlass*: " 'But how could you behave that way? It was stupidity'—'It has become difficult enough for me too.' "[21] [*Es ist mir auch schwer genug geworden*]

3. Less than eighteen months later, in the winter 1884–85 *Nachlass* to *Z* we read: "—but Zarathustra, said the serpent, you clever one, how could you behave that way! That was stupidity!—It has become difficult enough for me too.' "[22]

4. And less than thirty pages later, in the same winter 1884–85 *Nachlass*, one reads: "But you clever one, how could you behave that way! It was stupidity'—'It has become difficult enough for me too.' "[23]

5. Finally, in the published 1885 part IV of *Thus Spoke Zarathustra* one reads the following, in the section called "The Ass Festival": "And you, said Zarathustra, you wicked old magician, what have you done! Who should hereafter believe in you in this free age, when *you* believe in such gods-assininities?

It was stupidity what you did; how could you, you clever one, commit such a stupidity!

O Zarathustra, the clever magician replied, you are right, it was stupidity—it has become difficult enough for me too."[24]

That these five quoted passages which recur in modified form over a three-year period are connected is clear. Notice that the events, speakers, circumstances, and content change, however. What is unclear, moreover, is how or why any of these *Nachlass* fragments may be said to shed *any* light on the published *Zarathustra* remark. And my sense is that the remainder of the *Nachlass* bears much the same relationship to the published works, a thesis I cannot hope to demonstrate here, of course. The methodological point suggested should be clear, however: substituting *Nachlass* for published materials confuses an explanation with that which requires one.

Nevertheless, lumpers have often suggested that the *Nachlass* is "representative" of Nietzsche's thinking. It seems to me that this is either trivially true or misleading. For it is trivially true to say that Nietzsche's rejected draft notes "represent" his thinking, because the term "represent" may merely mean "what he thought." If they are Nietzsche's thoughts, they represent Nietzsche's thinking rather than someone else's. But notice that even this is oversimple and misleading, because some of the *Nachlass* consists of pages of the writings of *others* which Nietzsche dutifully copied, for example the dozens of pages of Baudelaire he copied in 1888. Are Baudelaire's thoughts to be construed as Nietzsche's thoughts? And if not, how do the former "represent" the latter? More typically, however, there are three distinguishable senses in which Nietzsche's *Nachlass* has been said to "represent" his thinking:

1. Sometimes the *Nachlass* "represents" his thought in the sense that the published writings and *Nachlass* are virtually identical, e.g., the notes surrounding *Die Geburt der Tragödie* are almost *verbatim* the published text. There are virtually no editorial revisions in this case.

2. Sometimes Nietzsche's *Nachlass* has been said to "represent" his thinking in an inappropriate sense, in the sense that he produced these plans and/or entries at time *t* but elected *not* to pursue them further at time t_1, i.e., Nietzsche deliberately abandoned them, as he did the five prefaces for five unwritten books Nietzsche prepared for Lou Salomé, or the *Wille zur Macht* plan of March 1887 which he abandoned in February 1888, or the bulk of the entries published under the *Der Wille zur Macht* title.

3. Sometimes the *Nachlass* "represents" Nietzsche's published thought in the sense that the notes are raw materials which are modified, typically substantially, in the published oeuvre, as in the *Zarathustra* chain I quoted earlier. These are the hardest cases and ones for which no algorithm will serve. Such entries should be treated with great care.

These three distinctions or something like them seem to me basic. I predict more with hope than with confidence that future Nietzsche studies will take them into account, so that sense (2) of the term "represent" will not be conflated with senses (1) and (3).

Before concluding these philological reflections it might be useful to review the general shape and fate of Nietzsche's projects during the summer and fall of his highest hope and deepest despair, his last summer in Sils Maria, 5 June 1888 to 20 September. Here are its highlights, in outline:

1. Nietzsche had begun to gather some of his notes together in early May, 1888, for a new work to be titled *Der Fall Wagner*. He works on these notes, writes many new ones, and by mid-August has a finished version to show his publisher as well as his admirers, chiefly Heinrich Koeselitz (a.k.a. Peter Gast). By mid-September printers' copies are ready.

2. At the same time, having reached Sils in June, he now begins to write a somewhat different work whose end result is as yet not clear to Nietzsche himself; for he is at work from June on not only on *Der Fall Wagner* but on a set of notes which he thinks, at first, will be called *Müssiggang eines Psychologen* but then relents and later decides on the title *Götzendämmerung* instead.

3. At the beginning of September 1888 Nietzsche segregates his entries into those which will appear as *Götzendämmerung*. He excludes from them what will eventually appear as entries 1–28 of *Der Antichrist*; and at the same time he replaces the conception of a project called *Der Wille zur Macht* with that of a new work in four parts, to be called *Umwerthung aller Werte*.

4. The book *Der Antichrist* is worked on. It contains the twenty-eight mentioned entries which were not included in *Götzendämmerung*; and sections 29–62 are written. Nietzsche leaves Sils on 20 September unclear about the shape of the *Umwerthung*. Sometimes *Der Antichrist* is to be part one, to be followed by a second title, *Der Immoralist*. The suggestion occurs to Nietzsche for the first time that perhaps *Götzendämmerung* is the synopsis of his views, his "philosophy" in outline form.

5. *Ecce Homo* is begun on or about October 15, his forty-fourth birthday. He works on it continuously, along with *Der Antichrist*. *Ecce Homo* is revised for the last time and sent to the printer on 2 January 1889.

6. From the end of November *Der Antichrist* displaces the *Umwerthung* as the title of that "major" planned work. In the end, even the *Umwerthung* subtitle is dropped in favor of "Fluch auf das Christenthum." And, as is well known, *Der Antichrist* does not appear in print until 1895, in the edition Elisabeth Förster-Nietzsche supervised. It appears in volume eight of the Naumann edition, mistakenly as Book One of *Der Wille zur Macht*. Finally, the first edition of *Ecce Homo* is not published until 1908, twenty years after its composition.

I take it that the philological evidence shows that by the end of Nietzsche's stay in Sils Maria no *Hauptwerk* called *Der Wille zur Macht* was forthcoming, and that by the year's end no *Hauptwerk* of any sort was forthcoming.

A lumper who views Nietzsche's *The Will to Power* as the distilled essence of his thought, its alembic, may nevertheless wish to avail himself of a distinction to avoid having to set his privileged text aside. He might adopt the strategy often urged by poststructuralist thinkers—from Barthes to Foucault and Derrida—and distinguish the author of Nietzsche's texts from the efficient cause of them, namely, from the historical person Friedrich Nietzsche. The term "author" is in this case a quasi-technical term, the complex product of the interaction of text and audience/critic. An "author" is an abstract object, as it were, only contingently connected to the "writer" who stands as the text's efficient cause. Viewed in this light, the "author" Nietzsche is—among other things—the producer of *The Will to Power*. Eighty years of commentary has produced a state of affairs in which Nietzsche's name is linked to that text. It is a part of his canon after all therefore.

It is unclear what to make of such a gambit. One might reply by saying that mistaken attributions of "authorship" are also a central element in canon formation, and are, in consequence, subject to revision. Consider, for example, the number of dialogues and letters mistakenly attributed to Plato—the author—in the past two hundred years which have subsequently been read out of the canon. Moreover, if "Nietzsche's" diary—*My Sister and I*—which was demonstrably spurious had instead become the subject of commentary, would Nietzsche have become its "author" too? And, finally, what is one to make of the *author* Nietzsche who had set aside the notes and outlines of *The Will to Power*? Is this to be a permanent contest of authors, Nietzsche versus "Nietzsche"?

I have gone on at such great yet regrettably superficial length about the *Nachlass* because most lumpers shall need to treat those materials as final versions if they are to get an ontology of will to power or eternal recurrence out of Nietzsche and perhaps if they are to collapse *übermenschen* into higher humanity.[25]

Most commentators who treasure the *Nachlass*—most lumpers—do so because it is there that the representational, foundationalist Nietzsche is to be found primarily, the Nietzsche who does *not* conflate art and philosophy, the Nietzsche who worries about the way the world's intelligible character is itself to be characterized, the Nietzsche who worries about facts and perspectives, truth and reference, the Nietzsche who worries about which virtues we should value and what we ought to strive for. And that Nietzsche writes relatively straightforward declarative sentences rather than endless hypotheticals and subjective conditionals.

Splitters, I have suggested elsewhere, need not be seduced by this picture. They may instead honor Nietzsche by placing his published work at the head of that philosophical genealogy which says that there is no ultimate contrast to mark genealogy off from ontology, no point in asking about the way the world is in itself apart from what we make of it. That is the Nietzsche who speaks with many voices in his many published texts, not with a single voice governing every concern. This "postmodern" Nietzsche does not merely reject the view that "philosophy" is a natural-kind term; rather, he is the thinker who also gave us a genealogical account of how we came to believe that philosophy must name a natural kind, that it must have a transcendental standpoint and a metahistorical agenda. He is, in short, the philosopher who showed in his own published writings what philosophy is, has been, and perhaps can only be—its own time reflected in thought.

Notes

1. Arthur C. Danto, "Philosophy as/and/of Literature," Presidential Address, APA Eastern Division, December 28, 1983; reprinted in *Proceedings and Addresses of the American Philosophical Association* (September 1984), pp. 7–8; in *Grand Street* (Spring 1984); and in *Literature and the Question of Philosophy*, ed. A. J. Cascardi (Baltimore: Johns Hopkins University Press, 1987), pp. 1–24.

2. Richard Schacht, *Nietzsche* (London: Routledge and Kegan Paul, 1983), p. xii. These observations are not meant as a direct criticism of Schacht's valuable book. Given his task, to write a book in "the arguments of the philosophers" series—a Herculean task which took him the better part of a decade—it is natural that he should be drawn to the "book" which I shall argue below consists of those notes Nietzsche elected neither to publish *nor* to work up for publication. In further defense of Schacht and other "lumpers" who precede him, it is worth remembering that we did not have an adequate textual basis until 1979 on which to set *The Will to Power* notes aside, when the Colli-Montinari edition was first completed. By that time Schacht had been at work on his study for nearly six years. Hollingdale and Schlechta—who had earlier pleaded that "Nietzsche" ought to mean the published corpus only—were voices crying in the wilderness. They had no authoritative text—as we now have—on which to base their urgings. Schlechta—for example and with more than a touch of irony—published his selections from Nietzsche's *Nachlass* under the title "notes of the eighties" (in his famous three-volume Nietzsche edition), and his selections derive *entirely* from *The Will to Power* notes, the very items Schlechta would have us (rightly) discount!

3. Schacht, p. xiv.

4. Martin Heidegger, *Nietzsche*, trans. David Krell (New York: Harper and Row, 1979), pp. 8–9. My italics.

5. Alexander Nehamas's excellent, challenging book, *Nietzsche: Life as Literature* (Cambridge, Mass.: Harvard University Press, 1985) contains the same ambivalence as Kaufmann's. While it should not affect the thrust or force of Nehamas's overall argument—with which I am in unreserved sympathy—he, too, relies heavily on the *The Will to Power* on those occasions when it alone will get the argumentative job done. This is especially true, for example, in chap. 3, "A Thing is the Sum of Its Effects," whose title and argument would probably collapse without *The Will to Power* as the primary source material. Nehamas then relies heavily on this chapter in subsequent ones—for example in his discussion of eternal recurrence in chap. 5—as when he argues, for example, that for Nietzsche to change anything is, for any X, to change everything. But—I repeat—Nehamas's fine book could have been argued to its conclusions without the *Nachlass* with virtually equal force.

6. Harold Alderman's thought-provoking *Nietzsche's Gift* (Athens: Ohio University Press, 1977) comes closest to expressing this point of view in English-language commentaries, as do some of my own recent and past writings.

7. This is Walter Kaufmann's characterization of eternal recurrence, in the "Editor's Notes" to *Thus Spoke Zarathustra: Fourth Part*, in his widely used *Portable Nietzsche*. It reads:

> Nietzsche wants the eternity of *this* life with all its agonies—and seeing that it flees, its eternal recurrence. As it is expressed in sections 9, 10, and 11 [of part IV], the conception of the eternal recurrence is certainly meaningful; but its formulation as a doctrine depended on Nietzsche's mistaken belief that science compels us to accept the hypothesis of the eternal recurrence of the same events at gigantic intervals.

8. It is important to mention that the lumpers/splitters distinction does not cut with equal force for each theme in Nietzsche's writings. Put simply, without the *Nachlass* it is virtually impossible to read eternal recurrence and will to power as first-order descriptions of the way the world is in itself, as a description of the world's intelligible character. (For eternal recurrence, for example, see my *Nietzsche's Existential Imperative*, Studies in Phenomenology and Existential Philosophy (Bloomington: Indiana University Press, 1978), chap. 3; and Alexander Nehamas's "The Eternal Recurrence," *The Philosophical Review* 89 (July 1980). Perspectivism, in contrast, can perhaps be read as a "theory of knowledge" whether one relies on the published or unpublished remains. The concept of the *übermensch* is the most difficult in many ways, including the philological dimension, precisely because—while it is central to the book Nietzsche regarded as his most important one, *Thus Spoke Zarathustra*—the notion virtually disappears in the published and unpublished manuscripts of 1886–89. In consequence, it is not the case that being a lumper is a necessary condition for reading the *übermensch* as an ideal type, a realizable goal manifesting certain "virtues."

9. Alderman's and Nehamas's books address this issue in different ways. I try to address this issue as well in "The Deification of the Commonplace: *Twilight of the Idols*" (this volume).

10. I refer to the *Werke: Kritischegesammtausgabe* and the *Studienausgabe*.

11. Kaufmann and Hollingdale translated these materials long after they had appeared in E. Förster-Nietzsche's biography of her brother (2d ed. versions) and after Kröner had incorporated them into the *GA*.

12. Many items are pertinent here, including *KGW* VIII:1, "Vorbemerkung der Herausgeber," all of *KSA* 14; but especially relevant is Mazzino Montinari's "Nietzsche's *Nachlass* von 1885 bis 1888 oder Textkritik und Wille zur Macht" in his *Nietzsche Lesen* (de Gruyter, 1982), pp. 92–120, as well as his entry in *KSA* 14, pp. 383–400.

13. See, for example, *KSA* 14, pp. 29–35.

14. Montinari suggests this in his *Nietzsche Lesen* and documents it very well.

15. *KGW* VIII:1 and the literature cited there tell that tale well.

16. The careful reader will have noticed a discrepancy between the 374 entries I refer to and the 372 entries I claim Nietzsche numbered. The discrepancy is Nietzsche's, not mine. He inadvertently repeated two numbers in selecting *374* entries for further polishing. Hence he thought he had selected *372* entries, while he had in fact selected 374.

17. *KSA* 13, *KGW* VIII:2, fragment 12 [2].

18. R. J. Hollingdale makes this point in his excellent study *Nietzsche: The Man and His Philosophy* (Baton Rouge: Louisiana State University Press, 1965), p. 298. He claims that Nietzsche had instructed his landlord to dispose of—as waste—manuscripts for which he had no further use as he left Sils in September 1888; that Durisch instead "brought out armfuls of this paper and invited them [i.e., interested visitors] to help themselves"; that this fact was reported in the 1893 (autumn) *Magazine für Literatur*; that Elisabeth put a stop to this at once after hearing the news; and that "when the *Will to Power* was prepared, it was among the 'manuscripts' from which selection was made."

Michael Platt and I have tried to reconstruct this scenario, with mixed results. To begin with, the autumn 1893 *Magazine für Literatur* article does not say precisely what Hollingdale claims it does. Rather, it is Fritz Kögel's account of his accidental discovery of an (at that time) unpublished variant of the preface to *Twilight of the Idols*, a page he discovered while perusing the *proofs* Nietzsche had left at Sils. Moreover, neither the name nor behavior of the landlord is described as Hollingdale alleges. As far as Platt and I can determine, Hollingdale's source must be Carl Albrecht Bernoulli, who recounts a similar but by no means identical tale in his *Franz Overbeck und Friedrich Nietzsche: Eine Freundschaft* (Jena: Eugen Diederich Verlag, 1908); see esp. pp. 301–302.

19. *WP* 1067. *KGW* VII:3, pp. 338–339; *KSA* 11, pp. 610–611.

20. *KGW* VII:1, 2 [41] and 3 [1].

21. *KGW* VII:1, 12 [1] 114.

22. *KGW* VII:3, 31 [52].

23. *KGW* VII:3, 32 [9].

24. *Z*, The Ass Festival, 1.

25. I do not wish to suggest that being a lumper is a necessary condition for treating the *übermensch* as a human ideal, because some splitters are bewitched by the same idealization project. I do think it is a *sufficient* condition, however. That is, if one views the task of philosophers to be that of giving an account, among other things, of the generic features of experience, the origin, nature, and limits of knowledge, and how we ought to live our lives—if, that is to say, one is in the grip of a picture of philosophy as the search for a permanent neutral matrix addressed to timeless questions, in Rorty's sense—one is inevitably destined to read the *übermensch* as the goal of human striving or as a recipe for achieving greatness. It should also be stressed that whereas one cannot easily extract an ontology from Nietzsche without *The Will to Power*, one can certainly extract an "ideal type" view of the *übermensch* without that nonbook.

A previous version of this paper appeared in *The Journal of the History of Philosophy* 24 (January 1986). It was delivered as an invited address under a different title to the Nietzsche Society on October 18, 1984, in Atlanta, Georgia, at its annual meeting held in conjunction with the Society for Phenomenology and Existential Philosophy. An earlier version still was delivered at a symposium of the American Philosophical Association's Western Division, in April 1984, on "Nietzsche and Schacht's Nietzsche." I want to take this opportunity, therefore, to thank the APA's program committee and the program committee of the Nietzsche Society for their respective invitations.

The research for this paper was made possible through agencies to which I should like to express my gratitude: The John Simon Guggenheim Memorial Foundation, the National Endowment for the Humanities, the American Council of Learned Societies, and the Academic Senate of the University of California, Riverside.

Bibliography

Primary Sources

Friedrich Nietzsche. *Kritische Gesamtausgabe Briefwechsel*, ed. G. Colli and M. Montinari, 24 vols. in 4 parts (Berlin: Walter de Gruyter, 1975ff.).

————. *Kritische Gesamtausgabe Werke*, ed. G. Colli and M. Montinari, 30 vols. in 8 parts (Berlin de Gruyter, 1967ff.).

————. *Werke in Drei Baenden*, ed. Karl Schlechta, 3rd ed. (Munich: Carl Hansers, 1965).

————. *The Antichrist* (1895, written 1888), trans. Walter Kaufmann, in *The Portable Nietzsche*, ed. Walter Kaufmann (New York: Viking, 1968).

————. *Beyond Good and Evil* (1886), trans. Walter Kaufmann (New York: Random House, 1966).

————. *The Birth of Tragedy* (1872), trans. Walter Kaufmann (together with *The Case of Wagner*) (New York: Random House, 1967).

————. *The Case of Wagner* (1888), trans. Walter Kaufmann (together with *The Birth of Tragedy*) (New York: Random House, 1967).

————. *Daybreak: Thoughts on the Prejudices of Morality* (1881), trans. R. J. Hollingdale (Cambridge: Cambridge University Press, 1982).

————. *Ecce Homo: How One Becomes What One Is* (1908, written 1888), trans. Walter Kaufmann (together with *On the Genealogy of Morals*) (New York: Random House, 1967).

————. *The Gay Science, with a Prelude of Rhymes and an Appendix of Songs* (1882, fifth book added 1887), trans. Walter Kaufmann (New York: Random House, 1974).

————. *Human, All Too Human: A Book for Free Spirits* (1878), trans. Marion Faber, with Stephen Lehmann (Lincoln: University of Nebraska Press, 1984).

————. *Human, All Too Human* (1880), vol. 2, vol. 7 of *The Complete Works of Friedrich Nietzsche*, ed. Oscar Levy, 18 vols. (London: George Allen and Unwin, 1911).

——. *Nietzsche: A Self-Portrait from His Letters*, ed. and trans. Peter Fuss and Henry Shapiro (Cambridge. Mass.: Harvard University Press, 1971).

——. *Nietzsche Contra Wagner* (1895, written 1888), trans. Walter Kaufmann in *The Portable Nietzsche* (New York: Viking, 1968).

——. "Nietzsche: Notes for 'We Philologists,' " trans. William Arrowsmith, *Arion* 1 (New Series) (1973–1974), 279–380.

——. "Nietzsche on Classics and Classicists," trans. and selected by William Arrowsmith, *Arion* 2 (1963), part I (Spring), 5–18; part II (Summer), 5–27; part III (Winter), 5–31.

——. *On the Advantage and Disadvantage of History for Life* (1873), trans. Peter Preuss (Indianapolis: Hacket Publishing Company, 1980).

——. *On the Genealogy of Morals* (1887), trans. Walter Kaufmann and R. J. Hollingdale (together with *Ecce Homo*) (New York: Random House, 1967).

——. *Philosophy and Truth: Selections from Nietzsche's Notebooks of the Early 1870's*, trans. and ed. Daniel Breazeale (Atlantic Highlands, N.J.: Humanities Press, 1979).

——. *Philosophy in the Tragic Age of the Greeks*, trans. Marianne Cowan (Chicago: Henry Regnery Company, 1962).

——. *Schopenhauer as Educator* (1874), trans. James W. Hillesheim and Malcolm R. Simpson (South Bend: Gateway Editions, 1965).

——. *Selected Letters of Friedrich Nietzsche*, ed. and trans. Christopher Middleton (Chicago: University of Chicago Press, 1969).

——. *Thus Spoke Zarathustra* (parts I–III, 1884; parts I–IV, 1891), trans. Walter Kaufmann, in *The Portable Nietzsche* (New York: Viking, 1968).

——. *Twilight of the Idols* (1889, written 1888), trans. Walter Kaufmann, in *The Portable Nietzsche* (New York: Viking, 1968).

——. *Untimely Meditations* (the last published 1876), trans. R. J. Hollingdale (Cambridge: Cambridge University Press, 1983).

——. *The Will to Power* (first versions published 1904, 1910), trans. Walter Kaufmann and R. J. Hollingdale, ed. Walter Kaufmann (New York: Random House, 1967).

Secondary Works on Nietzsche

Allison, David B., ed. *The New Nietzsche: Contemporary Styles of Interpretation* (New York: Dell Publishing Company, 1977).

Bergoffen, Debra B. "The Eternal Recurrence, Again," *International Studies in Philosophy* 15 (Summer 1983), 35–46.

Brinton, Crane. *Nietzsche* (New York: Harper and Row, 1965).

Copleston, Frederick. *Friedrich Nietzsche: Philosopher of Culture* (London: Burns, Oates and Washburn, 1942).

Dannhauser, Werner J. *Nietzsche's View of Socrates* (Ithaca, N.Y.: Cornell University Press, 1974).

Danto, Arthur C. *Nietzsche as Philosopher: An Original Study* (New York: Columbia University Press, 1965).

Del Caro, A. "Anti-Romantic Irony in the Poetry of Nietzsche," *Nietzsche-Studien* 12 (1983), 372–378.

Deleuze, Gilles. *Nietzsche and Philosophy*, trans. Hugh Tomlinson (New York: Columbia University Press, 1983).

de Man, Paul. "Action and Identity in Nietzsche," *Yale French Studies* 52 (1975), 16–30.

———. *Allegories of Reading: Figural Language in Rousseau, Nietzsche, Rilke, and Proust* (New Haven: Yale University Press, 1979).

———. "Nietzsche's Theory of Rhetoric," *Symposium* 28 (Spring 1974), 33–51.

Derrida, Jacques. *Spurs: Nietzsche's Styles/ Eperons: Les Styles des Nietzsche* (Chicago: University of Chicago Press, 1978).

Faguet, Émile. *On Reading Nietzsche*, trans. George Raffalovich (New York: Moffat, Yart and Company, 1918).

Foerster-Nietzsche, Elizabeth, ed. *The Nietzsche-Wagner Correspondence*, trans. Caroline V. Kerr (New York: Liveright Publishing Company, 1921).

Gelvin, Michael. "Nietzsche and the Question of Being," *Nietzsche-Studien* 9 (1980), 209–223.

Gilman, Sander L. "*Incipit Parodia*: The Function of Parody in the Lyrical Poetry of Friedrich Nietzsche," *Nietzsche-Studien* 4 (1975), 52–74.

———. *Nietzschean Parody: An Introduction to Reading Nietzsche* (Bonn: Bouvier Verlag Herbert Grundmann, 1976).

Harper, Ralph. *The Seventh Solitude: Man's Isolation in Kierkegaard, Dostoevsky, and Nietzsche* (Baltimore: Johns Hopkins University Press, 1965).

Hayman, Ronald. *Nietzsche: A Critical Life* (New York: Oxford University Press, 1980).

Heidegger, Martin. *Nietzsche*, vol. 1: *The Will to Power as Art*, trans. David Farrell Krell (New York: Harper & Row, 1979).

———. *Nietzsche*, vol. 2: *The Eternal Recurrence of the Same*, trans. David Farrell Krell (San Francisco: Harper & Row, 1984).

———. *Nietzsche*, vol. 3: *Will to Power as Knowledge and as Metaphysics*, trans. Joan Stambaugh and Frank A. Capuzzi, ed. David Farrell Krell (San Francisco: Harper & Row, 1986).

———. *Nietzsche*, vol. 4: *Nihilism*, trans. Frank A. Capuzzi, ed. David Farrell Krell (San Francisco: Harper & Row, 1982).

———. "Nietzsche's Word: God Is Dead," in *The Question Concerning Technology and Other Essays*, trans. William Lovitt (New York: Harper & Row, 1977).

Heller, Erich. *The Artist's Journey into the Interior and Other Essays* (New York: Harcourt Brace Jovanovich, 1976).

————. *The Disinherited Mind: Essays in Modern German Literature and Thought*, 3d ed. (London: Bowes and Bowes, 1971).

————. *The Poet's Self and the Poem: Essays on Goethe, Nietzsche, Rilke and Thomas Mann* (London: The Athlone Press, 1976).

Heller, Peter. *Dialectics and Nihilism: Essays on Lessing, Nietzsche, Mann and Kafka* (Amherst: University of Massachusetts Press, 1966).

Higgins, Kathleen. "Nietzsche on Music," *Journal of the History of Ideas* (October-December 1986), 663–672.

————. "Nietzsche's View of Philosophical Style," *International Studies in Philosophy* 18 (Summer 1986), 67–81.

Hollingdale, R. J. *Nietzsche* (Boston: Routledge and Kegan Paul, 1973).

————. *Nietzsche: The Man and His Philosophy* (Baton Rouge: Louisiana State University Press, 1965).

Hollinrake, Roger. *Nietzsche, Wagner, and the Philosophy of Pessimism* (London: George, Allen and Unwin, 1982).

Howey, R. L. "Some Reflections on Irony in Nietzsche," *Nietzsche-Studien* 4 (1973), 36–51.

Jaspers, Karl. *Nietzsche: An Introduction to the Understanding of His Philosophical Activity*, trans. Charles F. Wallraff and Frederick J. Schmidt (Chicago: Henry Regnery Company, 1965).

————. *Nietzsche and Christianity* (Chicago: Henry Regnery Company, 1961).

Kaufmann, Walter, *Nietzsche: Philosophy, Psychologist, Antichrist*, 4th ed. (Princeton: Princeton University Press, 1974).

————. *Tragedy and Philosophy* (Princeton: Princeton University Press, 1968).

Lea, Frank A. *The Tragic Philosopher: A Study of Friedrich Nietzsche* (London: Methuen, 1957).

Magnus, Bernd. "Eternal Recurrence," *Nietzsche-Studien* 8 (1979), 362–377.

————. "Nietzsche's Eternalistic Counter-Myth," *Review of Metaphysics* 26 (June 1973), 604–616.

————. *Nietzsche's Existential Imperative* (Bloomington: Indiana University Press, 1978).

————. "Perfectibility and Attitude in Nietzsche's *Übermensch*," *Review of Metaphysics* 36 (1983), 633–659.

Miller, J. Hillis. "Ariadne's Thread: Repetition and the Narrative Line," *Critical Inquiry* 3 (Autumn 1976), 57–77.

Morgan, George Allen, Jr. *What Nietzsche Means* (Cambridge, Mass.: Harvard University Press, 1941).

Natoli, Charles M. *Nietzsche and Pascal on Christianity* (New York: Peter Lang, 1985).

Nehamas, Alexander. *Nietzsche: Life as Literature* (Cambridge, Mass.: Harvard University Press, 1985).

O'Flaherty, James C., Sellner, Timothy F., and Helen, Robert M., eds. *Studies in Nietzsche and the Classical Tradition* (Chapel Hill: University of North Carolina Press, 1976).

————. *Studies in Nietzsche and the Judaeo-Christian Tradition* (Chapel Hill: University of North Carolina Press, 1985).

O'Hara, Daniel, ed. *Why Nietzsche Now?* (Bloomington: Indiana University Press, 1985).

Pasley, Malcolm, ed. *Nietzsche: Imagery and Thought, A Collection of Essays* (London: Methuen, 1978).

Perkins, Richard. "The Genius and the Better Player: Superman and the Elements of Play," *International Studies in Philosophy* 15 (Summer 1983), 13–23.

Pfeffer, Rose. *Nietzsche: Disciple of Dionysus* (Lewisburg: Bucknell University Press, 1972).

Reichert, Herbert William. *International Nietzsche Bibliography*, compiled and ed. Herbert W. Reichert and Karl Schlechta, revised and expanded (Chapel Hill: University of North Carolina Press, 1968).

Rolleston, James. "Nietzsche, Expressionism and Modern Poetics," *Nietzsche-Studien* 9 (1980), 285–301.

Rosen, Stanley. "Nietzsche's Image of Chaos," *International Philosophical Quarterly* 20 (March 1980), 3–23.

Sasso, James. *The Role of Consciousness in the Thought of Nietzsche* (Washington, D.C.: University Press of America, 1977).

Schacht, Richard. *Nietzsche* (London: Routledge and Kegan Paul, 1983).

Schrift, Alan D. "Language, Metaphor, Rhetoric: Nietzsche's Deconstruction of Epistemology," *Journal of the History of Philosophy* 23 (July 1985), 371–395.

Schutte, Ofelia. *Beyond Nihilism: Nietzsche Without Masks* (Chicago: University of Chicago Press, 1984).

Shapiro, Gary. "Nietzschean Aphorism as Art and Act," *Man and World* 17 (1984), 399–430.

Solomon, Robert, ed. *Nietzsche: A Collection of Critical Essays* (Garden City: Doubleday, 1973).

Stambaugh, Joan. *Nietzsche's Thought of Eternal Return* (Baltimore: Johns Hopkins University Press, 1972).

Sterling, M. C. "Recent Discussions of Eternal Recurrence: Some Critical Comments," *Nietzsche-Studien* 6 (1977), 261–291.

Stern, J. P. *A Study of Nietzsche* (Cambridge: Cambridge University Press, 1979).

————. *Friedrich Nietzsche* (New York: Penguin Books, 1978).

Strong, Tracy B. *Friedrich Nietzsche and the Politics of Transfiguration* (Berkeley: University of California Press, 1975).

Weigand, Hermann J. "Nietzsche's Dionysus-Ariadne Fixation," *The Germanic Review* 48 (March 1973), 99–116.

Wilcox, John T. *Truth and Value in Nietzsche* (Ann Arbor: University of Michigan Press, 1974).

Yovel, Yirmiyahu, ed. *Nietzsche as Affirmative Thinker: Papers Presented at the*

Fifth Jerusalem Philosophical Encounter, April 1983, Martinus Nijhoff Philosophy Library, vol. 13 (Dordrecht: Martinus Nijhoff, 1986).

Secondary Works on Specific Texts

The Birth of Tragedy

Arnott, W. G. "Nietzsche's View of Greek Tragedy," *Arethusa* 17 (1984), 135–149.

Barrack, Charles M. "Nietzsche's Dionysus and Apollo: Gods in Transition," *Nietzsche-Studien* 3 (1974), 115–129.

Calder, W. M., III. "The Wilamowitz-Nietzsche Struggle: New Documents and a Reappraisal," *Nietzsche-Studien* 12 (1983), 214–254.

Clegg, Jerry S. "Nietzsche's Gods in *The Birth of Tragedy*," *Journal of the History of Philosophy* 10 (October 1972), 431–438.

Groth, J. M. "Wilamowitz-Möllendorf on Nietzsche's *Birth of Tragedy*," *Journal of the History of Ideas* 11 (April 1950), 179–190.

Hinden, M. "Nietzsche's Quarrel with Euripides," *Criticism* 23 (1981), 246–260.

McGinn, R. E. "Culture as Prophylactic: Nietzsche's *Birth of Tragedy* as Culture Criticism," *Nietzsche-Studien* 4 (1975), 75–138.

Mansfeld, Jaap. "The Wilamowitz-Nietzsche Struggle: Another New Document and Some Further Comments," *Neitzsche-Studien* 15 (1986), 41–58.

Silk, M. S., and Stern, J. P. *Nietzsche on Tragedy* (Cambridge: Cambridge University Press, 1981).

Zuckerman, Elliott. "Nietzsche and Music: *The Birth of Tragedy* and *Nietzsche Contra Wagner*," *Symposium* 28 (Spring 1974), 17–32.

Other Early Writings

Clark, Maudemarie. "On Truth and Lies in the Extra Moral Sense," *International Studies in Philosophy* 16 (1984), 57–66.

Cooper, David E. "On Reading Nietzsche on Education," *Journal of Philosophy of Education* 17 (1983), 119–126.

Freydberg, B. "Nietzsche's Socratic Task in 'Vom Nutzen und Nachteil der Historie fur das Leben,' " *Man and World* 18 (1985), 317–324.

Scharff, Robert. "Nietzsche and the 'Use' of History," *Man and World* 7 (February 1974), 67–77.

Daybreak

Danto, Arthur C. "Thoughts of a Subterranean Man," *Times Literary Supplement* 4148 (1982), 1074.

The Gay Science

Lingis, Alphonso. "The Language of *The Gay Science*," in *The Philosophical Reflection of Man in Literature*, ed. Anna-Teresa Tymieniecka (Boston: Reidel, 1982), 312–320.

Uscatescu, J. "Nietzsche and the Death of God: Centenary of *The Gay Science*," *Folia Humanistica* 20 (1982), 743–754.

Thus Spoke Zarathustra

Aiken, Henry David. "Introduction to *Zarathustra*," in *Nietzsche: A Collection of Critical Essays*, ed. Robert Solomon (Garden City: Doubleday, 1973), 114–130.

Alderman, Harold. *Nietzsche's Gift* (Athens: Ohio University Press, 1977).

Beatty, Joseph. "Zarathustra: The Paradoxical Ways of the Creator," *Man and World* 3 (February 1970), 64–75.

Byrum, Stephen. "The Concept of Child's Play in Nietzsche's 'Of the Three Metamorphoses,' " *Kinesis* 6 (Spring 1974), 127–135.

Conway, Daniel. "Nietzsche's Oblique Promotion of Moral Excellence: A Philosophical Interpretation of *Thus Spoke Zarathustra*" (unpublished dissertation, University of California, San Diego, 1985).

Del Caro, Adrian. "The Immolation of Zarathustra: A Look at 'The Fire Beacon,' " *Colloquia Germanica* 17 (1984), 251–256.

Goicoechea, David, ed. *The Great Year of Zarathustra (1881–1981)* (New York: Lanham, 1983).

Gooding-Williams, Robert. "Literary Fiction as Philosophy: The Case of Nietzsche's *Zarathustra*," *The Journal of Philosophy* 83 (November 1986), 667–675.

———. "Metaphysics and Metalepsis in *Thus Spoke Zarathustra*," *International Studies in Philosophy* 16 (1984), 27–36.

———. "Recurrence, Parody and Politics in the Philosophy of Friedrich Nietzsche" (unpublished dissertation under the name "Williams," Yale University, 1982).

Gordon, Haim. "Nietzsche's Zarathustra as Educator," *Journal of Philosophy of Education* 14 (November 1980), 181–192.

Harries, Karsten. "Boundary Disputes," *The Journal of Philosophy* 83 (November 1986), 676–677.

Heidegger, Martin. "Who is Nietzsche's Zarathustra?" trans. Bernd Magnus, in *The New Nietzsche: Contemporary Styles of Interpretation*, ed. David B. Allison (New York: Dell, 1977), 64–79; originally published in *Review of Metaphysics* 20 (March 1967), 411–431.

Higgins, Kathleen. "The Night Song's Answer," *International Studies in Philosophy* 17 (Summer 1985), 33–50.

———. *Nietzsche's Zarathustra* (Philadelphia: Temple University Press, 1987).

Jenkins, Keith. "The Dogma of Nietzsche's Zarathustra," *Journal of Philosophy of Education* 16 (December 1982), 251–254.

Krell, David Farrell. "Heidegger and Zarathustra," *Philosophy Today* 18 (Winter 1974), 306–311.

Lampert, Laurence. *Nietzsche's Teaching: An Interpretation of Thus Spoke Zarathustra* (New Haven: Yale University Press, 1986).

———. "Zarathustra and His Disciples," *Nietzsche-Studien* 8 (1979), 309–333.

———. "Zarathustra's Dancing Song," *Interpretation* 8 (May 1980), 141–155.

Miller, C. A. "Nietzsche's 'Daughters of the Desert': A Reconsideration," *Nietzsche-Studien* 2 (1973) 157–195.

Miller, J. Hillis. "*Gleichnis* in Nietzsche's *Also Sprach Zarathustra*," *International Studies in Philosophy* 17 (Summer 1985), 3–15.

Morris, Phyllis S. "The Laughing Lion: Nietzsche's Vision of the Overman," *Humanities Review* 15 (Autumn 1961).

O'Flaherty, James C. "The Intuitive Mode of Reasoning in Zarathustra," *International Studies in Philosophy* 15 (Summer 1983), 57–66.

Okhamafe, Elmafedia. "Zarathustra and Heidegger's Call of Conscience," *Philosophy Today* 28 (Spring 1984), 77–82.

Pangle, Thomas L. "The 'Warrior Spirit' as an Inlet to the Political Philosophers of Nietzsche's Zarathustra," *Nietzsche-Studien* 15 (1986), 140–179.

Parkes, Graham. "The Overflowing Soul: Images of Transformation in Nietzsche's Zarathustra," *Man and World* 16 (1983), 335–348.

———. "The Wandering Dance: *Chuang Tzu* and *Zarathustra*," *Philosophy East and West* 33 (July 1983), 235–250.

Pashman, Jon. "The Pale Criminal," *Man and World* 4 (May 1971), 169–173.

Quigley, Michael. "Which Allegory for Religious Truth: Plato's Cave or Nietzsche's Zarathustra?" *The Thomist* 42 (October 1978), 625–648.

Reinhardt, Karl. "Nietzsche's Lament of Ariadne," *Interpretation* 6 (October 1977), 204–224.

Robbins, Leonard. "Zarathustra and the Magician, Or Nietzsche Contra Nietzsche: Some Difficulties in the Concept of the Overman," *Man and World* 9 (June 1976), 175–195.

Schutte, Ofelia. "The Solitude of Nietzsche's Zarathustra," *Review of Existential Psychology and Psychiatry* 17 (1980–81), 209–222.

Shapiro, Gary. "The Rhetoric of Nietzsche's *Zarathustra*," *Boundary Two: A Journal of Postmodern Literature* 8 (1980), 165–189.

Sillis, John C. "Nietzsche's Homecoming," *Man and World* 2 (February 1969) 108–116.

Thatcher, David S. "Eagle and Serpent in *Zarathustra*," *Nietzsche-Studien* 6 (1977), 240–260.

Weiss, Allen S. "The Symbolism and Celebration of the Earth in Nietzsche's *Zarathustra*," *Sub-Stance* 22 (1979), 39–47.

Williams, Robert J. [Gooding-Williams, Robert] "Recurrence, Parody and Politics in the Philosophy of Friedrich Nietzsche" (unpublished dissertation, Yale University, 1982).

Beyond Good and Evil

Lampert, L. "*Beyond Good and Evil:* Nietzsche's Free Spirit Mask," *International Studies in Philosophy* 16 (1984), 41–52.

Strauss, Leo. "Note on the Plan of Nietzsche's *Beyond Good and Evil*," *Interpretation* 3 (Winter 1973), 97–113.

Zanardi, William J. "Nietzsche's Speech of Indirection: Commentary on Laurence Lampert's '*Beyond Good and Evil:* Nietzsche's Free Spirit Mask,' " *International Studies in Philosophy* 16 (1984), 53–56.

On the Genealogy of Morals

Bergoffen, Debra B. "Why a Genealogy of Morals?" *Man and World* 16 (1983), 129–138.

Nehamas, Alexander. *Nietzsche: Life as Literature* (Cambridge, Mass.: Harvard University Press, 1985), chap. 4, pp. 106–132.

The Twilight of the Idols

Thatcher, David S. "A Diagnosis of Idols: Percussions and Repercussions of a Distant Hammer," *Nietzsche-Studien* 14 (1985), 250–268.

Ecce Homo

Altieri, C. "Ecce Homo," *Boundary 2* 9 (1981), 389–413.

Gasche, R. "Autobiography as Gestalt: Nietzsche's *Ecce Homo*," *Boundary 2* 9 (1981), 271–290.

———. "Ecce Homo or the Written Body (Nietzsche's Analysis of Himself)," *Oxford Literary Review* 7 (1985), 3–24.

Layton, Max Reuben. "In Defense of *Ecce Homo*," *Gnosis* 1 (Spring 1973), 82–88.

Silverman, H. J. "The Autobiographical Textuality of Nietzsche's *Ecce Homo*," *Boundary 2* 9 (1981), 141–151.

Tunstall, G. C. "Autobiography and Mythogenesis—the Case of Kaiser, Georg, and Nietzsche's *Ecce Homo*," *German Life and Letters* 37 (1984), 105–111.

The Nachlass

Brann, Henry Walter. "Nietzsche's 'Nachlass': Remarks on Alderman's 'Nietzsche's Masks,' " *International Philosophical Quarterly* 13 (June 1973), 271–273.

Magnus, Bernd. "Nietzsche's Philosophy in 1888: *The Will to Power* and the *Übermensch*," *Journal of the History of Philosophy* 24 (January 1986), 79–98.

Other Writings

Blair, C. "Nietzsche's Lecture Notes on Rhetoric—A Translation," *Philosophy and Rhetoric* 16 (1983), 94–129.

Brann, Henry Walter. "A Reply to Walter Kaufmann's 'Nietzsche in the Light of His Suppressed Manuscripts,' " *Journal of the History of Philosophy* 3 (October 1965), 246–250.

Engel, S. Morris. "An Early Nietzsche Fragment on Language," *Journal of the History of Ideas* 24 (April-June 1963), 279–286.

Kaufmann, Walter. "Nietzsche in the Light of His Suppressed Manuscripts," *Journal of the History of Philosophy* 2 (October 1964), 205–226.

Contributors

Frithjof Bergmann is professor of philosophy and anthropology at the University of Michigan. He is the author of *On Being Free*.

Arthur Danto is Johnsonian Professor of Philosophy at Columbia University. He is the author of *Nietzsche as Philosopher* (1965). His two most recent books are *The Philosophical Disenfranchisement of Art* and *The State of the Art*.

Lars Gustaffson is the well-known Swedish novelist. He is also adjunct professor of philosophy and Germanic literature at the University of Texas at Austin. He is the author of *Sprache und Luge* and *The Death of a Beekeeper*. Prix European *Sprache und Luge* and des Essais Charles Veillon, 1983.

Kathleen Higgins is assistant professor of philosophy at the University of Texas at Austin. She is the author of *Nietzsche's Zarathustra* (1987).

Bernd Magnus is professor of philosophy at the University of California, Riverside. He is the author of *Heidegger's Metahistory of Philosophy, Nietzsche's Existential Imperative* (1978) and, most recently, *The Postmodern Turn: Nietzsche, Heidegger, Derrida, Rorty*.

Christopher Middleton is David J. Bruton Centennial Professor of Germanic Languages and Literatures at the University of Texas at Austin. He is translator and editor of Nietzsche's *Selected Letters* (1969) and the author of many volumes of poetry and essays, including *Two Horse Wagon Going By and Pursuit of the Kingfisher*.

Alexander Nehamas is professor of philosophy at the University of Pennsylvania in Philadelphia. He writes extensively on Plato and on literary theory, and he is author of *Nietzsche: Life as Literature* (1986).

Richard Schacht is professor of philosophy and also of criticism and interpretive theory at the University of Illinois at Urbana-Champaign. He is the author of *Nietzsche* (1983), *Alienation, After Hegel*, and *Classical Modern Philosophers*.

Gary Shapiro is professor of philosophy at the University of Kansas in Lawrence. He is the author of *Nietzschean Narratives and Hermeneutics: Questions and Prospects* (co-edited with Alan Sica).

Ivan Soll is professor of philosophy at the University of Wisconsin in Madison. He is the author of *An Introduction to Hegel's Metaphysics*.

Robert Solomon is Quincy Lee Centennial Professor at the University of Texas at Austin. He is the author of *From Rationalism to Existentialism, the Passions, In the Spirit of Hegel*, and *From Hegel to Existentialism*.

Index

249